W9-BON-277

The Perfect Mistress, For Small Men with Large Ambitions

Paula Marckx

authorHOUSE®

AuthorHouse™ UK Ltd.
500 Avebury Boulevard
Central Milton Keynes, MK9 2BE
www.authorhouse.co.uk
Phone: 08001974150

First published by AuthorHouse   6/22/2010

ISBN: 978-1-4490-7382-4 (sc)

This book is printed on acid-free paper.

*This book would not have seen the light of the day
without a little help from my friends.*

*I am grateful to
Guillaume van der Stichelen for his advice and assistance
Elisabeth Khan for translating part of my Dutch-language biography,
Paula Marckx, Helemaal Bloot*

Johan van Herck for his graphical assistance

*And to
Dr. Jeff Hoeyberghs for his technical assistance*

Contents

Chapter 1
Boomerang

Me at the age of fourteen

I just had fantastic sex with a man who was a little more than half of my age, who could seduce every girl and woman he wants – a plastic surgeon of all people – I was just over 80, and he called me the perfect Mistress. He just made me realize that it was that what I had been most of my life.

Had I grown up in a marginal family? Not quite. My father was born and raised in a very catholic surrounding. He did turn out into an oversexed bull. He and my mother stayed together for the children's sake, the general excuse, trying as well as they could, in a hypocrite unreality, to educate (?) us in the puritan well behavior manners of the thirties and forties. This led sometimes to hilarious situations, meaning hilarious now, at that period it was dead serious. My sister Blanche was thirteen years older than I was. In her early twenties her favorite lecture where the

1

famous novels of Hedwig Courts-Mahler. Those novels had always the same plot. The leading character was a baron who employed a governess for his children. In every book of the serial, another baron fell in love with another governess. At the last page, he gave her a kiss on the cheek. End of the story. However, the girl of thirteen that I was at that time was not supposed to read such a vicious literature. Blanche was supposed to hide her books far away from her little sister.

My mother was a very prude woman with two lesbian sisters. The world lesbian was not common knowledge in those days, those women were simply called women for women. If the classical term was not an average daily word, the outcome was the same. My aunt Caroline, my mothers gay sister kept the very trendy bar Top Hat on the Italielei, the favorite hung out for that kind of women. In the afternoon, they came in for a drink while their husbands were at work. Most of those women were married to very respectable business men who had not a clue what their wives were doing while they were in their daily meetings. On busy days my mother often led a helping hand. Not that mom was considered one of them. Sex in whatever packing material it came was to be highly avoided as far as she was concerned. However, she liked a drink or two – in those days middle class people didn't have alcoholic drinks in their house – so she was more than pleased to go to a bar where there where plenty of drinks and a lot of laughs. When I had time of at school mom or one of the regulars picked me up and Top Hat became my second home. That is how I met Fabienne Zeller, wife of a top manager of Ziegler, a notorious maritime company, who took a crush on me. Not that kind of crush that would lead to forbidden games, just plain sympathy. Fabienne, or Faby as she called herself, had a steady girl friend, Maria, a ballerina at the Opera House. Fabienne was French, her family lived in Paris. She intended to spend a weekend with Maria in her hometown. Even so, to travel alone with her girl friend was too obvious. A third travel mate was more than welcome. She asked my mother if I could join them. My mother said yes. I was not yet fourteen years old.

The little girl that was not allowed to read the harmless story of a Baron in love was sent to Paris with two lesbian women! No harm done. My mother didn't realize what Women for Women could do. Her ignorance was nearly moving. To me, it was an adventure with what I considered ordinary girl friends. My sexual education was not that far developed. It was not developed at all. The first evening after our arrival in Paris we spent Chez Moune, the largest, internationally known lesbian bar/brothel of La Ville Lumière. Fabienne and Maria had the time of their life. But not for long. They had a hell of a time keeping all those women in heat away from me. Finally, we left. I still see myself running in the gangway of the metro station trying to get rid of a woman chasing me, as if I was game on the loose. We changed quarters and moved to Madame Arthur, another place to be, but this time for transsexuals. There at last they left me in peace. My mother never knew where her baby spent her first days abroad. Later in life when I remembered my childhood, I couldn't help thinking of a song by Jacques Brel called Bruxelles.. It is about his parents before they were married. They were at the back seat of a tramcar making a show of themselves hugging and kissing. Brel's conclusion was: Et alors on s'étonne que je ne suis pas sérieux (and then everybody is surprised that I am not serious). And so I entered the great big world where big wolves were waiting for the innocent sheep that I was. Alternatively, how an innocent sheep turned into a perfect mistress?

When I was fifteen, aunt Caroline, one of the lesbians, told me that I was going to make it in life. Not the way she did, a lesbian recognizes another lesbian, and I was not gifted. However, she predicted that men were going to fall for me. Not exactly for a marriage license, but to have me wined and dined, to treat me as a lady and to get as much sex as time permits. I only had to meet the right men, and I did. If aunt Caroline would still be alive, she would have been proud of me.

****

My first encounter with world history took place as I was taking off my clothes for a painter. I was seventeen. The good man conveyed my then limber body onto the canvas, but what was a passion for him was pure penury for me. It was 1943, the war was coming to an end and just like everyone else I was trying to survive, but in an era of prudishness and modesty it was anything but obvious to undress in front of a stranger. Even the family doctor had never seen me naked. Fortunately, Lode Seghers was an artist with strong ethics and a solid reputation. And if he noticed I was nervous, he never let on.

That I found myself in this situation had everything to do with the home front. My father was a man for whom no woman was safe, but for my mother the consummation of matrimony was a scourge. She was most likely frigid. I derived this conclusion from her words, "Let him take his filth elsewhere." So as long as he left her alone she was happy. Yet, she did have two children and not by way of immaculate conception. My sister Blanche was probably conceived during the wedding night, when Mother was just doing her duty and allowed Father to approach her in order to physically complete the marriage. I came along years later, a trick of my mother's to save the marriage. Through another child, she would tie Father, the breadwinner of the family, more securely to herself, she hoped. After living alongside each other for years, there were few lefts of their marriage. As far as the rest of my family was concerned: one side was thoroughly God-fearing, the others were freethinkers. My mother belonged to the freethinkers.

Father and Mother married right before the First World War. Mother was pregnant when Father fled to England, leaving her behind. As a consequence he would foster a great love for that country for the rest of his life. When he returned after four years he had become a stranger to both mother and child. Mother had been happy all that time without physical love, while Father had received such ample gratification in England that, once back, he could no longer do without.

I still think with gratitude of the Antwerp Minerva plant because that's where Father got a job after I was born. That's how he could afford a car of his own when few other people could. When the Second World War became a fact even in Antwerp, I found it thrilling. We were about to flee to Spain in our automobile. "But am I appropriately dressed?" I asked my mirror image. Perhaps my clothes were comfortable enough, but not sufficiently pretty. "Mother, where is my gray dress?" But Mother didn't get a chance to reply. From the foyer my father roared, "Paula, stop dawdling and get into the car!" Like many compatriots, Father had felt uneasy about the situation for a while now; the enemy threat was becoming too strong. It would be a long drive to Spain; there the enemy could not touch us. I took my seat in the Minerva where Mother, my big sister Blanche and Leopoldine with her husband were already waiting for me. With Father behind the wheel and myself in the back with the others, the car was pretty full. Leopoldine was Father's girlfriend. She was our relative, so it wasn't immediately obvious. She was my godmother's stepdaughter and owned a beauty parlor in our neighborhood. My father always took me along when he went to see her, as his alibi. No matter how much I wanted to grow my hair, it was not allowed. Time and again, Leopoldine plied her scissors, and Father was saved. After my umpteenth trim, those two were playing in the Garden of Eden, leaving me in the care of Leopoldine's husband, a men's stylist. Either he condoned his wife's actions, or else he was terribly naïve, but I never knew if Leopoldine's husband had any suspicions about his wife or my father. The Minerva puffed its way slowly but surely along the country roads. "Now this is an adventure," I thought. I had never left Antwerp this far behind me, and there was something cozy about it, as well. It gave me that safe childhood feeling. That feeling, however, had started with a drama: when I was little, we had two dogs at home, Bobby and Jenny. They were my great playmates. When my father suddenly gave them away one day to friends who were looking for a pair of watchdogs, I was inconsolable. In fact, I never forgave my father. Mother took me along to the fish market every week. There someone would pick a baby eel from one of those huge baskets. I carried it home in a little pail, and had hours of fun with the tiny creature. I let it wriggle in every direction, slide down from the curb, climb back up... until it gave up the ghost. However, every time my sadness was short-lived. The following Friday there was another fish market, and I was given a new baby eel.

My father's voice scared the Dickens out of me: "Get down, get down the damn it!"!" Father shouted, "Jump out of the car and roll yourselves into the ditch!" All his passengers did, almost instinctively, as he commanded. No sooner did we lie down in the muddy ditch than bombs were landing all around us. German Stuka planes were dropping their explosive charges on civilians, as well, because there were some soldiers among us. Our own army was almost totally lacking in coordination at the time. Luckily, the attack ended well. We got over the initial shock, waited for our clothes to dry, and re-boarded the car. Once we reached France, though, the Germans completely blocked our path; the enemy had caught up with us. Mother feared the worst, but I was almost relieved. The reason: we had eaten up all our provisions, and I was starving. Now that the Germans were forcing us to go back where we came from, we'd pass those same farms again where people could feed us. The war had become a lot less exciting to me by now. We heard shooting, and to our left and right, in front of us and behind, bombs kept falling.

Our car became just one link in the long chain of refugee cars that had turned around after the brutal encounter with the Germans. Our adventure had lasted just under two weeks, and it would take days before that chain was back where it had started from. On the road, we witnessed a lot of looting. Not by criminals with a police record: the average man in the street looted and robbed for providence and self-preservation. War became a situation suddenly ruled by different norms than what one had grown up with. Occasionally, we saw how cars ran out of gas and how their drivers had to continue on foot. Unfortunately, the abandoned automobiles acted like magnets on greedy passersby. Anything that wasn't too hot or too heavy was carried off, and nobody as much as lifted an eyebrow. Grabbing whatever you could grab was even fun in a way, and the war once again became a thrilling adventure.

Once back in Antwerp my father first nicely dropped his lady love and her husband back to their place, and then it was our turn. After roaming around for two weeks we were finally back on steady ground. In those days, we lived in the middle of the Jewish neighborhood, the so-called Jewish Quarter. I was born there and in my childhood, I played on the street with lots of Jewish children. During the day, I went to the nuns' school, at night I sometimes shared their kosher dinners. We frequented each other's homes, and if an argument erupted now and then, it certainly had nothing to do with our ethnicity. However, after our escape to France I sensed a change, and not just because we had grown older. Suddenly, some of my little friends were no longer there. Where could they have gone?

It didn't take long for the remaining children to appear with a yellow star sown onto their jackets. I was upset. Why didn't I receive such a nice yellow star? I didn't realize how lucky I was. And nobody was allowed to listen to the BBC on the radio. Anyone who got caught disobeying this order promptly landed in the local jail. School changed, too. Languages were no longer taught and English songs were strictly forbidden. We saw the Feldwebels pass in their gray-green uniforms. These German soldiers were not even major nuisances, but the school gate was no longer a safe place. The Catholic girls' school had a half day off, not on Wednesdays but on Thursday afternoon. On those Thursday afternoons, the gray-green occupier would disappear into the bushes with young girls. Seeing one of those girl's waves about a chocolate bar later, I knew just what was up.

Feldwebels seduced even elementary-school children with chocolate, a very scarce delicacy. However, I didn't walk into their sugar-laced trap, because I had received sex education. Not from adults but from my peers who spiced up their initiation into reproductive science with the most diverse fantasies. One thing, however, these precocious kids unanimously agreed on: from "dirty manners" came babies. So watch out for that Feldwebel with his chocolate bar.

Chapter 2
Bon Chic, Bon Genre

Me and Myriam walking on main street in Antwerp

As soon as I had my clothes back on and finally dared to look at the painter in the eye, I noticed that he didn't look so bad after all. He was thirty-something, tall, stylishly dressed, and pleasantly casual so that after a while I felt quite at ease with him. I told him about my mother, my father, and my future, which now depended on the pay, I'd take home. After hearing all of this, Mr. Seghers promptly walked over to a drawer, took out a bunch of banknotes and placed the impressive sum of 800 Belgian francs in front of me. I was speechless with surprise, but inside my head, there was this jubilation: "O my God, this is a whole month's wages!" Incredible, I

8

had earned my first paycheck and was all set for a whole month! What do you say to that, Daddy?!?

More posing sessions followed, even after I had attempted to explain the true nature of my work to Mother. However, I can't remember her listening attentively to my words, and she never of her own accord asked questions about the what, where, or how. To Father I still wasn't talking.

My frequent visits to Lode Seghers had me make the acquaintance of people about whose existence, I had been unaware before. Before the Second World War, Antwerp was a well-known hub of the lumber trade and merchants from Prussia regularly came to town. Some of them had managed to find the way to the painter's door. Seghers painted their portraits. When the war broke out, the first officers of the German army, too, happened to be from Prussia. The failed coup that would later take place against Hitler, by the way, was plotted by Prussians. Some of Seghers' military clients had been painted by him only recently as civilians. Now they came to him in uniform and that would get my painter into trouble. The resistance group that called itself the White Brigade began to consider him a collaborator. Being an artist, Seghers, who also taught at the Antwerp Academy of Fine Arts, didn't pay a whole lot of attention to what happened outside his sphere of interest. The painter painted on, even if his clientele was wearing the wrong uniform.

The German occupier had to dig in his heels. Because the Russian frontline was so immensely long, the German army needed a lot more soldiers than expected. Moreover, their soldiers were not equal to the extreme cold and many died because of the arctic weather. Germany, therefore, drafted young and old in to defend the Reich. This in turn caused a labor shortage in the German factories, including the arm's factories. Eventually, the Kriegskommandantur came up with a solution: they forced young people in the occupied countries to go and work in Germany. Only those who were students were excused from this obligation.

The resistance had initially looked askance at the cordial ties between Lode Seghers and his German friends but luckily that situation soon changed. Resistance people realized that this affable man had no evil intentions and so did not present any danger. That same resistance now approached him with a plan that almost rivaled the plot of Schindler's List in audacity: Lode would have to enroll as many young men as possible as students at the Academy, so they could escape forced employment in Germany. Although these youngsters weren't Jewish, this act of resistance could just as well have cost Lode his life. Despite the danger, he agreed to the request. Hardly, a single one of these youths had any notion of how to hold a paintbrush, and some of them never even showed up at the Academy. However, the plan succeeded brilliantly and none of these "students" were sent to Germany.

Due to the temporary nature of my job as a nude model, Mr. Seghers tried to offer me more security: "I can arrange for you to become a steady model at the Academy," the good man said. I objected: undressing for one man was the limit of my chutzpah. Imagine doing the same for a whole class of young, mostly male students. The painter understood my protest and accepted my refusal.

Even so, this meant that I had to look for new earnings. On stage for instance, that appealed to me. In the center of town was the largest Music-hall of that moment, The Rubens, called after our famous painter but nothing to do with fine art. TV was non existent in those years, so the show in the Rubens was very popular. Every Saturday night they had a competition where new singing talent could take their chances. A little like nowadays talent hunting with one huge difference: in modern times, there is a professional selection before anyone is allowed to go on TV, at the period where I am talking about there was no question of a previous interview. The candidates were requested to arrive, with their score, at the theater at 7 pm (the show was at 8 pm), register and without any rehearsal with the orchestra they were put before the lions at about 8.30. I had no singing voice at all, never had and never will, but that was the least of my problems, I wanted to be on that scene. At that time, the BBC had a wonderful hit ' When the deep purple Falls'. People from the occupied countries were not supposed to know that song, as it was strictly forbidden to listen to the English radio. But who cared. Listening to the BBC was doing our bits to win the war. I found myself the score and up I went. However, although I could not sing, I had a micro and everybody understood what I was saying, and in what language: English! The audience was filled with German Officers, Before I realized what was happening to me a couple of tough guys ran on stage, grasped me and pulled me behind the curtains. The men were grayish. They figured us already behind bars, and being in prison by the German army was not exactly something to look forward to. Cann't you sing something in German, they asked in despair. I was always good in memorizing songs, even if they were in a foreign language, and notwithstanding I didn't understand a word of it. Zarah Leander was by that time the sweetheart of the forces, and I knew her favorite song: Mein Leben für die Liebe: Jawohl. (My entire life is dedicated to Love: Oh Yes!) So that is what I was going to sing, still without a voice. However, I was in such a bad temper because I wasn't unable to sing my beautiful English song that I brought it with all the furor I had in me. Exactly, what the lyrics needed. I received a standing applause and was selected number 1. I received about two dollars and an engagement at the theater. Nevertheless, that is not exactly what my parents had in mind. I had to find work in an office. A serious job. So what the hell....

As luck would have it, Myriam, our greengrocer's daughter and a good friend of mine, was offered a position in a semi-official organization that aided the hungry in Brussels. I had been friends with Myriam for a while now, but in elementary school, and even before I had never had real friends. During recess, I always stood at the edge of the schoolyard. I simply didn't belong with them, much I wanted to. Maybe it had something to do with the fact that my mother never allowed me to bring classmate's home to play. It was too much trouble for her as it caused extra work, and she didn't exactly look forward to that. When I related at the beginning of my story that Jewish children walked in and out, that is not completely correct. We played together on the street, and I went into their homes, but the closest they came to mine was when my mother stood on the sidewalk watching us. I have no recollection of any child ever entering my place, not even my boy or girl cousins.

Myriam and I met in the first year of the commerce classes where I was supposed to acquire the basic knowledge for my future job at City Hall. She actually was my first real friend. Her parents owned the corner vegetable market, and she would take me home after school. She was a very pretty girl with long, blond hair, and I was happy she chose me because I looked up to her enormously. I thought it very normal that when men were around, their attention always went to her first. There were always men hanging around us because she was a born flirt, which I was not at all. Her boyfriend's pal would become my friend; this way there were always four of us, even if it was only for one afternoon or evening's outing. I think this is the reason why I never thought of myself as good looking —Myriam was the prettiest, even to my eyes. She knew that very well. Yet she remained the regular "country girl" even in Brussels. Eventually, she'd give up a dream life with an American businessman to start a family with a market vendor. At that time, she broke all ties with the past, including myself. Only once in my life did I run into her again, at a department store; that was twenty years later, when I was pregnant with Alexandra.

"Winterhulp" ("Winter Help") was founded to aid children and the poor during the war by handing out soup, milk, vitamin pills, and warm clothing. The organization was heavily sponsored by the Colonial Lottery, which would later evolve into the National Lottery. The Winterhulp head-quarters were in Brussels and Myriam was going to do administrative work there, and if I wanted, I could go with her. Brussels! This city was the equivalent of a foreign destination to me! Of course I wanted to go. We were put to work and assisted wherever we could. However, as the name Winter Help suggests, there wasn't much to do in summer, so we had plenty of time in those days to reconnoiter the capital. The atmosphere of the capital led us to dreams of a delightful future filled with riches and success, but Winterhulp was but a lowly rung on the ladder, and so we came up with a plan: we placed an ad in the newspaper La Dernière Heure, and had it typeset in bold: "Jeunes filles de bonnes familles cherchent n'importe quel travail."

(Young ladies from good families looking for any type of work.) This attempt at classy French made us feel important, and how proud we were when we set eyes on our printed advertisement. We rented a post-office box and waited anxiously for what was to come.

The weather was fine, and the side walk café's on the Place de Brouckère very appealing. That's where we spend our afternoons, and it must be that we didn't pass unnoticed, to be completely honest we must have looked like a couple of hookers sitting there with our lemonade watching every man that passed by wondering if he could be the one to introduce us in the upper life where we were dreaming of. That is how we met Gino and Matteo, two middle aged Italians, who were active in the black market circuit. Every late afternoon we met at the same café. They were not mainly flirting they were also talking business. One day we heard them saying that they were in urgent need for a load of French wine to sell to the German Army. Because we had no better to do I suggested that we could try to find

12

some. They must have been desperate because they send us on a mission. In Antwerp, I found publicity from a certain Mr. Fontaine, who lived in a street of the same name in Borgerhout a suburb of Antwerp. It was a rather stuffy place, but Mr. Fontaine agreed to see us. He certainly hadn't expected a couple of teenagers but when I told him that it was meant for the German Army he listened more closely. I suppose he took us for two Mata Hari's, but yes he had a stock of read wine, and yes he was ready to sell it. Overwhelmed with joy we took the train to Brussels to tell our new friends that their trouble was over. They couldn't believe their eyes, but the transaction went through and we were sent on another mission with some success. Meanwhile Myriam fell for Gino, I too, but I didn't stand a chance. When Gino thought the time had come. he took Myriam to a second class hotel in the neighborhood. Because we were always the four of us together. Matteo decided to take me to. And so I found myself in a third class hotel room with a man I only liked as a good friend but certainly not to lose my virginity on. When, while starting to address me, he told me with flame, which could have to do with his Italian nature, that my hips were made to have a lot of children , the little interest which I may have had vanished on the spot and when he came nearer to undress me, I took an ash tree that was at hand and threw it at his face. I left Myriam with her lover boy and out I went.

The unthinkable happened: we received lots and lots of responses. We made a stack of the less-than-serious ones before chucking them into the wastebasket, but one reaction really caught our eye: the fashion house Natan requested us to pay them a visit. We had never heard of Natan, or any other fashion house, for that matter. However, the address was familiar because we knew Louise Avenue from our city expeditions and were aware that it was the epitome of class. Our French skills were somewhat lacking, which led to certain level of linguistic confusion, but an employee of the fashion house inspected and approved of us. Mr. Natan, the boss, was Jewish. It would have been too much to expect for him to make a personal appearance in his store now. So Myriam and I were trained by his associates. We had to put on a dress, after which it was examined if our bodies could show off the garment to advantage. Then we had to get onto the catwalk in order to learn how to walk gracefully, how to place our feet, back and forth, for days in a row, until we felt as if we had traveled to Rome on foot. In the entourage of a fashion house like this one, there were always a number of young men who carried out all kinds of small tasks.

Some of these helpful boys introduced us to the priciest spots in Brussels. Furthermore, we underwent a crash course in the French language, another prerequisite for us to move in upper-class circles. Our new life brought about some other situations: the husband of a client, a man in his forties, set his sights on Myriam. He lived on Louisa Avenue, not far from the fashion house, and dropped in regularly. Myriam was terribly charmed by his attentions and besides, Roger was very handsome. However, after a few dates in downtown Brussels, the gentleman was ready for something more. Myriam, who didn't have a lot of experience yet, looked favorably on an initiation by a man like Roger. Thus she agreed to a rendez-vous in a little hotel on the rue Defacqs, a street that gave to Louisa Avenue near Natan's. Roger, however, who had a very jealous spouse, couldn't think of a suitable pretext right away, until his Malinois shepherd dog brought succor. Roger told his wife, he was taking the dog for a walk, and brought the animal to the hotel. The ruse worked and after the first tryst, he saw Myriam several more times at the same hotel, and each time the Malinois came along... until Roger took ill; he was temporarily immobilized due to the flu. The dog, missing his exercise, started to moan and became ever more restless. "I'll take him for a walk," Roger's wife said and took the animal out to calm it. The walk led them by the rue Defacqs, but when the dog reached the hotel, he would walk no further and pulled the leash to be taken inside. The woman, who wasn't born yesterday, cottoned on; and so the romance between Myriam and Roger came to an end.

Chapter 3
The Yanks Are Coming

Me and my brother-in-law

As we participated in many events, our standard of living kept improving. Through the clientele of our fashion shows we got to know, apart from the posh set, another type of folk: the black-marketing men who came to select expensive couture clothing with their wives. It was pretty certain these gentlemen treated their ladies to price gowns as a sop, as they clearly enjoyed surrounding themselves with the models on duty. This happened in select Brussels restaurants, but also in Antwerp. Antwerp businessmen had a good taste and loved to go out in Brussels, while the so-called upper crust from the province came to Antwerp to buy provisions. The black-market circuit was a veritable men's world and for most of them that black market was the only way to make money. Most of all, they were a fun gang that didn't fear even the Germans, as they did business with them. I recall a certain black-marketing man who went to lunch in a restaurant near the Antwerp Central Station. He ordered chicken. The waiter informed him that they were out of chicken as he had just served the last portion to a German officer. The latter was about to enjoy the fowl at a nearby table. However, the black-marketing man stood up, walked over to the German's table plate in hand, speared the chicken and transferred it onto his own plate, saying, "This is mine." Upon which he returned to his own table with the loot and proceeded to gobble up the bird. The restaurant owner turned ashen with fear, but the German himself allowed things to take their course; this Fritz knew all too well that anyone who could afford lunch in this restaurant must have been very well connected indeed.

Nighttime was always party time in the taverns of Antwerp's "Latin Quarter," an area around the theater now called Bourlaschouwburg. Except for Friday because that was "Bourse day." Then the action moved to the surroundings of the centuries-old bourse building. Real stock-exchange activities no longer took place here; there was only the shipping exchange left. This was the area of the Borzestraat, Pruynenstraat and Twaalfmaandenstraat, that gave to the Meir. You can best imagine the bourse area as a quadrangle with little streets that one could enter on one side, and that ended up at the bourse on the other side. In those streets were several cafés, all of them without exception run by women in the prime of life. The ladies enhanced their business by attractive and intelligent cocktail waitresses.

These girls were not paid any wages, but could live very well off the tips of rich customers, who consumed rivers of champagne and spirits and happily parted with generous gratuities. A café like that was no more than the ground floor of a single dwelling. Those who spent their money there valued their privacy, and so they had curtains and drapes that were pulled shut at night. However, these were definitely not covert brothels. The entrances to both the café and the living quarters were never locked, and what is more they were usually kept wide open; ultimately, anyone was allowed to see what went on there, and few women walked into the bourse café's anyway. The male customers were mostly regulars who crawled from café to café within the bourse quarter. You could call the girls who operated there, "European geishas'. They formed the lovely backdrop and created the relaxed atmosphere for businessmen to... do Business. Which didn't mean that there were not eventually love affaire going on. Aids were unknown to us, it was only years later it came into our lives, as far as I can think I wouldn't be surprised if immigration had something

16

to do with it. Condoms ? Never heard of it – they would be introduced to us by the American army at the same time as nylon stockings, I don't remember any girl in town who wouldn't sleep with one of the liberators in order to get her hands on one of those precious items. If somebody thinks that sex was hardly known in those good old times, he had better thought twice. "Geishas" sometimes went into trouble and were expecting, but they had special sex education, not from a book but from real life girls, mostly their friends. Most of them ended up well and went into business for themselves or married a man of means. As a young girl I went there, just like a number of other girls, to have fun and to win some extra money. Nowadays it would be unthinkable that top business men would stop whatever they were doing in the early afternoon to meet each other at a bar of a "Bourse" café to make fun, continue doing business until it was time to go home for dinner. Meanwhile champagne was ordered as if it was ordinary water, and the girls who attended had a generous fee on each bottle that was opened.

Brussels, too, had its weekly bourse day, not on Friday but on Wednesday. Sometime in the sixties, this way of conducting business ceased to exist. After the post-war euphoria, business became a question of efficient offices, with no more than a work lunch in a good restaurant. It was in those bourse-day cafés that my friend and I, amid the champagne, learned how business was done. I never stayed long in Brussels because I didn't really care for the place. After my modeling work, I preferred to return to my "Sinjoren" city as soon as possible. With my newly found, black-market-dealing Antwerp comrades, I felt at home.

My sister Blanche resembled Mother, in that she, too, impassively underwent whatever happened to her. Blanche had only one goal in life: to marry the first Tom, Dick, or Harry, who'd ask her. Marriage was popular and my sister was good-looking, so there was no dearth of suitors. However, as soon as she brought home a boyfriend, things always went wrong. The young man in question was soon confronted with the fact that marriage could turn out to be a lot more than sweet words and honey: arguments, dominance, and helpless acceptance of a partner's cheating were always present with us. As a result, those boys always got cold feet. In total, I've seen eight of them come and go. Fortunately, the ninth one had seen even worse at home and married my sister. Blanche and Harry had no furniture. And alas, just like the box that passed for their coffee table, their marriage wasn't much either. Good-natured Harry was an average guy from a blue-collar family. He looked normal, not handsome, not ugly, a decent run-of-the-mill chap. As a laborer he'd saved up some dough and married a woman with whom he opened a café by the harbor. Nevertheless, he had nothing but trouble with his wife and finally divorced her. Then he met my sister, a woman devoid of any ambition but leaving our home. An easygoing woman, she was not causing problems, something, which filled him with immense gratitude. He felt as if he had exchanged hell for heaven. Out of both financial necessity and also Flemish sentiment, he had joined the VNV, the Flemish National Union. The VNV was an initiative of Staf De Clerq, who wanted to bring about, via a radical program, an authoritarian people's state after the example of Nazi Germany. VNV members had a choice: go to fight at the Russian front, or perform boring administrative tasks at one of the headquarters. Harry opted for the latter, but his membership caused a shockwave in our very religious family. We already had two openly lesbian aunts, a "derailed" daughter—that would be me—and now our father was also stuck with a son-in-law who not only worked for the Germans, but walked around very visibly in the wrong uniform. He was a "black" and that was the stamp put on him by society.

My Brussels adventure could not last. The BBC broadcast ever more code names for the resistance and soon it was rumored that the Allies were on the way. One fine June day we heard they had actually landed in Normandy. This did not happen without the requisite bombings. The bombing was to support the advance of the units that had come ashore and was aimed mostly at the railways. A large number of bombs were dropped wherever German troops were preparing to leave for the Russian front. However, the nearby front was moving in the wrong direction for the Germans. It was moving south to the Bastogne area in order to defend the Atlantic wall, and also west in an ultimate attempt to destroy the (to them) enemy or at the very least push them back into the sea. Everything that moved however,, was being shot at, including the train to Brussels that I boarded so often to go to my job at Natan's. As soon as I became aware of the explosive situation I suddenly balked at that trip to Brussels. "I? Getting on that train again? Not for all the gold in the world!" I'd rather stay home than catch a bomb on my neck. Thus my wonderful life as a fashion model came to an end.

I, too, was subject to the mood that was clearly observable everywhere: waiting, in suspense and also some fear, for what was to come. At night, the parties in the Latin Quarter and the bourse area continued undiminished, but the conversation had changed. The war had more or less passed by everyone in this company, but now it was sitting at the bar with us. Everybody talked about one thing only: when that war would finally be over. Bets were placed on the day that the Allies would arrive in Antwerp. This air of tense expectation could be felt even on the street. Liberation was in sight, but at the same time the future was very uncertain to all of us. It would take until September for the Tommy's to arrive in Antwerp, but most of its inhabitants had no idea who these Tommy's where. The vast majority of people in Antwerp had never laid eyes on a Brit and even less on a Canadian or American, except for the movies where all Americans were cowboys constantly shooting Indians to pieces. One had been better beware of these weird characters!... But there was the adventure in the air. People were assiduously counting the days and never before had they listened in such massive numbers to the BBC. The BBC's signature tune became the greatest hit of 1943/1944 And the Germans? They had long ceased to check who was listening to the forbidden radio station; they had other worries.

Chapter 4
War Is Over – Peace Is Near

And then it happened. The Tommy's and Canadians were at the city's edge. Except for a few daredevils, nobody ventured out of doors because bullets were flying. And who else would surface, but the boys and girls of the Resistance. Now they suddenly seemed to appear out of nowhere, to the despair of the few Germans, who had stayed behind. Fruitlessly, as if drowning in quicksand, the German soldiers flailed, kept under shot by the Resistance. Now the Allies could fall on their prey, and no sooner had the struggle started then it was over.

Allied tanks could now roll into Antwerp triumphantly. The streets that had been so empty just a while ago now filled up with cheering crowds. Especially the pictures of young girls, I was one of them, sitting on top of the tanks and lying in the arms of the liberators, became part of history.

Once it became clear that we no longer had anything to fear from the Germans—at least that was what we thought—the euphoria turned into something else entirely. The civilians' years' worth of suppressed frustration and anger now turned itself against those who had been living it up with the occupier. This went very far, often too far. Some people, for instance, now wrongly identified themselves as resistance fighters. While their real colleagues were still fighting, the fake resistance heroes' only goal was to teach the collaborators a lesson. They broke into their homes, smashed the furniture to pieces, looted wherever they could, dragged the collaborators out into the street, and shaved off the women's hair. The empty lions' cages of the Antwerp Zoo were promoted to jail cells. The collaborators' neighbors lustily participated in this explosion of blind revenge. But who was a real resistance hero and who was a collaborator? I have witnessed some dramatic misunderstandings.

I remember Ida, a young woman who lived across the street from me. She worked at Thys, the most renowned tearoom on the Keyserlei. During the German occupation, the clientele consisted mostly of military officers. Civilians could not afford to frequent this place as everything was rationed and much too expensive. Because the business was known for its fresh wares, the unsold pastries had to be discarded each night, and my young neighbor was given permission to take them home. Ida, who was very kindhearted, always shared the treats with the people on her street. Sometimes the neighbors would already be waiting for her as she came home from work. "Ida, come out immediately!" three men in trench coats, who had taken up positions in front of her house, now commanded. They banged their fists on the door. Behind the three a small cluster of locals formed. "We know you were fraternizing with the Germans. It's time for your punishment. Show your face or we'll break your door!" It took a little while before the fearful woman picked out from behind the curtain of a tiny upstairs window. One of the men noticed her, grabbed a cobblestone and smashed in the window. A scream . Some more silence followed. Only when the downstairs windows were broken as well, Ida came out like a timorous little mouse, her hands clasping her temples in fear, sobbing, and scared to death. She was trembling all over her body. One of the three guys grabbed her roughly and lifted her onto an open cart. A few overzealous neighbors were there to receive her and tie her hands with a thick rope. In the meantime, two of those brave trench coats, followed by a group of greedy neighborhood women and men, had already invaded her home. And while the cart took off, presumably toward the lion's cage, you could hear from the street how her possessions were disposed of. Objects of value changed ownership with lightning speed. The rest was stomped or smashed to pieces and thrown out the broken windows onto the street. Even my family and I participated in this goings-on, brainwashed as we were by the inflammatory language of repression. The same way we had also joined in the pillaging during our flight in Father's Minerva. And while we were emptying the houses of collaborators, actual or not, my sister's house on the other side of town was plundered. She, of course, was married to a "black." That "black" was the symbolic opposite of the White Brigade, the Resistance. Brother-in-law Harry promptly disappeared into the lion's cage, and so did Father, the incorrigible Anglophile. Father had to come along because his son-in-law had visited the house wearing his black uniform, so he too had to be pro-German, according to the furious mob. It is almost cynical when nowadays Jews, who were not yet born by then blamed politicians who were not born by then either that nothing had been done to save Jews from the Holocaust. Nobody seems to understand that none but the persons directly involved knew about the horror that had been going on in those extermination camps during the war when

21

numerous Jews, gypsies, gay's who's only misfortune had been that they didn't belong to the type of Aryan one lunatic and his staff had in mind. I still remember I was very jealous of the beautiful yellow stars that my Jewish playmates had to wear very visible on their coats or whatever, they were wearing. I thought it was very chic and wondered why I had to do without one. Little could I imagine that those stars were my girlfriend's passports to the German gas chambers..

And then there was the fate of the painter Lode Seghers. With a lot of brouhahas, he was arrested in his patrician dwelling on "den Oever" and taken to the Begijnenstraat where the prison was and still is. Because his neighbors had clearly seen how he received regular visits from more than one German in uniform. After three days, however, he was released. It was all too obvious that Seghers was "clean" but he had been arrested for appearance's sake. However, he was urgently requested not to show himself in the city again, as it had become be too dangerous for him due to the reprisals. He moved to Brussels, and it would take ten years before I would see him again.

I was unemployed, but fortunately not for too long. One of my aunts owned a tavern nearby an Antwerp garrison where English officers and their troops were stationed. These military men regularly came and enjoyed a pint of Belgian beer at my aunt's. I was nineteen by now and when I dropped by, one captain Philip Turner apparently took a shine to me. After some sweet talk, he asked what I did. I didn't need a vast English vocabulary to reply: "Nothing." He offered me a job in his office. If there is such a thing as a gift from heaven, this must be it, I thought gratefully. I was hired by the Royal Engineers, and soon I spoke their language like a waterfall. The whole staff turned out to hail from the same neighborhood and without knowing it I was talking like an authentic cockney, the very broad dialect of a working-class area in the heart of London. The result was not only a heavy accent but also some very colorful expressions. If they said, "Get up those apples and pears," I knew I was expected in the office on the upper floor.

However, anyway, I had a job, and I was earning money, to both my mother's satisfaction and mine. I stayed with these Brits until their building on the Belgiëlei was closed. This came about as their regiment was ordered to move to Germany. From Philip Turner, my wartime boyfriend, I never heard again.

The merry evenings in the Latin Quarter and near the bourse got underway once more. The people were the same, but they, too, now worked for the British army. The one-time connoisseurs of German cigarettes now specialized in British military hardware. Their houses had not been plundered because they inhabited villas in the posh suburbs. But, sadly, even they had not been quite delivered from German war violence. A certain Werner Von Braun had designed a device that had brought new hope to the German army. His invention was a rocket that delivered a true nightmare under the names of V-1 and V-2. Both London and our Antwerp port became the main targets of this new weapon. Flying through the air, Von Braun's brainchildren made a buzzing sound. When the buzzing stopped you knew they were about to come down. The V-1 and V-2 arrived daily. Day after day, we heard first buzzing, then nothing, and after that, an earsplitting explosion. A great number of civilians were buried under enormous heaps of rubble. Most of the victims were either found dead, or were never found at all. The reason was that the rockets would pulverize their victims with the immense heat that was generated by the blast. Everyone knew at least one person who had not survived an attack, or had "gone missing."

This new, severe threat did produce more solidarity among the population. Those who owned a bomb-proof basement invited their neighbors to take shelter there. That was also the case with our house. "They're buzzing! They're buzzing! Dolf, Victorine, may we join you?" Neighbors near and far begged my parents for a spot in the safety of our basement, which was harder to hit for the V-1's and V-2's. We occupied part of a house belonging to a sculptor. His sizable house had an equally large basement, which in no time at all, resembled the catacombs. Especially at night it was often packed to capacity. "It's dodgy, man, I can no longer sleep a wink up there," quoted Marcel, a man who lived a few blocks away. "Just imagine: you're in deep sleep, you don't hear the buzz, and before you know it you're with Our Lord!"

As strange as it may sound, it was quite cozy in that bomb shelter. Whole families nestled under blankets and everyone just made the best of it. It was there we actually learned the news of the war's end. However, the happy tidings we'd heard on the radio only penetrated our awareness for real when we marched into the inner city at night and saw the streetlights being lit at midnight. For four whole years, we had lived in the dark, with drawn curtains, the inflexible curfew, and mostly, with fear. Now we stood on the street in the middle of the night and saw all those lights ablaze! People who were still indoors tearing open the drapes and let the lights of their living rooms shine forth. It was finished, the war was over.

Chapter 5
Meat on our plates

Me and my war boyfriend Philip Turner.
Extreme left: Mariette, the girlfriend of aunt Caroline

We had to get used to our new, liberated lives. Just when most people had found their way back to the gradually well-stocked stores, and there was decent food on the table, came "Operation Gutt." Camille Gutt, a liberal politician, had been the Belgian finance minister before the war. Because of his Jewish roots–his real name was Guttenstein—he was one of the first to flee to Great Britain when war broke out. He had the power of attorney over the cashbox of the National Bank and was responsible for the payment of the salaries of the other Belgian ministers who had followed him. Even the average Belgian who had fled to England was not to want for anything, although reality did not always match this precept.

25

In attaining such a powerful position, Gutt had made quite a few political enemies. Especially with minister Jaspar he tended to collide constantly. At the onset of the war, Marcel Henry Jaspar was the minister of Public Health. In this capacity, he was also responsible for the refugees. He stayed in Paris in order to co-ordinate the flow of refugees from there. When Paris was occupied, Jaspar, too, fled to Great Britain where he formed a new government together with Camille Huysmans, the fugitive mayor of Antwerp. Four Belgian ministers, Gutt among them, had already preceded him and formed a Belgian government in exile. To his dismay, Jaspar was no longer welcome in that little group and ever since, no love was lost between Gutt and Jaspar.

After the war, Gutt was again needed in Belgium to put things back on line. He had his own vision on the matter. "Here," he said, "a whole nation has been profiteering, four years long" It was obvious that the communication media had suffered tremendously. In order to get all that money into government hands, he decreed that every Belgian had to turn in all his or her money, and would receive 2,000 new Belgian francs in return. This drastic measure knew no precedent, but Gutt had underestimated the average Belgian. No sooner recovered from the shock, then the little Belgian took on Gutt: many multiplied the size of their families two- to tenfold. On paper, all babies turned into adults requiring capital. Whole new branches of the family tree were invented, who all were entitled to those 2,000 new Belgian francs. And anyway, the official proof of this extensive genealogy had conveniently been lost in the war. And so, many managed to recover a good deal of their assets in Gutt's new money. All's well that ends well.

There was more than enough work in the reconstruction of the country. And also with the liberators, because they, too, needed all kinds of things. Just think of anything needed for construction, transportation, provisioning. There was, for instance, a daily need for fresh produce, but they could not possibly have all those items shipped from their own countries, that would have been too expensive and time-consuming. So the Allies needed to call on our local suppliers. Businessmen were clever enough to assist them with this, for a price. The black-marketing's men huge hoarded of wine were also much in demand with the liberators. On the other hand, the allied servicemen were making money on the side selling all kinds of things to our businessmen, stuff that actually belonged to the army, but that was just a detail, in their eyes.

In any case, one could now openly work for the liberators, without any fear of the Germans. And as soon as the economy was smoothed out, money started rolling again. In addition to the bourse and the Latin Quarter, a new entertainment area had sprung up, with new establishments in the Anneessensstraat, a side street of the Keyserlei near the Central Station. The Anneessenstraat soon acquired the popular nickname, Ruination Street. (Too) much money was spent there, and that was largely due to the rousing melodies of the string bands. Gypsy string bands played and sang to the guests: "Life is beautiful if you only know how to live it…" Jos van der Smissen's band was very well known there, van der Smissen was such a great virtuoso that an American officer offered him a contract with the Metropolitan in New York. Van der Smissen refused, as he suffered from fear of flying! From this day forwards, the Anneessensstraat was the place to be seen for the wealthy families. One of the establishments was called Chez Thérésie, where gorgeously dressed young ladies encouraged the customers to consume as much as possible. And so they did.

The English and Canadians stayed on for a little while after liberation, and a regiment of American troops had been installed in barracks on the other bank of the River Scheldt. The Americans called the barrack's Top Hat, after one of the hippest entertainment temples in the United States. A lot of effort was invested in the Scheldt. Fortunately, the port had remained intact; in fact, it was the only European port that was immediately operational in 1944. Now the Allies wanted to expand it even further. In any case, ships could freely enter the port once more, which was of vital importance for the economy. The Americans were no longer considered by the average citizen as coming from a foreign planet. Top Hat had become a kind of a suburb from Antwerp, numerous teenagers from the city experienced in the quarters their first romance. Their parents turned a blind eye on it, after all they were our friends and their daughters always returned home with delicacies that we even didn't remember it existed. I was one of the girls, just after they arrived and before the end of the war, I was introduced to the barracked by an officer that I met somewhere in town, don't know where, don't know when. I still remember how after years of starvation, I eat my first donut sitting on the edge of his bed. He tried what most men would try in such a situation, without much luck, I was too much brain washed about the consequences, little Americans to turn up.

My beau tried to change my mind by showing me something I even didn't know it existed, a condom. It scared the hell out of me. He explained that when he put that on his penis nothing harmful would happen to me. It didn't convince me. What if that strange thing was lost in my body? So I remained on my guards and Richard, the officer in question couldn't do anything that giving me serenades, hoping that would help. Practically everyday I went to see him and everyday he sang to me: You made me love you, I didn't want to do it. Of course he loved me, he came out of the battle fields. He would have loved everybody wearing a skirt (girls nor women didn't wear trousers at that time). There had been some moments that I had been near to surrender, at this point when flying bombs came over, we had to run for shelter, and he took me in his arms to protect me. That felt very good. However, by then there was always sheer panic, the Top Hat population was running all over the barracks, and I could hardly imagine making love for the first time in my life in front of an entire division of the American Army. After the war Richard was stationed in Germany, and I never heard from him again.

Myriam still was my close friend. Meanwhile we had moved our stomping grounds from the bourse to the Century Hotel on the Keyserlei. Its cuisine was so exquisite that it would certainly merit a few stars in the present-day Michelin Guide. Even in wartime, the menu had already been excellent. Young and ambitious as we were, we were drawn to it like flies to treacle. During the war, however, we never dared to set foot in this place, because it was common knowledge that girls who were spotted here usually had something going on with a German officer, and we did not wish to be identified with that type of young woman. Now that the war was over and the Germans were back in Germany, there was nothing left to be afraid of. The Century Hotel lured us with its charms. How important we used to feel, sitting in those plush armchairs while a headwaiter in full regalia would bring our coffee. Coffee! All we had to drink during the war was a horrid herbal infusion. However, to be honest: in the Latin Quarter and the bourse area, we had practically lived on champagne. It was the usual state of affairs there. Indeed, I remember Myriam and myself being so conditioned by that champagne that we'd have considered it beneath us to order a mere soda in a regular café. Nevertheless, here, in the splendid lobby of this magnificent hotel, a cup of coffee was just the thing. One time we sensed two middle-aged gentlemen eying us. After a while, one of them approached us and offered us…a coffee. However, we felt too self-conscious to accept his offer just like that, so Myriam and I held an emergency consultation. We huddled together like conspirators and, shielding her mouth with her hand, Myriam asked. "Do you see any other girls here?" I glanced about me in the manner of an undercover agent. "No." Myriam laughed: "It's all right, then." Reassured, she relaxed in her chair, adding, "You know, the girls who used to come here earlier all had their heads shaved!" There was no harm in chatting with an American, I thought: "That guy won't hurt us; it's so crowded here he'll have to watch his manners." Giggling, we decided that nothing prevented us from accepting the man's generosity. Now we could end our secret conference. We really felt safe in the cozy, busy hotel lobby where a musician was hammering out the latest English tunes on the grand piano. Our answer to the friendly offer was an unanimous yes. This was to be our first encounter with Warren Lutz and his colleague Al Emmett, two American business men who had been sent to Antwerp to restart General Motors at the Noorderlaan. Warren and Al behaved like gentlemen, and when they suggested giving the hotels' restaurant a try, we were all too happy to grab that rare opportunity. Warren Lutz was instructing us on the cooking of meat, and especially how it ought to be carved in order to get the most out of his flavor. For us, who had hardly seen any meat in four years, that was an almost surrealistic conversation. After that period of war, we would have eaten anything that was put in front of us. It took every bit of self-restraint not to lick the last drop of gravy of our plates in this classy restaurant ! Fortunately we managed to control our baser instincts and were invited on a second date by Al and Warren.

Chapter 6
The Sky Is The Limit

The beginning of the Club Med in Calvi (France)

The dates began to follow one another quite rapidly, taking the shape of drinks and dinners, but also of evening in Ruination Street. This situation suited the gentlemen well. Ruination Street was next door to the Century Hotel where they were staying, and consequently, Myriam and I made the acquaintance of not just the lobby and the restaurant of the hotel, but the rooms as well. You couldn't call it a passionate relationship, just one thing leading to another. We liked each other, the men were lonely without their wives, and we had steady boyfriends who were looking after us.

Through Al, I discovered something I had seen at my Top Hat Period but still never had used before, the condom. I did know now it was of general use by now, that it existed and could be obtained at the pharmacy, but I would have never dared to purchase a thing like that. I am certain my Belgian boyfriends would have looked askance at me had I turned up with something of that nature. "Leaving the church before the singing" (the withdrawal method of birth control), was the order of the day; the men adhered to it as much as possible, and after that, the women had to take care of themselves. Abortion was rampant. The addresses of doctors who did "it" and of female "angel makers" *(back-alley abortionists)* circulated both in the schools as well as at high-society tea parties, where Champagne

30

took the place of tea, as showing off one's spending power was decidedly in.

Even more GM associates arrived in Antwerp. They were to make preparations for the opening of the first showroom on the Noorderlaan, and it happened right in front of Myriam and me. We had become part of it as a matter of course. There were Warren and Myriam, and there was Al and I. Two times two made a foursome, and nobody asked any questions, not even when we were present at important meetings. Warren was director-general of the local GM establishment and Al was his right hand. Myriam and I had no official title in the business, but as we were involved in everything we knew the ins and outs. Suddenly, Al had something to tell me: "Darling, you know I'm married…" I felt black cloud gathering, "…and my wife is ill." Oh, is that all, I thought. He's looking for excuses because he's cheating on her, the poor dear! Unfortunately, he was speaking the truth, and one day, the wife's condition became so serious that Al had to return to the U.S. I shed quite a lot of tears at his departure, but he promised to come back. Meanwhile, I could go everywhere with Warren and Myriam, even to Paris. Nor did Al forget me: he regularly sent boxes of delicious foods, cigarettes, and nylon stockings. Nylons were a rarity and I wore them like jewels. However, Al was unable to tell me when he would return; his wife's health was constantly going up and down.

Apart from missing my American boyfriend, I had few worries. In addition to the outings with Warren and Myriam, I regularly frequented the Latin Quarter and the Bourse area. There I would see the same clientele, now joined by some new faces: port managers and professionals. Lawyers and notaries had discovered there was good business to be done in these establishments, and they came more and more often to get a piece of the pie. Now that war was over, the port of Antwerp was once more operating at full capacity, and its managers brought with them that typical harbor atmosphere. Coupled with the Burgundian nature of the people of Antwerp, that atmosphere injected lots of life into these entertainment areas, which were doing better than ever. I was very sensitive to that port-city atmosphere as it caused waves of nostalgia in me. I see myself as a toddler, holding hands with my mother, standing on the embankment of the River Scheldt. "Child," she said, "I would so much like to make a long voyage." But her financial circumstances never allowed it, so she could travel only in her mind to all the exotic destinations the ships were heading for. Mother

31

and I would observe with special fascination the departure of the Congo liners; that was what most affected her. Undoubtedly it was here, by the banks of the Scheldt, that my love for the city and its port was born.

Myriam and I had discovered a pub in the Seaman's Quarter. A Greek captain whom we knew from the Bourse area had taken us there one night. Greeks abroad tend to stick together like glue. Thus, Café Rhodos on the Verversrui was the gathering place of just about every Greek setting foot in Antwerp. The result was a colorful assortment : Greek families with their offspring, the crew of Greek ships that were moored here, and the neighborhood hookers who came to catch their breath between customers, aided by a cup of Greek coffee. They all danced together, shoulder to shoulder, to the tune of Greek folk music. We had loads of fun in Café Rhodos and ever since that night we went there regularly. One night we had taken along Jef Verbist. The man was a highly respected notary in Antwerp, and a real party animal. Verbist earned loads of money and spread it around most generously. He was always dressed to the nines, he was a beloved fixture of the nightlife, but nobody expected to see him in the Seaman's Quarter. I still recall how the eyes of Jerry, the Greek landlord of Café Rhodos, lit up : "A notary in my café, a real notary!". If Jerry had a red carpet, he would have rolled it out immediately, but there was no need for it: after a couple of ouzos, Jef was dancing shoulder to shoulder with a Greek sailor and a hooker. The other patrons, in a circle around the dancers, enjoyed the spectacle and clapped their hands rhythmically. I still here Verbist, who had worked up a prodigious sweat by that time, shouting "Opa ! This place is just terrific." The fun lasted until the door flew open, and we heard a voice call out, "Police Control !" Anyhow, this type of control was not that terrible in those days: more often than not the policemen ended up at the bar, a glass of ouzo in hand. However? Jef Verbist would rather not be seen there. A wooden staircase led to the living quarters and to the roof. In a second, landlord Jerry showed him the escape route : "Mr. Notary, this way, quick!". He grabbed the gentleman by the arm and nudged him toward the stairs. Meanwhile, a regular was already on his way to the neighbors to warn them that company was on the way. Myriam and I, with another volunteer pushed the inebriated Verbist up to the stairs to the roof, and from there entered the neighboring house. After which we could step out onto the street as if nothing had happened. We were still panting when the police saw us come out. However? We were emerging from the private dwelling of a dockworker's family with lots of children, and so we could not be charged with anything. "It was his lucky day" a patron remarked afterwards, "The neighbor on the other side runs a brothel...". Just to say that I had a fun, carefree time while Al in America was tending his wife on her sickbed.

The first time I traveled on my own, my destination was Chur in Switzerland. During a dinner dance at the hotel restaurant, I met Karl Heckendorn, an industrialist from Basel who was staying there with some friends. Heckendorn fell in love with me and before the holiday was over we were a couple. Karl was more a holiday sweetheart. We were together for two years. The relationship consisted mainly of letter writing and also some pleasure trips. Whenever Karl went away with friends, for instance to France, he would send me an airline ticket, so I could join him. This way we also traveled to Germany and Austria.

Vienna at the time was still divided in an American, British, French and a Russian zone. I specifically remember the caviar being delicious there, so delicious we would have it even at breakfast. Actually, I could have eaten it all day long. And it wasn't expensive, either; caviar was the only means of barter the Russian soldiers had to trade for necessities. This allowed us to eat caviar to our heart's delight for next to nothing. When I was in Heidelberg with Karl, I discovered in a *Stube* an automatic cologne dispenser. Driven by the entrepreneurial bug my Antwerp Bourse friends had infected me with, I proceeded on my return to make the rounds of Antwerp pubs, to ask if, perhaps, they would care for such a contraption. And indeed, there was plenty of interest. I contacted the supplier, asked for and received an appointment, but there was a problem: the firm was in Berlin, and that city was blockaded by the Russians. The only way you could actually enter Berlin was via the "air bridge" organized by the Americans. Airlift or air bridge was the name for a temporary air connection with Berlin in full Cold War. So the city was partitioned into American, British, French and Russian sectors. There was a road leading to the western Allied parts to provision them. When these parts introduced a shared, new currency, Stalin cut off the supply road in frustration. From June 1948 through September 1949, the Americans basically had no choice but to set up the airlift: every three minutes an airplane landed in Berlin, and fortunately I managed to find a way to get on board. In Berlin, I stayed at the Kurfürstendamm. At the end of it stood the heavily bombed

Gedächtniskirche, barely preserved; it was a place where you could still taste the war.

I made a deal with the cologne-dispenser firm, and subsequently had some success in Ruination Street, the Bourse cafés and the Latin Quarter, where many taverns wanted to have this contraption. Piece of cake, I thought. Just when I considered how easy it was to make money, black clouds gathered on the horizon in the shape of racketeers. They at once confronted me with a choice: turn over my dispensers to them, or else. They threatened me directly and I felt they were serious. I soon learned that just about the whole vending-machine trade was in the hands of gangsters, and because I was not exactly interested in a physical settling of accounts, I took the certain to the uncertain and abandoned my lucrative business. This was also the end of my first attempt to gain a foothold in the business world.

As soon as I could walk, my mother had trouble keeping me in line. She used to go for a drink now and then at the Vlaamse Kaai, where in those days, there was still a dock with ships, and, of course, water. I had the annoying tendency to run repeatedly to the edge of that dock, so my mother decided to sign me up for swimming lessons at age 5, before I could drown. That was only possible at the AZC, the Antwerp Swimming Club, in the Lange Gasthuisstraat. The swimming teacher on duty was Maurice Blitz, rather well known as a water-polo player. Together with his brother Gerard he won silver in the 1920 and 1924 Olympics! According to my mother's decision, I was dangled in the water regularly, by a hook held by Maurice Blitz who meanwhile kept yelling at me how to move my little arms and legs. It worked. I learned how to swim, although I'd never really turn into a water animal. In the meantime, Mother was having a good time in the swimming pool's cafeteria, so we kept on going there. Maurice was always to be found there as a friendly face, but when the war broke out, he disappeared from our site. Although his last name sounded like German, he had Jewish roots. That was quite common, as many Jews had originally come from Germany. In any case Maurice, in his forties by then, had to go underground. I was overjoyed for unexpectedly run into him on the street one day, after the Liberation. Thank God he had survived. I ran up to him and gave him a heartfelt hug. "Oh you silly thing, look here, I'm going to cry in a minute!" he teased, but I saw his eyes were tearing up for real. "I'm just here for a visit, but I actually live in Corsica," he said. "I'm a bartender in the holiday resort of Calvi." I smiled, happy that things were going well for him. "Why don't you drop by some time, eh?" he added. I had no idea if I'd be able to do that, but in any case, we exchanged addresses.

A girl from one of the pubs came and sat next to me in my familiar hangout near the old Bourse. "Paula dear, I'm just dying to go away for a bit, I don't care where, but I have to get out of here!" No sooner had she uttered those words than I felt a pleasant current running through my body, because of course I immediately thought of Maurice Blitz's new abode! We combined our savings and soon Jenny and I were sitting in the plane to Nice, from where we continued by ferry to our destination: Calvi, Corsica. We financed our trip with the tips we had hoarded. On busy days, we liked to help out at the Bourse pubs so that we'd collected a tidy sum in no time at all.

Calvi, situated on a bay, is a historical town built around a fortress. Blitz worked at a resort that was called Club Méditerranée due to its location. Club Méditerranée was indeed nicely situated in the middle of the bay but the resort was not much more than a number of primitive tents , inherited from a previous owner who ran a sports club. The club was intended mainly for French workers. From 1936 onward, when Leon Blum introduced the paid vacation, they could spend their leisure time there. Club Méditerranée had now been supplemented with a few American army tents. There were a couple of open-air showers that most of the time didn't work. The guests dined at long wooden tables with bowls full of olives. We didn't stay long because the hard benches were uncomfortable to sit on. Maurice welcomed us from behind an improvised wooden bar, his workstation. Maurice was there with his son Gérard, also a water-polo player, and his daughter Didy, a Jill-of-all-trades at the camp. Her two toddlers had plenty of room to play and grandpa Maurice adored his grand kids.

If the amenities were disappointing, the guests were anything but. They were, for the most part, unmarried Frenchmen in their twenties. Here and there, one came across a Brit, but we were the only Belgian girls. On the weekend, a boat arrived from Nice. All of us stood on the quay to welcome the newcomers and at the same time wave out those who were leaving, even if that was sometimes less pleasant. Jenny and I soon had such a close friendship with the guests that it felt like saying goodbye to our own relatives.

The boat from Nice was a major attraction. Furthermore, Maurice organized beach games. Simple though they were sometimes, they were always fun. Everyone felt so at home in the camp that it didn't occur to anyone to change for dinner. We simply dined in our swimsuits.

Some days before our departure, Maurice organized an endurance competition. The intrepid participants would be taken to the old town in a van and would have to return to the camp... swimming. The distance, as the crow flies, was nearly three miles. Among the twenty candidates were three girls. Blitz wanting an international competition, he had persuaded some Englishmen to participate, and we too, were in demand. Jenny didn't know how to swim, so I alone was left. Moreover, a French buddy was pressing me so hard that I couldn't possibly refuse. I even felt challenged to defend my country's honor, and so I became the fourth girl on the list of candidates. I was taken aback by Maurice's promotional talents, because when we arrived in Calvi, it was crowded beyond belief. The whole town had turned out to see the crazy people who were about to swim across the bay.

"The four girls in front!" Blitz shouted. His protective reflex toward the weaker sex appeared to be in overdrive, and again I felt I was being put to the test, this time as a representative of that weaker sex. Behind us stood the twenty young men, rearing to go. In the water lay little boats manned by local youths. They would follow us and pick us up when we became exhausted. The crews lacked any kind of experience whatsoever, and the boats were just about ready for the dump, but we still managed to feel good about it. Poof! The starting pistol was fired and we all jumped into the brine.

In the beginning, it was not too bad, after all I did use to belong to a swimming club, and had swum across the dock in Antwerp. However, this was a different kettle of fish. Soon it appeared as if I was not moving even one yard ahead. A tree on the shore that I was keeping my eye on remained stubbornly in the same position. And it was damn hard to stay in the course. Splashing sounds behind and beside me indicated that some swimmers already had enough of it, and I saw them being pulled on board the little boats by their arms and legs. This swimming is taking forever, I thought, while I carried on, panting. After the three other girls had given up, I was the only female left in the race, and after what seemed like hours, just when I thought my lungs were about to burst, land came in sight. A little later I could see the spectators awaiting the arrival on shore. The remaining male swimmers were preparing for the "end spurt." I could hear how they extracted the last bit of strength from their nimble bodies. I'm sure the best man won, although I don't remember who that was. After their much-applauded arrival, I kept on swimming bravely by myself. Suddenly, my French friend came running back into the water to encourage me. He was not allowed to help me, though, or I would forfeit my prize. The rules said that the swimmers had to reach the shore under their own power up to the spot where they could stand up in the water. So my friend shouted me onward: "Allez Paula! Encore un peu. Presque fini!" (*Go, Paula! Just a little more. Almost done!*). I was totally out of breath when I heard him yell: "Tu es arrivéeeeeee!" (You're theeeere!). I felt him pull me up by my arm. My totally waterlogged feet finally touched firm ground, but no sooner did I realize that I had made it, then I collapsed with exhaustion back into the water. My legs were no longer able to carry me. Filled with masculine pride, my friend lifted me up and carried me over to the jury in his arms. Still somewhat dizzy, but proud as a peacock, I received my diploma of "nageuse de demi-fond" (middle-distance swimmer). I had saved the honor of the females *and* of Belgium.

Not long afterwards, the Club Mediterranée Association was officially founded in Paris. Club Med, the lifework of Maurice Blitz, his son Gérard, and their associates were a fact. In 1950, the first Club Med village opened its doors on the Balearic Islands, preparing the way for the further conquest of the world.

Chapter 7
In Search Of A Man

Some months after my Corsican adventure, Al wrote to say his wife had passed away. He would return to Antwerp to continue his work for General Motors there…and to see me. What a strange feeling, I thought suddenly, to know that Al is a free man now. The situation opened up new perspectives. Once upon a time I had declared to my father that I was going to make it in life, and marriage to a man like Al could be a giant step in that direction. So I eagerly awaited his return and especially his phone call. With the crucial moment expected to arrive any time now, Al suddenly seemed to have disappeared… Days passed before Al finally gave a sign of life. He asked if he could talk to me. His words made me very nervous, and it seemed like Al had turned into someone else. I reassured myself: of course it is because, recently widowed, he's been going through a lot. When I saw him enter the Bourse café where we had agreed to meet it was not like before. Al had indeed changed and we suddenly seemed like strangers to each other. He approached me timidly: "Hi, how are you?" I nodded, I was O.K., although I knew right away I was not. Al was friendly enough, but not really enthusiastic, I thought. He continued: "You need to know this: I've married Alice, a good friend of my wife's. She was so supportive." If the sky had a roof, it was caving in on me at this moment. I was totally perplexed, speechless. I spent quite a while in that Bourse café, staring in front of me. I never even noticed that Al had left. Did he say anything else? Did he stroke my hair? Smile? I didn't know. I felt separated from reality; the world looked to me like a misshapen bowl. Some time later I thought: if he had told me earlier how close he was with that woman, I might have understood, perhaps, but now… I stood in front of the mirror in my parents' living room, and I remember shouting at that mirror: "Cowardice, Mister Al, is something I never could tolerate!" I sank into a chair and burst into tears. Yet, life went on. Earth does not stop turning in spite of stinging, searing heartache. The rhythm of daily life slowly took me back into reality and somehow I found the strength to take my life back into my own hands. For years, Al lived in Antwerp with his second wife. I even ran into them regularly, alone, in Ruination Street. At the end they remained good friends, until their return to America.

38

That short period of time when I was contemplating marriage had triggered something in my head. I had been a party animal for years, but my vow to my father, to go further than he in life, had lodged itself deeply in my mind. In order to reach my goal, I knew I had to go in search of a man who answered certain criteria. Unfortunately, all the men in my circle of acquaintance were married, and those who were not probablyweren't marriage material, anyway. So, I needed to expand my field of operations.

Maybe Suske can help, I thought.

At the corner of Ruination Street and Station Street, there was a large brasserie. Suske, the owner, had been raised as an orphan by one of my aunts, which made us somewhat related. He was forty by now, still a bachelor and into special things. As in printing counterfeit money. He accomplished this feat in his apartment above the brasserie on a printing press he had somehow managed to get hold of. Suske got caught regularly and spent time in jail equally often. His little suitcase containing pajamas and slippers was always packed and ready for the next occasion. Arriving in the big house for the umpteenth time, he would call out cheerfully, "Guys, I'm back," but each time he would be back at his station in no time at all. Probably, nobody took him seriously as a counterfeiter.

One day, Suske was sitting in a café in the Lange Lozana Street. With a big bag of fake money, he was waiting for a man who failed to turn up. Suske wanted to phone the latecomer, but thought it too dangerous to do so from the café. So, he decided to go and find a payphone, and in the meantime he stashed away the bag full of money on top of the wall-mounted water tank of the café toilet. However, the little restroom window was open and a neighbor could see what was happening there from her balcony. She promptly notified the police: "Something fishy's going on in the toilet of the café." The law snapped into action, reached the place in record time, found the bag, and confiscated it. Upon returning, Suske noticed the bag was gone. "Has anyone here seen a bag?" he asked the people present in the café. With a twinkle in her eye, the landlady proceeded to tell him what had happened, whereupon Suske hoofed it to the police station, threw to open the door, and announced in loud voice, "Gentlemen, I've come to report the theft of my fake money." Thus, Suske ended up behind bars again.

When he did happen to be at his brasserie, I would go to Suske's for a drink on a Sunday. His café, by the way, was the only one on Ruination Street that was already open from noon. When I privately confided to him, I was ready for a man who was free, young, with lots of dough, and of good family, Suske immediately promised to help me. He kept his promise, and even mobilized just about the whole Station Quarter for the cause. Soon after, he called me with the message that my ship had come in. The "victim's" name was Frederic – Freddy – Grisar, a scion of the Grisar line, which was, like the Kreglingers and Osterrieths, a family of German businessmen who'd been living in Antwerp for many years and were counted among the top of the high society. The Grisars belonged to a number of families that had successfully swarmed out all over Europe since 1100. Freddy's father, Pierre Grisar, owned a large shipping company and chaired a great number of associations. His son and I would meet on a neutral territory, to wit, in Suske's brasserie. It ended up clicking, too, and Freddy and I continued to see each other. Even so, the man never mentioned getting engaged or married. It's probably me, I thought, I must be too impatient. Meanwhile I was passing my time with visits to the movie theater and sampling food and drink, mostly in Freddy's company. He wanted to follow in his father's footsteps, but somehow it didn't quite work out. I could see why: his father had a particularly impressive résumé; a man like that was not easy to emulate. I hoped my boyfriend would somehow find his way, professionally as well as privately, and the sooner, the better. Nevertheless, time passed and still there was no talk of an engagement. My patience ran out and I broke off our "relationship." When I told him, Freddy looked at me with a half smile, not really knowing how to react, but he didn't seem floored by my revelation: "I'll think it over," he said. To my surprise, he did. Eventually, he arranged to be given a villa in Kapellen by his father, where he and I could live together. It was also a way for his parents to slowly get to know me, although shacking up without the benefit of marriage was just not done in those days, not even in my eyes, and so I decided to discuss the matter with father Pierre.

However, nobody seemed to know where Pierre Grisar spent his leisure time. After quite a bit of sleuthing, I found out that he, a reserve officer, acted as a sponsor to the army cadets and would be present at their upcoming party. My sister Blanche and her "black husband," who had long since been released from the lion's cage, had a connection with the cadets through some military association, and this way I easily obtained an invitation. Elena, the wife of the sea captain who had introduced me to Café Rhodos back in the day, went to the party with me. I spotted him, as soon as we walked in: the great Pierre Grisar, a charming, chain-smoking, fifty-something and lover of female beauty. Through this particular hobby of his, we ladies soon landed at his table. Grisar cast his eye on my companion, who indeed was a looker, but my boyfriend's dad barely noticed me. After the requisite number of whiskies, he tried to get a date, but that didn't fly with the faithful Elena. "Serves you right," I laughed inwardly. This rejection made Grisar bite the dust, but me as well, because now I no longer had a pretext to meet with him again. My brain cells were working at a full speed, and I quickly whispered in Elena's ear, "Don't worry, I'll go to the rendez-vous in your place." The ruse worked, and I felt quite relieved to hear how she accepted Grisar's amorous proposition. Now I would be able to talk to him in private.

Chapter 8
Man Found.
Mission Accomplished

I can still see the look on his face when I, and not Elena, arrived at the rendez-vous. "What are you doing here?" he asked, inspecting me with great suspicion. Under his scrutiny, I felt like some kind of yucky insect. "Mr. Grisar, my friend does not wish to deceive her husband for anything in the world; she is Greek and feels very strongly about marital fidelity, that's why I've come in her place. I think you're a nice man, you see..." My confession seemed to please him and his gaze softened. With the addition of a couple of drinks, it turned into a nice evening. Grisar started telling jokes, time flew by, and I completely forgot the reason why I was there. When, days later, I did recall it, I could have hit myself. However, there was still hope: Grisar Senior had given me his office phone number that night, so I could call him there. Unfortunately, we didn't have a telephone at home; my only option was the pay phone at the grocery store. So be it, I thought, and nervously I dialed the number on the wall-mounted rotary phone. But, my goodness, it was not Grisar but a female voice that answered. 'M-m-madam, could I talk to Mr. Grisar? It's very urgent!" No sooner did she hear my name than she hung up on me. Disappointed, I walked out of the store, but the following day I tried again, and again the day after, and so I kept trying day after day to phone the man I was determined to talk to. I wouldn't give up until I had Frederic's father on the other end of the line. My stubbornness cost me a lot of nickels, but one day my luck changed, and I heard Grisar's voice. Unfortunately, his message was not very promising: "Look here, girl, I am a very busy man. Got it?" A click and the conversation was over.

Still, hearing his voice had given me fresh courage. So, every day I went back to the little store to give it another try. Two months passed. Sometimes, my persistence felt frightening even to myself, but that devilish claim I'd made in front of my father drove me to this phone stalking. I called Grisar's office every day at ten A.M., until, completely fed up with my little game, he at last deigned to talk to me: "Have your way, you annoying girl. Where and when?" I was triumphant, Grisar wanted to meet me! I did feel somewhat uneasy: my telephone calls had been part of my daily routine for months, and now that was over. However, I had won and that was what counted. Much later, he told me he had intended at that time to get rid of me once and for all…

The momentous encounter was to take place at Theresie's, an establishment in Ruination Street populated with classy dames who knew how to make men spend their money. Geisha's with deep pockets, I called them. Pierre Grisar had expected me to take flight after one look at this decadent goings-on, but that did not happen. On the contrary, I considered it a challenge!

Grisar's disappointment didn't last long. He very much enjoyed the geishas' antics. Soon he was in his cups, and it took a while for him to notice me again. I had remained sober, as nobody had offered me a drink. He wobbled in my direction and asked me to take him home. He lived in Quellin Street, which was walking distance. And so I left with Grisar draped around my neck like a sack of potatoes, and delivered him to his front door. The next day I called to find out if he was all right. This time he did not hang up, but thanked me extensively and even invited me to dinner. Things do change, I reflected happily. The date went smoothly and many others followed. The better I got to know him, the more my respect for him grew. Throughout my life, I have admired businessmen. My father, too, was an outstanding businessman and, despite our various differences of opinion, I always admired that side of him. Grisar was the best thing that ever happened to me. Before long I became his official mistress. In those days and in those circles, this was the normal procedure. Mistresses where part of marriages of convenience; they openly accompanied their men everywhere. The wives not only knew about it, but often had a young lover of their own. Without that I even realized it Pierre gave me a very adequate education in how to behave, and most of all he made me aware of the huge difference between being a girl friend of a married man and his perfect mistress. At his service and in command. That is how he wanted it – and so many other men with him, as I was going to find out. Pierre also gave me the wonderful feeling that we were not cheating. He learned me furthermore that being a mistress only suits women who are not looking for a commitment in a relationship. He learned me that being in love, doesn't necessary mean being jealous of another partner. In the contrary there could be a kind of secret understanding. A surplus value for everyone involved. Although he didn't say it in so many words, there was no question that he would leave his wife, and I accepted that. Before long Pierre and I were in love with each other, what do I say I worshiped him . And he, he was working on what was to become my future. If I would become a perfect mistress at that time, and later I had to do it according to certain rules.

Pierre could speak Dutch but was actually Francophone, and we conducted our lovemaking in the language of Molière. Apart from teaching me French, he took care to expand my cultural horizons, and like a true Professor Higgins, he wanted me to become his very own "Fair Lady." He believed in me and showed it, causing my self-confidence to grow day by day. My knowledge of a second and third language proceeded more slowly. I had a habit of mixing up French and English that caused Pierre to exclaim more than once in despair, "Before long I'll be talking like gibberish, to!" But that never came to pass. What did happen to be that I fell in love with my "professor" and his son disappeared from my emotional landscape. Frederic, by the way, had given up on his aim to follow in his father's footsteps. He enlisted in the Foreign Legion and was sent to Vietnam where he fought at Dien Bien Phu. Only much later I would learn that, thankfully, he'd survived that adventure.

Although Pierre Grisar was in his late fifties, he became my lover and my mentor. That he was the same Grisar who, during the war, was part of the Belgian Government in exile I came to know much later. Like every Belgian government minister of those days, including Camille Huysmans, he was a Masonic Grand Master. He was a perfect teacher, sharing with me the ins and outs of what transpired in his company, Grisar & Marsily. Through him, I learned all there was to know about the port and everything connected with it. I was with him when he had refrigerated hangars built for his Belgian New Fruit Wharf (a very daring business move at the time), and saw him create the American Belgian Association. At the time of the Suez crisis in 1956, I witnessed his distress when ships were forced to sail around the Cape of Good Hope. He expected this crisis to cause serious financial trouble for his company. Produce from the east coast of Africa was normally transported via the Suez Canal to the Mediterranean and onward to Antwerp. The closing of the Suez Canal meant that ships had to make a detour of thousands of miles, rounding the southern tip of

Africa, to reach Belgium via the Atlantic Ocean. The result was a gigantic loss of time and money, and the newly built storage remained empty until a political solution was found. The crisis could bring about the end of Grisar & Marsily, and the loss of hundreds of jobs for his employees. One day, Madame Grisar arrived at her husband's office and put a signed document in front of him. Surprised, Grisar stared at the paper, put on his silver-rimmed spectacles and read: "I hereby donate my jewelry collection, consisting of ...," followed by a long list of the priceless pieces in Mrs. Grisar's possession. Some were centuries-old, invaluable heirlooms. Grisar was deeply moved by this extremely generous gesture and warmly embraced his wife. As soon as I heard about it, I was ready to contribute my own modest savings, as well. However, Grisar magnanimously refused both our offers, and fortunately things turned out all right.

Problems had a very strange effect on Pierre; in times of crisis, he felt the need to visit prostitutes. Thérésie's would also do, as long as he could get rid of his stress, which apparently required some kind of feminine ministrations. Before any crucial business meeting, he first walked by the "girls in the windows" of the Korte Nieuwstraat, a short distance from his office. I put up with it; Higgins had educated me to accept it, but sometimes I landed in weird situations because of this compulsion. Like the time Pierre had stopped at a brothel near the railway station. It was an expensive place but this time they had sent him an exorbitant bill, for that sum, he could have treated the whole city of Antwerp to champagne. Pierre asked me to drop by the house in question and have them double-check the invoice. Nice, I thought, I have to do the dirty work! However, Pierre's intentions were above board; as a freemason he wanted to teach me how to respond to unusual challenges. And so I willingly headed for the bordello.

It was fairly early in the day, and I had to ring the bell several times before a sleepy-eyed girl appeared at the door. When I asked to see her boss, she mumbled something in a language I didn't understand, but suddenly I heard a man's voice asking from behind a curtain what the matter was. In response to her answer, two bodybuilder types in crumpled pajamas emerged. I still don't know who was more surprised, they, seeing a young woman in business attire at the door, or I, who had – with eyes like saucers - landed in a world so totally unfamiliar. I got over my awkwardness and explained the reason for my visit. The fellows grumbled and looked daggers at me. I had disturbed their sleep, not a laughing matter to them. I just remained standing there with the bill in my hand; it was all I could do, as I was rigid with fear. After some ponderous mutual consultation, they came to the conclusion that Pierre was quite a good customer, and solved the matter in their own way: they crossed out the last zero of the invoice amount, opened the door and told me to leave the premises at once. I didn't need to be told twice and hurried back to Grisar in a daze.

Chapter 9
My Fair Lady

Pierre Grisar

"Higgins" was pleased with the first performance of his "Fair Lady." His "education" was beginning to yield results. *"All the way, you and I"* now became our slogan. I also learned a lot about his business transactions, and all the while he kept polishing me, mostly without my even noticing it. An approving pat on the shoulder from him had become my main goal in life. As time passed, the glory days of the Bourse and the Latin Quarter had come to an end.

In 1954, an 18-year-old French girl named Françoise Sagan turned the literary world on its head. Her book, *Bonjour Tristesse* ("Hello, Sadness") was an immediate, international success, and she became the talk of the town. Françoise Sagan was the first author to describe sexual love from the woman's point of view. And if that was a revolutionary topic in those days, the fact that this was the brainchild of an eighteen-year old girl from a respected Christian family was the real shocker. Like everyone else I read the book and found it quite exciting. And with my newfound self-confidence I figured I could emulate it. I already had the whole story in my head: it was going to be autobiographical (I was still young but my life had been eventful) and in French! Everybody around me thought I was going nuts – I had learned some French by then but certainly not enough to write a book, they said. Pierre was the only one who believed I could pull it off, and so I started my heroic act. With the French Larousse dictionary like a faithful dog beside me, I sat down at the kitchen table, and I started to write. No, it was not easy, but I would show them what this Antwerp girl was made of. Progress was slow, but one fine day, to my own surprise, my romanticized autobiography was complete. I gave it the title, *La Route Sinueuse*, the Sinuous Road. It was about my love for Pierre, whom I had christened Philippe in the story. I generously included my other alliances, like the story of Alexander, an in-between boyfriend, who had invited me to his home in Scheveningen to ride horses. I had never been on horseback, but I'd kept mum about that detail. Once in Scheveningen, I tried to save myself by claiming I had forgotten to bring the appropriate attire. "No problem," he said helpfully, "You can borrow my sister's riding gear." And there I stood in the riding stable, in someone else's riding clothes, in person with a very large horse. I hadn't the faintest idea how to get on top of that animal. A stable boy who had trouble suppressing his laughter came to my rescue and gave me a hand. I placed my foot in his palm and swung myself all the way over, landing on the ground on the other side of the horse. After a few more attempts, I finally got it right and Alexander and I rode out to the dunes accompanied by a group of young ladies on horseback. Walk, canter, gallop, and many variations of this routine; the well-trained animals were indefatigable. Sooner or later, all the other girls fell off their horses, but I clenched my teeth, held onto the manes of Scampolo—that was the horse's name—and stayed in the saddle throughout that wild ride. In *The*

Sinuous Road Alexander asked me afterward: "Valentine, - the name I gave myself in the story, do you know why the other women fell? It's because they were scared, and a horse can feel that. You will make a marvelous rider some day," he said, "because you have no fear." In this somewhat pastoral way I had Alexander summarize the reality of those early days of my life. In the book I returned to Philippe (Pierre) after this interlude. After a fairly convoluted intrigue, Valentine got engaged to François, Philippe's son. The brand-new couple then went on vacation to the French Riviera. Upon their return, they learned Philippe was financially in dire straits (due to the Suez-crisis). Philippe's wife, convinced it was Valentine who had ruined her husband, left him. Although engaged to the son, Valentine longed to reunite with the father and revealed her true feelings to François. Her fiancé, chivalrous and generous to a fault, set her free, and she looked up Philippe who passionately embraced her. In passing, Valentine also found out that Philippe's financial problems had now disappeared; they married and lived happily ever after. The end.

Still following in Françoise Sagan's footsteps, I needed to find a publisher in Paris. It took some time before I figured out how to do that, but I became aware of a very famous French magazine in those days, *Les Nouvelles Littéraires* ("The Literary News"). Publishers would sometimes search for new, young writing talent in its pages, and so I came across an ad from the Parisian publishing house Hachette, which was indeed accepting new authors. I queried them and they asked me to send my work. Within one week, they replied that they liked it, and they asked me to come see them in their office in Paris. General consternation . I felt equally happy and panicky. I took the train to Paris and first made a stop at the salon of Fernand Aubry, hairdresser to the stars – I had read about him in a movie magazine. Only when I was certain I looked at my best did I go to my meeting at Hachette's. To my surprise, everything went smoothly from then on: I walked into the office and sat down at the invitation of the director, whose name I have long forgotten. He assured me he was happy to have me join his team, and handed me a contract to sign, on which I placed my signature with as much importance as I could muster. I walked out with a signed agreement in my pocket and the assurance that they intended to introduce my book as "Book of the Day" in their pavilion at Expo'58, the 1958 World's Fair that was about to open its doors in Brussels. This was much more than I had ever dreamed of, and I traveled home in the train feeling elated. Hachette wanted me to select a pseudonym; eventually, I came up with Perrine Marick. I had chosen the first name with great care. Literally, *perinne* means little stone, little Pierre (after my beloved) and Marick resembled Marckx but sounded more artistic.

Before long, I proudly held a copy of my book, *La Route Sinueuse*, in my hands. The publisher presented it to the press, and the papers called me "Antwerp's Françoise Sagan." It was indeed the story of a liberated young woman from Antwerp, but luckily they did not ask about my age, because I was already 33 at the time, and so no match for seventeen-year-old Sagan. However, I could relax: my ambitious goal had been reached. I was interviewed by Jan Walravens, at that time one of the editors of the daily paper, *Het Laatste Nieuws*: "Miss Marick, could you tell us who your favorite authors are?" Caught unprepared, I brashly stated: "I never read because, ... I don't want to be influenced by anyone." Thinking of my feet, I was. There were autographing sessions all over Belgium and also in Paris. Soon after, the World's Fair opened its doors and my book and I were drawing crowds at the Hachette pavilion.

Among those present was DinoVastapane, owner of the Martini firm, and brother of the flamboyant man who would, many years later, make the newspapers for his dealings with Sobelair. After visiting the Italian pavilion, Vastapane had come to have a look at the French one. The name "Martini" was well known in those days, not just as a brand name an aperitif but also for his mentorship of young talent in the French show business. Big names like Juliette Gréco and Françoise Hardy were among his discoveries. The company had offices in Brussels, first at the Avenue Joseph II, and later, of course, in the Martini Tower on the Place Rogier.

In Antwerp, Martini worked with Brasserie Métropole in the Leysstraat. Vastapane was the mentor of the French-language showbiz, but now he began to question me about my ambitions, and together with another gentleman, he proposed to promote my book. Thus I became Martini's first literary protégée. At my launch party in the Joseph II office, several Flemish journalists like Carlo Segers and Bernard Henry were also present. Henry was famous for his travelogues in the series "Visa pour le Monde" (Visa for the World). As I got to know these gentlemen better I'd go for a drink with them once in a while. At the bar, Segers said to me casually: "You should be a journalist, have you ever given any thought to that?" Of course I had thought of it, but I didn't know how to go about it! Henry came up with a solution: "We will back you, as long as you can manage to write six stories and get them published."

I was definitely interested because I loved to write. When I was very young, I used to invent whole movie scenarios in which I mentally cast all the big Hollywood stars. However, my parents had nipped my writer ambitions in the bud by trying to force me into an office job at the Town Hall. Journalism was not taught anywhere in Belgium at the time, but now Henry and Segers were giving me this opportunity, and provided me with sponsors who were ready to back my application to the Press Association in Brussels. If the plan succeeded, I would receive a press pass and become a real, professional reporter. However, first I had to fulfill my obligations toward the Martini firm. Not that I minded; after all, that allowed me to meet Paul Anka. We were introduced to each other at the bar of the Hotel Métropole. He was only eighteen years and had just released his world-famous hit, "Diana," . He was about to go on a tour of Russia and Egypt. Before the press hounds descended on him, I had the chance to have a little chat with him. Anka was a down-to-earth guy without any pretensions, and, it turned out, with Jewish roots.

Soon after, Vastapane took me along to Paris. First he took me for lunch at a restaurant Place Concorde. Next to our table Rita Hayworth was enjoying her steak. Vastapane knew her and we were introduced. I was sitting next to the famous 'Gilda' with her red hair as a flaming brand, and I was not even conscious that I was talking to a movie legend. She was very easy to approach. Maybe because I was with Vastapane she mistook me for a celebrity. Later he took us to "La Terrasse Martini" on the Champs Elysées. There I realized at the fullest the reach of Vastapane's realm; I heard him on the phone with Michel Piccoli, talking down to the famous actor, as if he were a little boy in need of his advice. He also oversaw the business angle of the careers of Anouk Aimé, Yves Montand, and Serge Gainsbourg. And my book? It was selling like hot cakes.

By now, Antwerp had forgotten all about Lode Seghers and his German friends. So the coast was clear for Lode to move back to the city. In the meantime, he had become a respected and well-connected art historian. After all these years, I ran into him while shopping and told him about Pierre Grisar. And I told Pierre about Lode. Pierre approved wholeheartedly of my friendship with an interesting man like Lode Seghers. And anyway, art had to be part of the education he was giving me.

Once the hoopla around the book had calmed down, I could focus on the promise of journalism. I needed to get six published assignments, which was not easy without a press pass. Nevertheless, Pierre and Lode were very helpful: Grisar&Marsily, Pierre's company, published a magazine, The Link. I could contribute to that for a start. Lode introduced me to Jos Van den Eynde of the daily Volksgazet. He, too, committed to accepting an article that would be published in the group's magazine, ABC. And then there were Lode's friends: Albert Maertens Director-General of Het Laatste Nieuws and Wilfried Somville, owner of the Gazet van Antwerpen. Lode also came up with interesting topics. One of his ideas was to devote an article to the hostesses of Expo '58. The idea of a hostess, the way it was used at the Expo, was unique in the world at that time. People had become accustomed to flight attendants, but women acting as hostesses at events were as yet non-existent. The organizers of Expo'58 had a hard time finding trained applicants. Only the daughters of the upper crust were sufficiently well versed in etiquette to play the role. So the hostesses were recruited from that social group. One of them was Ingrid Jansens; later she became director of the "Bouwcentrum" (Antwerp Convention Center). Another was Austrian-born Eva Maria, who made a career in Flanders as a singer of light classical music and married Ludo Dierickx, soon to be a "green" politician. During Expo '58 these young ladies and their peers, in elegant yellow uniforms, welcomed ministers, ambassadors and other personalities. I wrote my first article about them. Lode, just like Pierrre Grisar wanted me to make it in this world. Where he could help – with all his connections – was to have my articles published in Newspapers all over Europe. He wrote for a number of them as an art critic, but he had the impression, I was not quite ready for the job. After all I had no schooling experience, and he wanted me to be somebody special. I realize that but as a result he always corrected my articles, and finally it wasn't me anymore, and it gave me the feeling that I was a lousy writer. There were Pierre observed me from behind the screen Lode wanted to be part of it. It was not before I wrote my biography – together with Anne – that I realized that I knew how to write, and I did not need a trained man, or whoever to tell me how to do it.

My next subject was more complicated. ABC sent me to Morocco to interview a Belgian, Leopold Houben. He had been living there for ten years, from the moment that Tangiers had been declared a Free Zone at the Paris Conference. Fluent in several languages, Leopold, together with a few other Belgians, had been selected to supervise the police force. Because of his imposing physique, the locals called him "The Tall Belgian." Commander Houben was well liked among the Arabs; the following excerpt from my article explains why. I cite: *"Walking in the souks, Commander Houben shakes hands with the Mohammedan tradesmen who greet him by touching their hearts. They have cause for gratitude. He taught them discipline and made Tangiers the cleanest city in all of Morocco. He assigned the merchants a fixed place and fought corruption."* End of the quote.

I almost got cold feet at the time of departure because I had never been to Africa before! But I pulled myself together and flew to Casablanca where I wrote an additional story on "Everyday life in Morocco". From there I took a train to Tangiers. Moroccan trains had no less than four different classes and every non-African traveled in first class because "In the lower class you risk your life," I was told. But first class seemed kind of boring to me and in Casablanca station I sought out an official. I brandished a letter given to me by the editor-in-chief of ABC, and it worked : he gave me permission the visit the other classes accompanied by the conductor. For safety reasons the coaches of the different classes were not connected to each other. We had to wait until the train stopped in order to access a coach of a different class on the platform. I was traveling on a night train and outside it was raining cats and dogs, which made me feel rather uncomfortable. Whenever the train became too wobbly, it was impossible to hold on to the handrails because they were so greasy that my hands keep slipping off. Classes two and three were not to bad, but in class four I understood why it was considered so dangerous : there was no light in this part of the train ! I stayed close to the conductor who used a flashlight to get around. He beseeched me not to make any photographs; it seemed like he didn't feel too safe himself. The light of his torch fell on drunken sailors and other unpleasant mugs, with in between them black-veiled women, some breastfeeding their swaddled babies. In this fourth class, the conductor didn't dare to ask to see the tickets. He, and I, might have been thrown out of the moving train and nobody would have known about it. I felt relieved to be able to get back in my first class carriage at the next station. Finally we arrived at Tangiers. Commandant Houben was waiting for me, overjoyed to welcome someone bringing the latest news from his homeland. He invited me to stay at his house for a few days and I readily agreed: he lived in a lovely seaside villa. Rather unexpectedly, I scooped up a lurid story, and wasn't that the whole point of my trip ? The last evening of my visit I sat down to dinner with the family when the Commander was called to action. There was some trouble in the red-light district. My host invited me to tag along, which I gratefully accepted. Out of the blue, I got a close-up view of the brothels of Tangiers. When we arrived on the scene, nothing untoward was happening. All the girls sat nicely in their rooms. Occasionally, customers objecting to the house rules disturbed the peace, and the "Tall Belgium" was summoned to sort things out. My idea of North African brothels was influenced by the movies I had seen, like Pépé le Mokko, so I expected to see white slaves, but there was not a single white woman in sight. The Tangiers brothels were closed houses with local girls who were completely naked, except for their faces. It would have been immodest for them to show their mouths...

When I arrived back in Belgium. I had my six stories and was granted a press pass.

Chapter 10
High Society

My first steps into High Society

My life with Pierre went on as usual, in as much as our activities could be called "usual." Aside from our very passionate relationship, Pierre and I frequented all the trendy restaurants of the moment. That was part of the game plan: we had to be seen together. Many an evening ended in the Nocturne, a tavern in Ruination Street owned by Jos Vandersmissen, a gifted violinist who had become a something of a national monument.

Later, his son Walter would also become famous as a musician in Flanders. While Vandersmissen took a little break,

Lode Seghers, too, began to introduce me to his circle of acquaintances. Lode was handsome, had charisma, was funny and was always there for me when I needed him. Maybe that was the reason why, to my own surprise, I never fell in love with him: I never had to fight for him. However, Lode was in love with me, he told me later, from the moment, I first took off my clothes for him. Being a professional artist with high ethical standards, he never revealed his feelings toward a seventeen-year-old innocent. And as long as I was with Grisar, Lode remained a perfect gentleman. It was Lode, who would introduce me to the cream of Europe. This was something Lode and Pierre had in common; both wanted only the best for me. In return for his kindness, I became Lode's personal driver. I had a car and he hated driving. I drove him all over Belgium and across the borders, too. Not only did I enjoy the driving, but our trips together allowed me to cover interesting, and sometimes foreign, news items. I also discovered that the high society allowed only two other human "species" to penetrate their own, closely guarded circles: professional artists and journalists. We made the perfect team. The first noble family we went to visit was that of Count de Limburg Stirum; they lived in a Castle in Anzegem, West Flanders. On our way I had mixed feelings about all those noble lineages. Pierre's mother, baroness d'Heusch, had something to do with it. Proud as she was of her title, she had an unfortunate habit of saying "People who don't belong to the nobility are not born. Ils ne sont pas nés." . Fortunately my apprehension proved unfounded with the de Limburg Stirum family. I felt at home with them right away and Lode and the Count went along like a house on fire. Count de Limburg Stirum was a lover of the arts with exquisite taste who owned a valuable collection of paintings . While the gentlemen were talking about art, the countess and I played with the grand kids on the rug. The ambiance was extremely cordial.

As Lode's driver, I was adopted by all his friends and acquaintances. It was like the proverbial pebble in the pound ; thanks to Lode my circle was ever widening. Those friends and acquaintances then introduced me to their families and this way I met Princess de Ligne. Her husband was Count de Limburg Stirum's brother. The couple lived in Brussels on the rue de l'Abbaye, and together we tried out the restaurants in their neighborhood. Another relative was married to the daughter of the Count of Paris and lived in a castle in Heverlee; countless times their kids sat on my lap.

One day we received a missive from Princess Lilian, the second wife of King Leopold the Third. In the attic of her castle at Argenteuil there were hundreds of paintings by unknown 'masters' that had been collected by her mother-in-law Queen Elisabeth of Belgium. Queen Elisabeth was known as a great patron of the arts; she gave her name to the prestigious Queen Elisabeth Music Competition. She tried to support young painters by buying their works to give their budding careers a boost. These were the canvasses in the attic that Princess Lilian wanted to get rid of. However, first she needed Lode to tell her if there was anything of value among them. She had invited us for lunch and Lode, and I drove up the wide avenue leading to the royal domain. My car had a big sign that read, "PRESS." We were ushered into the large drawing room and asked to wait for the princess. Princess Lilian turned out to be a charming hostess. Near the sofa, we sat on was a large photograph of her with king Leopold. She talked nonstop, among others about her in-laws. What struck me was her obvious hatred that she made no attempt to dissimulate that day. Knowing that I was a journalist and could easily take advantage of her revelations, she surprised me by relating how Queen Elisabeth couldn't stand Queen Astrid, Leopold's first wife. Astrid was more popular than she, and that she found unbearable. Lilian went so far as to suggest that Elisabeth had wanted to trip her daughter-in-law while going down some stairs while the latter was expecting her son Baudouin. I've never been able to verify her story, nor her allegation that Queen Elisabeth supported young artists not so much for the love of art, as of the young men themselves, a love that did not necessarily remain platonic, either.

We went to pay our respects to King Leopold. He was having a stroll in the garden, but was about to leave for the royal villa at the seaside, so he would not have lunch with us. Lunch was served in a small, oval room. Princess Lilian, Lode, and we were joined by the princesses Esmeralda and Marie-Christine, nine and fourteen respectively at the time. I noticed that, contrary to what Marie-Christine would claim later, Lilian was very solicitous of her daughter. Lilian told us Marie-Christine liked to paint and was quite gifted, and she asked Lode if he would teach her.

On the menu were hopping shoots, my favorite dish. Hop shoots are available only for a week or two in spring, and that helps me remember what time of the year we had lunch at Argenteuil. After lunch, we went up into the attic. Princess Lilian put her arm around my shoulders, as if we were boarding-school friends and talked to a mile a minute while Lode was making his notes. Before we left, she invited us to another date, when Lode would present his findings. The princess had heard that Lode was friends with the historian, professor. Alexander Von Randa. She wanted to contact him regarding the writing of her biography. "And wouldn't it be great," she suggested, "for all of us to get together in my chalet in Austria to discuss things?" But when we returned a few weeks later as agreed, Queen Marie-Josée of Italy had come for a visit. We could see the two of them sitting in the garden but were beckoned away by a secretary who took charge of the matters we had come for. We went home and never saw the princess again.

In the late 50's a movement was started that aimed for the unification of Europe. It was called C.E.D.I., Centre Européen de Documentation et d'Information. The Belgian participants were Jacques Solvay, blanket manufacturer De Lovinfosse (of Manta, makers of the famous "Sole Mio" blankets), Father Maurice Janssens, economist of the Jesuits Wilfried Somville owner of the Gazet van Antwerpen, and Lode Seghers. One of their first meetings was held in Zurich and Lode had arranged for me to tag along as a reporter for the Gazet van Antwerpen. This time I did not have to drive; Lode's son Paul was our chauffeur. Paul, in his twenties, was handsome and a photographer. Father Janssens was the third passenger, a charming man with a potbelly that spoke to his enjoyment of the finer things in life. In this capacity, he pointed out all the best restaurants along our route, some of which we sampled, to everybody's satisfaction.

In Zürich, I saw a lot of faces I recognized from the newspaper, even though I wasn't always sure who was who, and I hear them talk about the advantages of the United States of Europe. The idea sounded quite simple to my ears, but of course it wasn't, as the future would bear out.

The Gazet van Antwerpen news desk was happy with my report, and I began to get more assignments from them and other papers. With this occupation, and the company of Lode and Pierre, I stepped into the new decade, the sixties. However, something happened one day that changed the course of my life.

One night, as Pierre and I were cuddling in bed in a small rendez-vous hotel, he suddenly tensed up and a look of terror appeared in his eyes. He gripped my arm and ordered me to take him home right away. I obeyed almost instinctively: I helped him dress and cross the street, supporting him all the way. I was afraid because, clearly, Pierre had become very ill. When we arrived at his door – each step seemed to take an eternity – he stroked my cheek before making his way inside with great difficulty. The next morning I heard he had died. He had been found dead in an armchair in his living room just half an hour after I had walked him home. Feeling death's approach, Pierre's only concern was to protect me to the end. He did not want me to be involved in a scandal, having been found in bed with a deceased married man at a hotel. Although my dear, sweet Pierre's last loving words had been for me, I was in total shock. I felt as if I had been hit by lightning. All those years, Pierre had been there for me, and it had seemed like it would last forever. Nevertheless, that's not how things work, after all, Pierre was 30 years older than I. With him gone, my whole world fell apart. The only thing I had left of him was his letters and lots of little notes in which he kept repeating that I had to succeed in life. When sex was exploding in us, he always repeated: All the way you and I. Nothing can stop us. Nothing was going to stop us Pierre. That man learned me, intentionally how to cope with humiliation – intentionally as I later understood, because he was not going to be always there to help me along- who learned me what affection and ambition were and so much more that is impossible to explain, and that you do not learn in any university. Little by little, I regained my strength. And yes, I would make something of my life… for his sake and for mine.

Chapter 11
At Home with the
Homeless of Good Breeding

At Salamanca : invited by the Spanish Government.Meeting with the first European lobyists. Next to me Countess Thurn and Taxis

It took another year before I heard anything more from the C.E.D.I. Lode Seghers, however, had assiduously traveled across a certain road in this company that had made the C.E.D.I. into a strong group. The headquarters, meanwhile, had been housed in Madrid, Spain. There's a historical reason for this choice: just before, and even more after the armistice, many Germans had fled their country. The real war criminals, the Nazis and so on, traveled on to South America to escape the death penalty. However, the rank and file, "ordinary" officers and soldiers who would otherwise have become prisoners of war, fled to the Iberian peninsula, and more specifically to Spain, where Franco was in power and offered them shelter.

The Germans would congregate in one of the Spanish capital's restaurants named Horcher, after its owner. Herr Horcher had abandoned the hospitality business in Berlin to start a new life here. Spain was also the new domicile of a large part of the exiled East-European nobility, including that of the former Austro-Hungarian Empire. These aristocrats no longer felt safe in their homelands that were now occupied by the Russians. Thus Spain had become home to several groups of people who'd had to leave behind their homes and properties, and often a lot more, in a hurry. Understandably they were dreaming of returning to their roots, despite the inviting climate and tax laws of Spain. All these people were extremely receptive to C.E.D.I.'s idea of a united Europe. And fortunately for them, Franco left the Spanish aristocracy, the *grandes*, alone; his daughter had even married a marquis.

The newcomers were well received in Spain and Franco not only tolerated the C.E.D.I. but even gave it special consideration. When Lode suggested, after my mourning period for Pierre, that we attend a C.E.D.I. congress together, I met a lot of people there whom I could now perfectly place, having learned all about them in the newspapers. The man who had accepted to preside over the Council was Archduke Otto of Habsburg. He was the son of Zita, the last Empress of Austria, who had lived for a while in exile in Belgium with her children. He had gone to school in Belgium and still had a soft spot for that country. And he, Otto Von Habsburg, would introduce me to other major players. With time, the aristocracy was becoming more modernized and independent. Among the noblemen who had joined the C.E.D.I was the Duke of Wellington, a descendant of the Trafalgar hero. Carlos de Bourbon, married to Princess Irene of the Netherlands, was also one of them, as well as ex-King Simeon of Bulgaria and Alexander Von Randa, the historian mentioned earlier. And then there were the likes of Willy Brandt and François de la Noë of *le Quai d'Orsay*, the French Foreign Ministry, or Stanley Clark, a close aide to Field Marshal Montgomery. The members would meet every month at the Escorial (a famous monastery/palace complex near Madrid, once the summer residence of the Spanish court). Franco's government had given them the use of its halls and on Sunday the whole group, led by Otto van Habsburg, attended mass there. In honor of the European group, the service was held in four languages: Spanish, French, English, and German. I had no choice but to be present. The priest had asked me to read from the Scripture...in Spanish. I did the best I could even though I didn't understand a single word I read. The papers announced our presence: *Congresistas del C.E.D.I. en Nuestra Ciudad* ("Members of the C.E.D.I. Congress in Our City"), and from Santiago de Compostela to Malaga, mayors received us at their town halls with a great ceremony. Something happened that I could never have predicted: Lode and I became lovers. I have to confess here that the love came mostly from his side. In my case, it was a great friendship. We spent most of our time together and usually shared a hotel room, and one thing led to another. I have a feeling we must have stayed in all the *paradors* and Palace Hotels of Spain, compliments of the C.E.D.I., with the room, flowers, fruit baskets, and drinks paid for by the Spanish government. On July 2, 1962, I wrote in the *Gazet van Antwerpen*: "The European Community must be developed further!" In any case, Europe was on the rise and in the closing session of the international congress, former French minister Michelet declared: "Europeans must not forget that, but for Spain, the Sorbonne in Paris and Oxford University would today be teaching the Koran instead of the principles of Christianity!" A provocative statement in 1962. Every month, Lode and I traveled to Spain, which we had begun to consider our second home. There were no freeways in those days, so we drove along French country roads, along gastronomical hotels and the delightful vineyards of Bordeaux. Lode was a connoisseur of fine wines and thanks to him, I developed a discriminating palate. Our favorite stop was the restaurant *La Mère Catherine* in Saint-Emilion. It's a pity that only afterward I fully realized how wonderful my life was at the time. In Spain, too, we had our favorite place. Just outside Madrid was the *Valle de los Caídos*, the Valley of the Fallen, where the fallen of the Spanish Civil War were buried. Spanish visitors and foreign tourists (still scarce in those days) alike admired the handcrafted mosaics that gave the place a serene, fairytale atmosphere. The creator of these mosaics was Santiago Padrós, a debonair Spaniard, who appeared to have emerged directly from the era of the *hidalgos*, the former landowning gentry of Spain. This artist, too, was a friend of Lode's. He lived in La Florida, a wealthy suburb of Madrid, with his wife Montserrat. Here, too, we became quite comfortable. We enjoyed having coffee with the Marchesa de Oriol. King Baudouin and Queen Fabiola spent part of their honeymoon at her villa. I remember her coming out to greet us on her driveway along with her ten children. Padrós and Montserrat organized perfect dinner parties in their garden. There were deer in the park, which merged fenceless with that of the neighbors, the marquis and marquise de Villaverde. The marquise was general Franco's daughter, and so I made the acquaintance of the generalissimo himself.

Franco was a dictator but there were serious differences between him and that other dictators, Adolf Hitler. Franco did not send people to death camps based on their faith or race; When I met him, I had already seen a good deal of Spain, but in the meantime I had joined the Association of Travel Writers, thanks to my mentor Bernard Henry, and I regularly contributed articles to American travel magazines. For one of those articles I had landed among Spanish Gypsies, who were no beggars nor thieves as they are often represented, but very accomplished businessmen. They had a virtual monopoly in the horse trade, and the horse markets of Jaen drew visitors and buyers from all over the country. I was their guest in the *cuevas,* the caves of Granada where the Gypsies lived cozily side by side with their sheep, goats and pigs. These cave-dwelling Gypsies told me what had happened to their people in Eastern Europe during Hitler's time, how tens of thousands had been sent to the gas chambers, just for being Gypsies. I still think it is deplorable that of all the war victims we commemorate, the Gypsies are the most overlooked. In Spain, these people were especially friendly and hospitable; they did not possess much but when I left, they always had a watermelon ready for me. As they handed it to me, they would say, 'Vaya con Dios'. Go with God. I still think of them with great respect.

My "important" meeting with Franco took place in his daughter's garden. I tried to suppress a smile when I saw the generalissimo, stripped of all his grandeur, calmly sipping his coffee. A far cry from the autocrat who could be seen on TV conducting affairs of state in full military regalia and surrounded by what could be termed his courtiers. This average little man in leisure clothing, slouching in his armchair, didn't at all come across as a great world leader. The daughter introduced him simply as her father. Among other things, we talked about the C.E.D.I., well known to him, of course, and I told him what I had already seen of Spain. However, unintentionally I also became privy to the *petites histories*, albeit not through Franco personally. A person of his entourage confided that Franco had a health problem that caused him to urinate only infrequently. As a result, his staff and the generals who regularly traveled with him between Madrid and Barcelona would make a beeline for the bathroom before each departure, as they knew he never made a sanitary stop on the 400-mile trip. In his daughter's garden Franco waxed eloquent about José Antonio, a popular hero admired by the Spaniards. His full name was José Antonio Primo de Rivera, but everyone affectionately called him by his Christian name, which also happened to be a bit more practical. José Antonio was the son of a dictator of the same name who ruled Spain between 1923 and 1930 and was a vehement opponent of Marxism. At the start of the Civil War, he naturally chose the side of the military. Nevertheless, in 1936 he was captured and executed soon afterward. He was only 33 years old. Franco worshiped him and during his regime a veritable cult of José Antonio was instated. In every Spanish church one finds a corner with an inscription commemorating the fallen of the Civil War, and always José Antonio heads the list. It was especially for him that Franco had the *Valle de los Caídos* built, the Valley of the Fallen. Tickled by my interest in his hero, Franco thought I should meet Pilar Primo de Rivera, Antonio's sister. She was fifty something when I met her in the early sixties, in her office on the Via José Antonio, named after her brother. It was the main street of Madrid, nowadays called *Gran Via*. Pilar Primo was a beautiful, dark-haired woman with large, dreamy eyes. After our first meeting, we'd regularly go for coffee, *churros*, and *tapas* in the cafeterias of various government offices. The Spanish unions were in command here, but they could not be in comparison to the unions in Belgium (or the USA). They were more of an autonomous personnel service that took care of both the higher executives and the regular employees. It was in one of these *cantinas* that Pilar told me the following story: the Spanish government had once suggested a strategic match between her and none other than Adolf Hitler. This way, they expected, Spain would occupy an important position in the fascist world, as soon as the Germans defeated. the Allies in 1941. This intelligent, charismatic woman who was the sister of Spain's greatest hero was their ace in the hole. However, Joseph Goebbels whispered in the Spanish delegation's ears that this plan could not work, as Hitler would not be able to produce any offspring. During World War One, he said, the latter had been hit by a bullet in the testicles. The lovely Pilar was eventually introduced to Hitler, but after learning this particular detail, she returned to Spain post haste. After the war she was put in charge of the "role of the Catholic woman," and this in a typically Spanish way: with lots attention to Spanish cuisine, dance and music. Pilar coached the staff of the "training schools" where Spanish women were taught how they could make family life as attractive as possible for their men. And although this plan has a very traditional ring to it, it was driven by a profoundly feminine strategy: finding at home all they used to crave, the men would no longer have to seek their entertainment in taverns and clubs;

One of my articles still in my possession is titled "What after Franco?" it's an interview with Manuel Fraga de Iribane, Spanish Minister of Information. The title proved that "the dictator," while even though hale and hearty, didn't mind people reflecting about what would happen after his rule. Because of my familiarity with Spanish topics, I was now being asked to write for the Spanish papers *La Semana* and *Actualidad Espanola*.

My love affair with Lode went on smoothly. When we were not traveling around, he came to see me on a daily base, either at my home where I lived with my mother, or at his own home where he lived with his wife and son, Paul. Paul was in his early twenties, a very good professional photographer and very handy. When Lode and myself went abroad on a mission, he often drove the car to our destination. Nobody seemed to see any harm in our 'friendship'. I have a feeling it came in very handy for Mary, Lode's wife, who was on turn very spoiled by her very rich Jewish boyfriend who up to a certain point took care of the entire family, I included. The sexual activities of Lode and I were restricted to the nights we spend at hotels in foreign countries. I can't remember that I enjoyed it. Looking back to it I hardly could understand what he saw in me. I suppose that to him this must have been the thing called love. Lode had me enrolled at the European College in Bruges, just a tad closer to home. Here, Professor Henri Brugmans was grooming future diplomats for a centralized European government, in hopes that a United Europe would soon materialize. I was among the number of those being coached. My reports about this experience were published in, among others, the Courier Journal of Louisville, Kentucky. For the Spanish press I wanted to deliver something special. I had heard the Russians were constructing the Assouan Dam in Egypt, and it seemed like a good idea to go and check it out. For some reason, I decided it would be a good idea to travel by car. I was in touch with André Scohy, who had been heading the Belga press agency in what was then Leopoldville, in the Belgian Congo, for many years. When the Belgians retreated from the former colony, he had moved back to Brussels much against his will, and had started working for the French-language Antwerp paper *La Metropole*. He and I clicked in the most serious sense of the word. Amorous activities were out of the question as I was simply not his type. André fell for exotic women and had married an African lady in Congo with whom he had a son. However, his wife and son had stayed behind when André returned to Belgium, and the man was

65

suffering from severe nostalgia. He frequented the exotic restaurants in Antwerp, hoping to find a balm for his wound. I often accompanied him to establishments that were not always of a superb level, but nowhere have I eaten more authentic ethnic food than in the cafés of the harbor quarter. André asked me out because he hated sitting alone at a table, and because it allowed him to hit on the local girls without drawing too much attention to himself. And I found it very refreshing to go out with a man who had no ulterior motives; men have no idea how tiresome it is for a woman to have to be constantly on guard! André was harmless and when he heard I wanted to go to Egypt, he came up with a brilliant idea. In the souks of Cairo, there was a merchant who belonged to the so-called fifth column, in other words, a spy. During the war these people provided intelligence mainly to the British in North Africa. Even today, they recruit agents in the countries where they live, and the fifth column is also hard at work in Iraq. I definitely had to meet that Egyptian, André thought, it would make a great exposé. He gave me the necessary information to find the man and also asked me to bring him back some cigarettes, as his favorite brand was sold there. And so I left for Egypt with a well-defined plan. I expected to see more if I traveled by car than with any other form of transportation, and in Brussels I put my little Fiat on the auto train to Milan. From there I drove myself to beautiful Venice and, thank God, arrived there without a hitch. In Venice I drove my car onto a ferry and drove off it in Alexandria, Egypt. I had informed the Egyptian embassy of my travel plans and when they heard I was a journalist they sensed the potential of extra publicity for their country and welcomed me with open arms. Mass tourism started in the seventies when loads of foreigners began to visit the land of the pharaohs, but in 1964 that was not yet the case. Fortunately I had been given some valuable words of advice. Because my car was a Fiat, I was told to stay in close contact with the Belgian embassy in Cairo. The Egyptian government had made a lucrative deal with the Italian automaker to build Fiat cars in that country under license. I remember the cars that were assembled in Egypt were christened "Nasser" instead of Fiat, in honor of the then Egyptian president. But they didn't have a license for the spare parts, that detail had unfortunately been neglected. So the spare parts had to be imported from Italy, which was an expensive affair. One of the consequences was that if a naïve traveler in Egypt left his or her Fiat unattended for a while, they were guaranteed to find it stripped. The stolen parts then found their way to the black market.

On my arrival in Alexandria, I was met by some Egyptian policemen who promptly stuck a piece of paper with lots of official stamps onto my windshield. The writing on it was all Arabic to me, but it had something to do with the fact that I was visiting under their government's protection and was not to be hassled. To reach Cairo, I had to drive through the desert. Those same officers saw me on my way, but once in the desert, I was all alone, not even a camel in sight. It's quite a distance from Alexandria to Cairo, and for the time being, I saw nothing but sand. Here and there, I came across a road sign in Arabic script, Allah only knew what was written on it, For safety's sake, whenever I was in doubt about which fork in the road to take, I would stop and wait until another car came by. It could take a while, and then the conversation, in English, went like this: "Where are you coming from?" "From Cairo," "O.K., so that's in that direction. And where are you coming from?" "From Alexandria." "Ah, so that's *that* way." (Finger pointing in the opposite direction.) Every now and then, my opposite number would speak a language I did not understand. The same conversation would then take place, only in sign language. Fortunately, there was a soldier in a military watch post about every three miles on my route. He noted the license plate number of any passing car and reported it to the next post. If the car failed to arrive there within a certain time span, a search party was sent out. I also found a gas station/eatery where the boy who filled up my tank proceeded to make me an omelet. He looked so happy to see someone at long last that I thought he was going to embrace me.

Eventually, I safely entered the suburbs of Cairo. My car had been coughing for a while due to an excess of sand and now gave up the ghost entirely. There I was, a western woman all alone in a car that refused to budge, surrounded by a crowd of Egyptians, who, I feared, were about to dismantle my car on the spot, and who were, in any case, shouting unintelligible things at me. I hadn't the faintest idea what to do next. However, a guardian angel, in the form of a man wearing a hat, walked up to me. It was the hat that did it; it was the only one in a sea of turbans. The guardian angel read the paper that was still stuck to the windshield of my car. It appeared to be sufficiently impressive for him to ask me in broken English if he might be of assistance. I gave him my name and asked him to contact the Belgian embassy. The man nodded and disappeared, and I was left again among the milling turbans who now smiled broadly at me. I smiled back but found the situation awkward and scary. After what felt like an eternity, a car with diplomatic insignia and a Belgian flag stopped beside my ailing little Fiat. I felt incredibly relieved, and even more overjoyed when two gentlemen got out of the car and explained to me that a tow truck was on the way, and that one of them would stay with my car until it arrived. Meanwhile the other gentleman would take me to the Belgian embassy where I could recover from my sandy adventure with a cup of delicious Arabic coffee. Even so, when the ambassador heard I planned to drive on toward the Assouan Dam, he tried to dissuade me. I had to promise him I would continue by train to Assouan. Meanwhile my car would be repaired at a Cairo garage; it would be all ready to go by the time I returned. I kept my promise to the ambassador and went by rail to Assouan, where a very unusual week awaited me. Because in Assouan, there were Russians...

Chapter 12
The Fifth Column

My little car who drove me through the desert

André Scohy, who sent me to the souks of Cairo to buy hasj, at the baptism of his baby son. Baby Stephan in the arms of his mother, the stripper. I was Godmother and Lode Seghers Godfather

After twelve hours on the train, I arrived in Assouan, the last town of Egypt. It didn't look very deserted because a lot of people live in those Egyptian cities. However, there were few that looked like me. I showered at my hotel and took a taxi, or something that was supposed to be a taxi, and went looking for my Russians. I found them at the Barrage or what was about to become a Barrage. The man who was at guard probably noticed that I was not exactly from the neighborhood. I managed to explain that I wanted to meet his boss and minutes later somebody stood in front of me who spook rather well German, probably picked up during the war. He introduced himself with a name that I could not pronounce and certainly not remember. Nevertheless, he was a Russian, no doubt about that. From the moment I saw him, he hardly left my side. He drove me to a large water that looked like a lake but happen to be large a tank in which thousand of hectoliters of water were pumped in order to stop flooding by the river Nile. It was to be called the Nasser Lake. Hundreds of people, Russians and Arabs labored in a heat that felt like a steam boiler, it was not hard to imagine how the slaves must have felt while building the Pyramids. The worst part was that he insisted on showing everything to me, on foot, and it was very, very large. They seemed to have no secrets, and anyway he must have understood that I didn't understand much of the situation. But it was impressive ! After four days, I started to believe that there was not coming an end to what he wanted to show me, and finally it was over. He changed clothes, up until then I only had seen him in shorts and a soaked T-shirt and invited me as a perfect gentleman – for a moment I had the feeling that he believed the entire town was his property – stepped in his car and drove to the monuments of Abou Simbel, who had not changed place at that time. He knew how to impress people. At last he put me in a wobbly little boat to visit the tomb of the Agha Khan on an island nearby. On the tomb was a red rose who was changed every day, order of the Beghum, the wife of the deceased. That ended my visit, I had my scoop and returned to Cairo and my car that was waiting for me. An Egyptian tourist police was going to look after me for the rest of my stay in the Egyptian capital. That came in very handy because I still had to look for my member of the fifth column in the markets of the city. And with all those booths it was not exactly that easy. The people of our Embassy were not very at rest with my entrepreneurship, it was 1964, but I asked them how 'hello' was said in the local language, they said 'saida' and away I went. From everywhere men, women and children ran at me but when I said 'saida' it was, as if I saw the sun breaking through in the shadow of the souks. Everybody laughed at me and said the only English word they knew : Welcome. I was offered left and right mint thee .

When they finally calmed down I asked , or my guide asked where I could find the man I was looking for. The only information I had was that he sold perfume that he made himself. I don't know yet how we happened to find him but finally we proceeded. He was seated in a kind of tent surrounded by beakers. There was a counter and a worn-out coach in his booth. To be a member of the fifth column it was necessary to know a few languages. The man spoke German. As a kind of introduction I had to ask for a certain kind of perfume. This would prove I was reliable. So I did. With a large gesture, the man invited me to lay down on the coach. Not to sit, but to lay down. My tourist police office stood outside the tent because I wanted to talk in person with my perfume man, but I hadn't expected a coach situation. I did what the man asked me to do and lay down. It was very hot. I had not many clothes on, and I was not much at ease when the man kneeled down next to me. He took a deep breath and started sniffing all over me. My legs, my arms, my neck nothing was spared. At the moment, when I expected him to jump on me, he raised and asked me to follow him. He went to his bottles and started to mix several kinds of color liquids. Finally, he put everything in a small bottle and offered it to me. The perfume was made according to the odors of my body. It smelled awful; If it was that what he had smelled on my body I was in bad shape. Before he left, he gave me the cigarettes where André had asked for. When I came out of the tent my policeman was waiting for me and took me sightseeing. He was a good looking fellow, the evening ended in a very charming way.

A day later I went back with my car in the desert where I started to feel like home, went in Alexandria back on the steamer to Italy and from there on I went back to Belgium.

When I gave the cigarettes to André he was thrilled with joy. He told me that he was in a serious dip but those cigarettes willing it would help. I wanted to know why these cigarettes were so special . Without hesitating, he said : they are hashish. Never more did I bring purchases from abroad for who ever asked me.

I saw André from time to time . Until I had notice that he was going to be father again; He wanted me as godmother. Mother of the child was an Algerian stripper. The child was going to be baptized in Paris and Lode was godfather. We were selected because we both were Catholics, and he wanted his son to be raised according to the catholic faith . I am ashamed to say that I wasn't very helpful to the little boy in that matter while his mother was touring Europe to show her unveiled art. Once when she was performing in Antwerp, she called me to look after Stefan because his nanny fell sick. Artists from that field of entertainment have a network of nanny's to look after their babies when their mother is working at night for their daily meal. I looked after him and that was it. About two years later I met him with his mother in their apartment in Paris. He had become a very handsome little boy. Since then I lost sight of them and of his father. When he was baptized in Paris his stepbrother, the half-breed son of André's one and only legal wife was present . A fascinating young man who loved to travel around the world to be witnesses of the baptisms of all André's children. André helped each of them financially. I cannot think where he had all the money from. However, this is none of my business. Once I asked him why he never divorced. He answered that in his catholic faith divorce was forbidden. Theoretically he was absolutely right.

By that time, my life was a bit confused. During my different travels, I had met in Milano a young, single engineer Giano Giovanini who was as strict about his freedom of status as I was. Giano was a good-looking man, the Italian dream of any girl of my age, and he seemed to fancy me. We made a deal. We were going to meet in Milano every first day of a new season for a relaxing weekend somewhere in Italy. We did so for a couple of years. And it worked perfectly. I had always some period to look forward to without strings attached. To know that every three months I had somebody to fall in love with, more so that it was mutual, was quite exciting.

He took me to the nicest places in Italy and introduced me to the Italian way of living. Which was an extra bonus, and instructive as well. I still fancy the ***** restaurant where Gino took me to in the main street in front of the Dom of Firenze. At the table next to us two couples were seated. Two ladies in their sixties looked after and dressed with terrific class. The men with them were considerably younger and seemed to have stepped out of a publicity spot of Ferrari. They were obviously the gigolo's of their companions but there was so much complicity and fun between them that I realized that it was what I wanted to have when I would be older. Wishful thinking of course . I knew that I would never have the money to pay for that kind of Chippendale Armani outfits on a regular base. I had not to complain about the men in my life, but in a way I had to be always available when they called for me. However, to be able to switch destinies, so that I could be in command and order a man around by saying : Drop everything, the master needs you. Wouldn't that be loverly..........

Chapter 13
Any Arms for Sale ?

*I, Father Janssens and Lode Seghers. Janssens
was the one who was looking for arms in Pakistan.*

In the 'Bundestag' with Willy Brandt

A Flemish very popular magazine offered me a job as their Spanish and Portuguese correspondent, which opened every official door to me. King Simeon of Bulgaria granted me an interview, and I still remember how His Majesty was waiting for me in the parlor of his villa. The interview that followed was fascinating and highly interesting. With lots of love, he talked about the country where he fled from and about the fact how pleased, he was to remain in contact with his countryman. Every one of them is welcome to my house, he added. And I insist of meeting them a person to a person. The heading of my article was "Invited by Simeon, the Tsar without a Country". The man also talked about his youth : 'I lost my father', he said, 'when I needed him most I was only six and his death still remains a mystery: officially, he died of a heart attack, but it could be that he was murdered' . It was obvious that he was still feeling very ill at ease with this part of his life. ' Father' he added ' once made a statement that still is very doubtful. He said : My generals are German minded, my diplomats are English minded, the Queen is Italian minded and my people Russian minded. I am the only one who is neutral'. Some people took this very evil and never forgave him this pronouncement.

Simeon went on : 'This was the country that I inherited at the age of six: the regents were fusilladed and mother, who was an Italian princess flew with her two children to Madrid, to the villa where we are, for the moment. Later Simeon married and meanwhile the political climate changed in such a way that he could return, as a King in exile. From 2001 until 2005 he became by the name of Simeon Borisov Sakskoburgotski prime Minister of his country. At this very moment, he is an ordinary civilian.

The meetings of the CEDI went on. One day Lode was approached by Father Janssens, economist from the Jesuits. A war was about to brake out between Pakistan and India about Kashmir and Father Janssens asked Lode if he didn't know a way to get hold of arms for the Pakistani; he had received a request in that direction. Because there were several catholic missions in Pakistan Father Janssens had promised to look around. Lode had no idea where he could find that kind of stuff. However, while talking with some of his CEDI friends he learned that Portugal and Angola, who had been in a fight were in a cease fire period and possible they had a lot of arms as residue. We decided to travel to Lissabon to find out. Lode and I received a red carpet treatment and contacts were highly positive. I could not tell if finally the Pakistani got hold of the weapons as the war finally went on no longer than sixteen days. However, I do remember when, a couple of weeks later I met Father Janssens in the Convent of the Jesuit's in Brussels and while talking about our last sojourn in Madrid, I remembered him of our adventure with the arms for Pakistan, he looked at me outraged, brought his hand theatrically to his chest and asked : 'Me, weapons ?'.

Meanwhile my field of operation had been transferred to London, where Stanley Clark, the former right hand of Lord Montgomery, one of our friends, had been installed as PR-manager to Sotheby, the world famous auction house. Through Clark I had entrance in their departments and assisted at their auctions where millions of pounds changed hands from one minute to the other. Furthermore, I got acquainted with people from the wine department of Christie's, the other famous auction house. They were planning to open a branch office in Brussels and Michael Broadbent, the wine guru of Christie's hired me in order to make the Flemish translation of their catalogues. I was in for another challenge.

I kept on working as a reporter, traveled all over Europe, and met legends such as the Federal Chancellor at the time Willy Brandt. Later on I was asked where we had been talking about. Automatically it was supposed to be about the Wall of Berlin. I suppose we did mention it, but mostly Willy Brandt was interested in Europe and its future. He was very committed.. Sometimes I wonder :would those idealistic politicians from the sixties not turn around in their graves if they should be able to watch what happened to the Europe they once had in mind.

In Germany my attention didn't go merely to the politicians.

It went also to a famous alley in Hamburg, the Reeperbahn. Nowadays, it is a legend, in the sixties – and before – it was bitter reality. It was situated in St. Pauli. Paid love was forbidden in Hamburg so the ladies and gentlemen that were in sex business moved to a suburb of Hamburg to offer whatever, they had for sale. It became world famous. I wondered why. After the brothels in Tanger, I thought I had seen it all. How wrong could I be? The alley was separated from the rest of the world by revolving doors, where everybody could enter. And they did. I remember the first couple I met, an elderly one, probably from Bavarian because he wore a hat with a feather (a pinzel). They were walking through the alley and looking at the girls and boys behind the show cases, as if they were walking true a Zoo.

In the show cases where girls – and boys – trying to attract attention to their more or less naked situation. At the entrance was their female coach with a pile of towels which they handed to the men entering the houses in question. The curtains closed for the time of the intimate relationship. When the men came out they returned the towel to the woman at the door. I learned that on closing time the prostitutes were paid according to the number of towels that were in their baskets. When later Lode and I returned to our hotel room, he said that he wasn't ready for sex after what he saw. I couldn't blame him. I wasn't either.

Time for some more serious activities. While in Germany I had the opportunity to interview the daughter in law of Richard Wagner in Haus Wahnfried, the villa from Wagner in Bayreuth. Winnifer, who was a very friendly lady was the widow of Siegfried Wagner, the son of Richard. There had been quite a difference of age between the two of them , Siegfried was already far in his forties when he married Winnifer who was only seventeen. He was actually gay but to avoid a scandal his family had found him a bride. They were going to have four children. I was very pleased to meet her but my editor-in-chief insisted that I should take the opportunity to assist to the Festival of Bayreuth where they were performing De Ring der Niebelungen, the musical masterpiece of Wagner. This was another cup of tea. For somebody who wasn't exactly brought up with opera and classical music it was a horror. The public was composed of the most extreme fanatics that I have ever met. Far worse than the most extreme religious fanatics I could think of. During the daytime, I was in their midst to listen for hours to the very heavy music and in the evening the same crowd came together in Tavern Zum Eule, once the favorite hangout of Wagner himself, where every note was analyzed. I suppose something is wrong with my IQ or maybe my MQ –music quotient – but I still have more goose pimples when I listen to Amazing Grace than to music from Wagner or Beethoven. I was more than happy when it was time to leave.

I was ready to leave Europe for what it was and to go to travel to another continent. In the Middle East the Mandelbaum Gate was hitting the news. Nobody was allowed to trespass anymore, a situation comparable with the Wall of Berlin. I decided to find out for myself and while I was there have a closer look to Israel, Jordan, Syria and Lebanon because I felt sure that stories where there to be told.

Chapter 14
Arabian Coffee and
Kosjer in Israel

In Jordan with my guide and boyfriend Shehadeh Zananiri

It took me some time to make the necessary contacts and to obtain visa's.

A free lance journalist has to illustrate her stories. I considered myself a fairly good photographer. However, to be recognized by the photographic union, I needed an adequate university diploma. And I had no university diploma whatsoever. Full stop. My good old friend Lode – he wasn't that old – had friends on a high level at Agfa Gevaert, the world leader in the graphic industry. They ran since decennia a world famous, black and white and color photo school. The courses were about to start and with the necessary connections Lode managed to enroll me. What we didn't know was that it was a finishing school for photographer's with a solid reputation. At that time photo developing was done manually. The colored pictures of those days faded after a while. My class mates where women and men from all over the world.

Our first task was to make a picture of a tree. Opposite the main entrance of Agfa was a square with trees. One of them stood in the middle, and we choose him as a target. The photographic part of the assignment was not the problem, it was when we arrived at the lab that my problems began. We were instructed by the professor to develop the film in the warmest color we could imagine. As a help we received little square glasses in different colors. They were called magenta, fuchsia among others, it was all Chinese to.me . We were supposed to glide them over our negatives after which they were dropped in a bath of chemical substance to be steadied. My colleagues went to work but although in general I have a lot of imaginations I didn't have a clue how to start. On the other hand, it was not in my line of acting to admit it. I started to glide over the glass material, but probably I did it to fast or in the wrong direction . As a result after removing my picture from the bath it showed not one tree but an entire wood.

When the professor looked over my shoulder, he looked at all those trees, then at me and understood that I didn't know what I was doing. Fortunately he had a good sense of humor. He suggested that from there on I should be coached. Next day he entrusted me to a student with an Arabic name who invited me to follow him into the dark room.

Those dark rooms were a little larger than a fitting room. I noticed vaguely a developing machine, a bath filled witch chemicals and at the ceiling a small red lamp provided the necessary light. To make sure that our pictures would not be exposed to daylight if somebody unexpectedly came in Achmed, or whatever his name was, locked the door at the inside. This didn't disturb me until we had to wait for the development of a picture and my new friend started to explain where he came from. He was an Algerian, who had fought against the Pieds Noirs (the French, who had annexed his home country) He had been responsible for the fake passports for his fellow combatants. His enthusiasm when he told me how many hostile throats he had cut, was not less than frightening.. I couldn't help wondering if by any chance, he had acquired a taste for it. Some way or the other my pictures became developed, Achmed seemed pleased with my improvement, and I left the dark room without any damages.

I finished my schooling and went home as a happy girl with my first diploma. It is still in my drawer.

It was about time to leave for the Middle East. A letter from my travel agency nearly gave me a stroke. They told me that my plans had to be changed because they were unable to send me through the Mandelbaumgate from Jordan to Israel. To get rid of my frustration and my hysteric behavior the employee at the desk advised me to contact Madame Sabine, the only one who may be able to help. And that is how I met 'Chérie'

Madame Sabine was a Jewish lady who managed with firm hand a travel agency in the Diamond quarter of Antwerp. Firm hand was putting it too mildly. She was the nightmare of. every single airline company. Sabine never accepted no for an answer and because of the importance of her clients nobody would dare saying no to her. Everybody who entered her office, including me, was greeted with a cheerful 'Hello, Chérie', hence her nickname. Her 'Chérie's' where well taken care of. I told her my problem, she told me to relax and sure enough a couple of days later my tickets and travel papers were waiting for me. A car with a Coptic driver was going to pick me up at the airport of Beyrouth and an Israeli delegation would take over at the Mandelbaumgate

Everything went as planned. The situation in Lebanon was very calm it looked more like a tourist excursion. At the Syrian border, a Syrian driver relayed. He drove me to the desert for my first contact with the Bedouins, who were busy doing nothing in their tent a little away from the road. With my brand new diploma in mind I wanted to shoot a couple of pictures but my driver swore to God that those people were dangerous and tried to move on. I shouted so loud to stop the car that for a moment it seemed like he was not very sure who were the most dangerous, those Bedouins or me. He decided to make the best of a bad case and stopped. I stepped out of the car.

Children ran to us begging for 'bakschich, bakschich'. In Egypt, I had learned what this meant but I acted as if I didn't know what they were saying. With a large smile, I walked to the tent. In Arabian countries, everybody smiled when they saw a stranger, at least away back in the sixties they did. I hoped that when I smiled to them, they would accept me. In the tent, several people were seated in a circle on the floor, men at the back, women and toddlers in front. Nobody moved when I walked in. Even the children who ran behind me silenced. My driver kept to his car as if his life depends on it. I went to the person closest to me, a woman – I had no idea of her age, except for her eyes she was covered in a black dress, with a baby on her lap. I caressed him on his little head, a universal gesture, and she took my hand. At the same moment, an old man seated in the middle of the circle , probably the head of the tribe, stood up came toward me and invited me to follow him. He returned to his place and invited me to sit next to him. The atmosphere became more relaxed. A man approached with a china cup, filled it with coffee and offered it to me. It was not exactly in the best of hygienic conditions. For a moment, my driver feared that I was going to refuse to drink, which would be a great offense and no one could predict what would have happened next. Machetes and sabers were not far away. However, I didn't even consider refusing, I felt it as an honor, what it was meant to be. I had read somewhere that the best coffee in the world is made in those tents; It was true. When my cup was empty the servant took it from me, filled it up again and gave it to the old man who emptied it. The same little cup went to all the people who were present, dozens of them, most with their head full of flies – nobody seemed to care and drank – until it arrived back to me for another drink. Five times the same cup went around the circle and then the ritual was over. When I left all the children, laughing and full of joy ran with me to the car to say goodbye and wave me out. None of them asked for a bakshich anymore, but I am sure that my driver was more than happy to be rid of me when he trusted me at the border to his colleague from Jordan.

My Jordanian driver was a very handsome boy, the kind with whom any women would love to get lost in the desert. His name was Shehade Zananiri. I still remember how he stood there waiting for me. He was also a Copt, but with this one I had the feeling that I was going to have a great time. He brought me to my hotel in Jeruzalem and took me to his family, very decent people who found it a little strange that their son was driving around with a white woman. However, they seemed to like me, and I was invited to a chicken dinner. Eating chicken with fork and knives was considered impolite. I had to eat with my hands, and it tasted great. I was invited to return at the end of the year to spend Xmas with them in the Holy Place which I did. After which they entrusted their son to me, or vice versa, I am still not quite sure, and away we went.

During a week, we toured Jordan. The last day we drove to the Death Sea to float in the salt water. It was already dark when we returned to

Jerusalem., we passed the Mount of Olives, a fantastic view in the moonlight. During the week that passed by I had noticed that Shehadeh's car was not exactly in good shape. From time to time, we broke down and with the laborers from neighboring villages it had always been quickly solved, but at this late hour this was not so evident. A lot of wild donkeys were running around and a grey donkey in the dark surroundings on a mountain is not exactly what you want to meet in the middle of the night. To my relieve I noticed somewhere behind us the lights of another car. Shehadeh looked in the mirror and mumbled something in his own language, which meant problems because the boy spooks fluently English. I asked him what was wrong. He replied that he believed that the car belonged to the Royal Palace. Their headlights were going on and out. I asked Shehadeh what those men wanted. His answer was short and sweet : You! Meaning me. At first I thought I misunderstood, but then he gave me the general idea. It was common knowledge that the brother of the King had his body-guards kidnap women for bed and breakfast service. More bed than breakfast. After a couple of days, they were returned home. My home was rather far away so this was not exactly a pleasant prospect driving on the Mount of Olives in a shaky old timer with a driver who tries desperately to keep the sick motor running in order to keep away from bodyguards who are trying to keep up with you.

Finally, we arrived in Jericho where I noticed the blue lights of a police office on guard.. But Shehadeh ignored it and went full speed – manner of speaking – ahead, the other car still following us. Rather shaky I asked Shehadeh why he didn't go for help. He replied that it was out of the question. At that time of the night, a Jordanian in a car with a white lady would certainly end up in prison. So further we went to Jerusalem. A couple of miles outside the city, on a country road our car was slowing up. It was a nightmare. I figured car trouble. Shehadeh stopped. 'Something is wrong there', he said. 'I am going to have a look. Lock the car from the inside'. Away he went to the car which had been following us. I was expecting the worst, a gunshot or something, but after a little while my driver came back with a stranger, obviously the man from the car. I looked around to find something to defend myself, nothing . It was pitch dark. Shehadeh knocked at the window and told me to open the door. So I did. The stranger went in the back seat, Shehadeh returned behind the wheel, and we drove of. When I found my voice back I asked him what the meaning was from all this. 'His car was out of gasoline' he replied 'and in my country, we help people who have problems on the road'. The three of us entered Jerusalem, I was dropped at my hotel and the men drove away looking for gas oil. Obviously, my guardian angel had been traveling with me.

The next day Shehadeh brought me to the Mandelbaum gate. Rules were strict in the Middle East. I knew we liked each other, but a guide having sentimental intentions with a client was out of the question. Somehow I wanted to give him a signal that I had been more than attracted. When he said goodbye I ran with my finger over his spine. He shivered and clearly understood. This was not the last I was going to see from him. My luggage was neatly put down in the middle of the Gate and picked up on the other side by an Israeli custom officer. He offered me a bouquet of flowers. Madame Sabine had the right connections indeed..

At the custom's office, they looked at my passport and asked if I intended to return to Jordan. I replied that I would fly home from Tel-Aviv but wondered why they wanted to know. 'Should you return, I will not put a stamp in your passport, the custom officer replied. That way on the other side of the border it will seem that you have never been to Israel. With an Israeli stamp, you will never be able to enter Arab countries anymore. It didn't make much sense to me. After all a Jordan official had escorted me to the Israeli border. He saw me entering Israel. Sometimes it is better not to understand. It all happened in a very relaxed way. No aggressiveness . I didn't even notice that those Middle East people where I was in contact with disliked each other. They were all very nice. They knew I was from the press. However, nobody even tried to blacken each other.

I stayed at the King David Hotel in Jerusalem. I considered it as a favor that I was introduced to the very roots of the Jewry and the dreadful souvenirs of the Holocaust. It was a very special experience. It brought me back to my youth when I had lived between those victims without realizing it. Most of the Jews I met settled in Israel after World War II, some of them had never been in that war. However, they were still traumatized. They took me to the Kibitzes where I was the privileged witness of entire families working in the burning sun, from morning until night, to fertilize the soil. They hardly saw their children who were brought up in nurseries. Those men and women who had lived in the western world with all their privileges had given up good life to do unpaid hard work. Once a year they were allowed to buy one or two garments, unless a new farming machine was needed. This had priority.

The Rabbis from South America I met had very different attitudes. The Israelis who lived in the country were extremely religious. It was a mean of defense. They were far different from the Jews that came as a tourist. Motivation is different as interest.

On a Saturday, I decided to go on a ride on my own. I borrowed the car of my driver who was not allowed to drive anyway. I drove to Jaffa, one of the oldest seaports of the world. At the Jaffa Gate I read that it was forbidden to take pictures on Sabbath; I supposed that this applied to Jewish people, so I drove on. While I did so my car was regularly hit by gravel some people threw at my car. I hadn't realized that it was against the Jewish religion to drive on a Saturday. I considered myself a Christian, so I drove on to the beach of Eilat for lunch. The dining room in the very fancy hotel was crowded. A notice on the entrance informed me that it was forbidden to smoke on Sabbath. Main reason, on Sabbath it is forbidden to light a fire. I – reluctantly – follow legal orders but have problems to follow veto's imposed by religious authorities away of places of worship. I nearly broke my neck once in the Emerald Temple in Thailand when seated on the floor, as I was supposed to do, I tried to get up without pointing my toes to the Buddha – a blasphemy . However, in a public restaurant. No way!

A waitress seated me at a large table with a Jewish family and their children. Before long I was engaged in a very interesting conversation. After dessert, I asked the waitress for an ashtray wondering what was going to happen. She brought me one and I lighted my cigarette. My neighbors, including the children, turned way from me and ignored me for the rest of my stay.

I left Israel. At home I went to Cherie to thank her for her support. While I was waiting for her to show up, I overheard some of her clients, diamond people, arguing with someone at the counter about a trip they had to make to Zurich. There was no direct flight from a Belgian Airport, and they were complaining about it. They didn't like to do a transfer with their precious diamonds. When Sabine came in she joined the conversation and as usual came in with a solution. A private flight from our Airport in Antwerp. On a flash of inspiration, I asked Sabine if she would be interested in someone who flew for her : meaning what if I learned to fly. Sabine was always in for a decent challenge, and she agreed. The next day I went to the Airport of Antwerp to learn how to fly.

Chapter 15
Up in the Air

In Milano with my boy friend Franco Giovanini

The man behind the desk at the Flying School of the Airport of Antwerp didn't seem a bit surprised when I walked in and asked him if he could learn me to fly. Outsiders thought I must be crazy to even consider the possibility, we were in the middle of the sixties, but Jos Vermeiren, the man in question found it perfectly normal.. He asked me when I wanted to start, we made an appointment for the next morning at eight. And that was that.

It was a beautiful morning. On the tarmac, a Cessna 152 was waiting for me. My first flight was unforgettable. While Jos directed me how to handle one of the two controls sticks, we were flying over the harbor, an image that I will never forget. Nothing can be more beautiful than a port seen from the air. The water that flows to eternity, the activities around the ships, the atmosphere that sticks to your body, there is nothing like it. Each port has a heart, I felt it beating, it was great.

My first flight tasted for more. The days after I flew repeatedly. In the evening, we had drinks together, and more than one , with the instructors and the pupils who told the most incredible flight stories. One of them I experienced myself when I was given into the hand of a flying instructor called Ralf. I had heard he was a lady man. Quite good looking to. He was a good instructor as well. He taught me never to be afraid when flying an airplane, even if the instructor put his hand in your pants. When he did it for the first time I was startled. However, what could I do. It was either to accept it or an emergency landing. And I wasn't qualified. So what the hell. And to be exactly honest. It was exiting and a lot of fun.

Then I received a letter from Shehadeh, my guide from Jordany. He invited me to spend Xmas in the Holy Land.. I went. His family was very happy to see me again. Neighbors were invited. It worried me. Suddenly, out of the blue I became Shehade's fiancée. I was staying in a hotel nearby, but it was out of the question that Shehadeh came with me to my room. It simply was not done. I was taken on sightseeing tours, went to the Holy Mess in Bethlehem – quite a horror, it looked more than a fancy fair . It was Ramadan, there was no place I could eat during the day, and Shehadeh remained the perfect gentlemen, which didn't help very much. I had almost given up on him when it happened. It happened on an excursion to Ramallah. It was burning hot, it was noontime, I was hungry and refused to say another word to Shehadeh if he didn't come up with some food. Wishful thinking. Ramadan, you know. My 'fiançé' realized I was not joking. Suddenly, he saw the light. In Ramallah he had a boy friend who owned a restaurant. At this time of the day he was closed of course, but maybe he could fix up something. The house was locked but through a back door we found the owner. Shehadeh explained him what the problem was. There was a lot of arguing but finally the young man brought us to a small room at the back of the house. He closed the curtains, told us to keep quiet and after a while brought us a couple of sandwiches. This felt better. It was pitching dark and somehow rather romantic. Shehadeh must have felt it to and suddenly we were laying on the floor doing where I had traveled across thousands of miles for. At last. It was heaven. At the 'moment supreme' when I figured, as far as I could think straight, that we were alone in the world, outside somewhere in the garden a chorus of boys and girls started to sing the Flemish national hymn, which starts like that : 'He will never be tamed the proud Flemish Lion' . I nearly went in shock. What happened to be that the day before Flemish scouts who were attending the Holy Ceremonies in the Land of God had asked, and received, permission to put their tents in the garden of the restaurant where we were so happily making love on the floor. Later in life, when I hear this Hymn, I always remembered the two of us rolling in interrupted ecstasy.

I returned to Belgium quite satisfied with myself. My recent escapades, had not been unnoticed by Lode, He feared that I was getting bored by our regular trips to Spain, a country that I loved but that at little or no surprises anymore for me, so he came forward with a new territory to explore, Italy. He introduced me to Walter Gardini, Capo of the Servizio Stampa at the Ministry of Foreign Affairs, who, by the way, would become later Ambassador to Italy in Paris, and who would open all the necessary doors for me. Walter was a charming man. He took me quite willingly under his wings and learned me to live like an Italian. Never breakfast at my hotel, or at home, for that matter, that had to be done at a terrace on the Via Veneto. In Rome the place to be and to have dinner was the restaurant of the Slaughterhouse. The first time I was invited in there I was full of expectancy until I noticed what was on my plate : udder which brought me back to my childhood. Once a week, on Sunday, father gave mother her weekly allowance. Which wasn't that much. Next Saturday there was not much money left. The cheapest meat on the market was the udder. And that's what we got. I hated it.

But there were hilarious moments as well. One day we were driving in a suburb of Rome and Walter was driving too fast. On the corner of a street we were stopped by carabinieri. Walter stepped out of his car and started a lively discussion with the policeman. With my seasonal Italian boy friend I had learned basic Italian so I was able to follow the discussion. Walter tried to persuade the agent not to give him a fine which was impossible because the man had started writing on his official notebook. The conversation went on in order to find out how the situation could be solved. At the end of his wits Walter asked him what it was going to cost him. The carabinieri told him . Walter esteemed it far too much and asked if he had nothing cheaper. The agent considered the question for a moment and replied that the cheapest fines went to cyclists. How much are they ? Walter requested. It was a much lower fee. Walter asked if he could not have that one. Done, said the carabanieri and this solved the case. The agent had his fine and Walter's car had become a bicycle. I have a feeling that this is only possible in Italy.

It was not entirely fun. I had interviews to come up with. The one I specially remembered was the one with Maria Rubiola the PR of the Fiat company and personal assistant of Gianni Agnelli. It was a lady in her fifties, always dressed in black, tailor suits were not in for ladies at that time, never any makeup or jewels. But she was not to be underestimated, she was the decision maker. Important clients of Fiat were well aware of it. Emirs of the Middle East loaded her with expensive jewelry. But Maria didn't like jewelry. The jewels disappeared in the safe of Fiat with the name of the generous donor. I was in her office when a clerk came to tell her than some Arabian Prince had arrived unexpectedly. Panic all over , Maria screaming : Where is my ring, where is my ring ? And while somebody took care of the Prince another one hurried to the safe to dig up the precious jewel. When the Prince entered the office the ring was shining at Maria's finger.

In Milano I passed by the Grand Hotel Duomo not far from the Dom when I noticed an hysterical crowd shouting the name of the Beattles . The entrance was blocked by a couple of carabinieries but that Walter of mine had learned me how to deal with them. I showed them a paper, said something which referred to the Servizio Stampa Affari Esteri. And without any more questions I was given a floor and a room number, I knocked , a voice invited me to come in and I stood eye to eye with the Beatles. When I left them half an hour later safeguarded by carabinieri the youngsters nearly begged for an autograph.

When I returned to Belgium I found a message from Shehadeh saying that he was coming to visit me. It had been more than four months since we saw each other for Christmas and I was quite flattered that he had not forgotten me. What he hadn't forgotten either was that we were supposed to be engaged. Which was not quite how I saw it. But he was an handsome boy, a little young he was in his early twenties, and I was fifteen year older, and when I picked him up at the airport, I felt the same thrill as I felt in Jordan. In Belgium, there were no problems to be in the same hotel room, Shehadeh was more relaxed. We stayed together for an entire week and we said goodbye with a vague promise to see each other soon to make some arrangements or whatever.

I was anxious to fly solo vaguely dreaming about one day flying on my own to Jerusalem. However, my first solo flight wasn't that sensational at all.

One morning I was walking with my charming inspector to the Cessna ready to board when a middle aged couple stopped us. The man wanted to learn how to fly and his wife was getting hysterical because she thought it was too dangerous. Raf tried to calm her down by saying that this young lady – meaning me – was also a student and he suggested that they would wait for him until we were back. We flew away, and did a couple of touches and goes. I had learned that I had to look out for the roof of the hospital nearby, to fly from there to the Gevaert factory with his typical chimney and from there back to the airport. On the second landing at the Airport, we did 'touch and go' Raf told me to stop on the tarmac.. I did what was asked, he opened the door, went out and ordered : GO! I went of without realizing, at first, that I was out there on my own. I flew past my identification marks. Suddenly I realized that I was losing my way If I didn't come to my senses. Somehow I turned the plane to the direction where I came from.. Per fortuna I lived in the neighborhood so I was able to orientate myself a little. I noticed Gevaert and flew in that direction. I didn't even had time to make my prayers, priority was given to the look out for the runway. How I did it, I will never know, but finally I noticed runway 25 where I had to be. I went down determined to take off again and do the perfect show. But this was without taking my airplane into consideration. Runway 25 was a grass runway and when I landed I noticed that the plan wasn't reacting as it should do.. From the Tower I heard a familiar voice asking if something was wrong. Yes, I answered, I think I have a flat tire. Stay where you are, the voice from the Tower ordered, we come and get you. A few moments later the fire brigade of the Airport came picked me up and dropped me in front of the terrace crowded with people. My first solo flight was a fact. Later Raf told me that when suddenly I was out of his site. he wondered where I had gone to. I forgot to ask him if the gentleman that I met before was still as eager to learn to fly after he saw my demonstration.

Chapter 16
Troubled Waters

Needless to say that I was not quite ready to fly for Madame Sabine more so I never would be. Not that I was fed up with it, but I found myself pregnant. By Shehadeh of all people. I wrote him a letter that he was about to become a father. He was so filled with joy that I feared for a moment, he intended to kidnap me on a flying carpet. The idea enchanted me for a moment, worse things could have happened. However, whatever plans we were making, they were nipped in the but by Moshe Dajan. The six day war brook out and a rather unknown Israeli Minister of Defense took in Jerusalem, made it Israeli territory and wrote history. Going in of out of the country was for a long while out of the question . There was no communication what so ever. I had no idea that happed to my Romeo. One thing was for sure. His baby would be safe in Belgium and waiting for him whenever his father showed up. However rigid she was for herself, my mother was rather broadminded – with a daughter like me, she had to be – I decided to wait and see. However, I didn't have to wait long.

Things turned out quite differently. My niece Lily came into the picture. Lily – thirteen years older than myself, of the same age as my sister – married her childhood sweetheart Armand in the thirties and left for Belgian Congo – now called Zaire – where Armand found himself a job with the Belgian Government. I was still a child when I went with the entire family to wave her out at the dockside. It was overwhelming. We never had known someone before who went that far away from home. Lily and Armand were both from very humble families. The parents from Lily where housekeepers, the parents from Armand had a small shoemaker shop. In Leopoldville, where they were going to stay for several years it was a big luxury. The colonialists were pampered. Boys, Negroes of course, to look after their big houses, parties you name it. When they both returned home for a holiday, they were completely transformed. They made it and they made sure that everyone noticed it. It was also the first time that I came in touch with racism. The way they talked about their black servants was totally disgusting. They couldn't have children which they compensated by interfering with everybody else's.

They returned to Belgium when the battles started in Congo. They had to run away and settled in Antwerp where they drowned their family with good advices. They had nothing else to do. When Lily learned that I was expected a baby from a man with a black skin, it was more chocolate, but she didn't know she had never seen him, she was outraged. When she found out that the father was not able to join me, she came daily to my house, so called to comfort me, but I have my doubts. Finally, the entire situation was a little to much for me. In my family, nobody was ever ill, we didn't have a house doctor. When I didn't feel well Lily offered me to go to her general practitioner. A man she had met in the Congo, a colonialist and a racist just like she was. He treated me friendly and asked me to return. I did. He checked me up real good. A couple of days later I had a miscarriage. Lily said she was so sorry. And turned to other cousins with advice.

The situation escalated in the Middle East, and I didn't hear from Shehade again until many years later.

Life went on. Apart from the interview with Maria Callas in the Opera of Paris where she performed Norma and where I met her lover Aristote Onassis, and Oona O'Neill the wife of Charles Chaplin my European interviews were mostly made to order now, like the one of Maurice Bejart, when he presented his 'Le Sacre du Printemps' in the Monnaie in Brussels.

In order to publish art historical books mostly written by himself Lode Seghers had set up a company Ars Europea.. In the beginning of the sixties he had published a book about Mannerisms in cooperation with Prof. Bousquet, a French art historian married to the sister of Queen Sirikit of Thailand . We often went to see them in their home in Lyon. At the end of the sixties Lode wanted to specialize in books about the paintings of the Prado in Madrid. Lode was a very talented artist . From business, he didn't know a thing. His first publication was a disaster. The text translated by someone who pretended to be English was full of mistakes. The sheets were not properly dried and clung to each other. Impossible to put on the market. His second book looked much better. It was about a painting of Catherine de Medici with her girl friend, both with naked breasts. Catherine had the nipple of her friend between thumb and forefinger.

The picture was on the cover of the book. Two days later the vice squad, tipped by passengers for attack of decency ,came to the shop, an antique shop with a fine reputation opposite the National Bank, to remove the book. Lode went nearly behind bars. That did it. He closed his books and asked for a retirement fee. It was refused because he had connections with the Germans during the war. The man that had saved so many young lives was marked as a collaborator and until he died was refused assistance by the Government.

Meanwhile there had been some more changes in my life. A couple of years earlier, my father, in his late seventies left the house and went living at the other end of town with his sweetheart, a Czechoslovakian girl just over thirty. Not much later I heard they had a baby..

I also moved to another house with my mother.. I bought her a dog to keep her company when I was out traveling. Through Peggy, the little bastard in question, I met the vet Ralf Distave and was in for the most tiresome years of my life. Ralph was divorced and had the character of the lifelong bachelor. He seduced me on the spot . He was working like hell, often past midnight.

In his Vet Clinic in the neighborhood of Antwerp he took it for granted to call me in the middle of the night when I was fast asleep, to join him for a drink in his favorite club followed by several sexual fantasies at his home until the next morning. The man was as strong as an ox and didn't seem to need a rest. Which was not exactly my case. I was running around during daytime half asleep. Nevertheless, somehow I jumped out of my bed when he called, I was hooked, Since my love story with Pierre Grisar I didn't have a relationship that was so demanding. For several months my will was put in the fridge.

Since his bad experience with our authority Lode was no longer the same. His friends in Spain and Italy were also disappearing from the scene. The boy friend of his wife had died , and she was a fine haute couture seamstress with a lot of clients. She took good care of her husband, and we had become very good friends. The perfect mistress, remember. She knew that I had kept her marriage together. And if at the time it hadn't meant so much to her, now she valued it. I saw Lode regularly for a coffee in town or dinner at his house but the targets for my interviews had faded with Lode. I was looking for something new.

Ralf brought the answer when he returned from the States where he had been attending a Congress. He had discovered the telephone answering service, very popular in the States, but unknown in our country. The fact that he mentioned it to me seemed to mean that he preferred that I stay home in Antwerp, close to him and available. He did add that I would never consider it as I liked to much my journeys abroad. That settled it. I do not like that someone tells me what I am able and unable to do.

The problem was that such a service worked around the clock. Staff means money and I had no money. Lode came once more with the solution. He still had his office for his Ars Eurpea adventures. Our relationship had become totally platonic, but we still did remain very good friends. An office, next to his, was for rent and he suggested that I should take it. Alternately, we could make night shifts.

We didn't expect too much work in the beginning, and we may even be able to sleep once in a while. We only had to find staff for the week ends. Students and retired people could do the job. Lode had some friends left, and, he sent me to one of them who worked at the Flemish Economic League an Association of Employers. A very friendly man gave me a golden clue. If my employees didn't work longer than 1 hour and 55 minutes daily, I didn't have to pay taxes on them. That came in handy. Needless to say that that was impossible to check. My office was next to the one from the telephone company. Exactly, what I needed. Ralf had brought me some literature about American answering service companies but when I went to our telephone company to explain my plans I was told that linking telephones was considered wire tamping and was strictly forbidden in Belgium. If I didn't believe him, I should ask more information from his boss engineer Bally. To Bally I was a gift from heaven. For years, he had been trying to start such a project but was rejected by his superiors. In the shortest possible time, he gave ma a crash course in telephony – after a couple of days I used technical terms, as if I had used them my entire life – political strategy and touchiness and the promises that he would always be there for me, whenever I needed him. The decision maker for telephone matters in Brussels was a member of the socialist party. I had to find someone in Antwerp, who was taken for granted in that party. Jos

Van den Eynde, the editor in chief of the Voksgazet, the leading socialist newspaper for which I had worked occasionally as a journalist was the man to contact. I went to see Van den Eynde in his office in the Somerstraat and explained my problem. Van den Eynde was not merely a politician but also a businessman. He asked me if it was technical possible, I answered yes, he took his telephone called the socialist in Brussels and barked to him that he had someone in his office with an interesting proposition, and that he had to see me next day. Actually, Van den Eynde didn't bark, his was the way he expressed himself. However, 24 hours later I was seated in front of the right person, at the right place in Brussels.

Chapter 17
The Channel of Corinth

Life is beautiful. If you only know how to live it.

Every possible assistance was granted for my new venture.. Direct lines where a problem and I was advised to contact the member of Parliament Minister to be Rika de Backer, she lived in Antwerp, and if I could convince her I could be sure of the backing of the entire Catholic Party. One visit did it , which was only logical, she was part of the opposition. They wanted to Engineer Bally was so much enchanted by my successful intervention that he promptly sent somebody to my office to install telephones all over the place. In anticipation of direct lines, I could offer to my clients their own telephone number, that in turn they could offer to their clients as a permanent answering service. At the same period, a novelty was on the market, publicity papers which were put free of charge in everybody's mailbox. The first one on the market was a small publishing company with two employees. I went to them for publicity but when I came out of their door, I had a contract in my pocket between the manager and myself. He became my partner, and I had free publicity all over his paper. He was a very PR minded man who wanted to start our cooperation with a fancy party. I talked it over with engineer Bally who advised me to contact Bell Telephone. And that is how David embarked with Goliath. Dozens of candidates were queuing up to work for me. But first I had to look for customers. That was another piece of cake. To start up something new in Belgium takes ages. However, the first company that I contacted signed up. Noticing the response of the big chief I believed that I had discovered a goldmine. I was too early for my appointment and because Armand van den Bossche, the man that I was going to meet, was not in I went to park my car in a parking space. At the same moment Armand arrived, ran to me while he shouted 'Am I too late?'. A little while later my first contract was a fact. Williams, the company in question was specialized in refrigerating machines for supermarkets and soup kitchens all over Belgium and for the Antwerp Zoo. We had a list of their technicians. Should their clients have problems after office hours they could call us, and we could send them who ever they needed? My new staff was briefed and of we went.In the beginning, we had no staff to operate at night, so I did the permanence myself and slept between my telephones.

On a Saturday night at around two o'clock I had a guardian of the Zoo on the line. He panicked. The fridge broke down in the penguin quarters, the ice was melting, the animals didn't know anymore where to turn to and neither did he. On top of all this they expected a new load of animals in the morning, and all of them were used to icy temperatures.

I looked and found a technician on duty at the other side of the country, and I had the distinct feeling that he thought I had been drinking when I mentioned penguins. However, finally he got the picture, he drove to Antwerp and solved the problem.

It was not that easy to find customers. I had no money to pay night staff, so I stayed every night at the office. On Saturday night, I went in with my sandwiches only to come out on Monday morning. Sometimes Lode came in to replace me.

This went on for a couple of months. I had turned to the show business industry where I managed the diary of local celebrities as Louis Neefs, Ann Christie and Wannes van de Velde, it helped to pay the rent, but that's all what it was. Then a man walked in who was looking for a company just like ours. He lived out of town and needed to send telexes to his business relations abroad. He had no telex of his own, neither did we, but I could send them at the Telephone office next door. He gave us a check as prepayment but when we went to the bank he happened to be uncovered.

I nearly had a stroke. I called him on top of my nerves, and he brought us the money in cash. I had no idea what kind of business he was in, I suppose it was something tricky. Before long he happened to be loaded with money and our most important client . With the two of us, Lode and me, we were working around the clock and our economical problems belonged to the past. I hired my first employees.

After this stressful period – I also had Ralf to go out with and in between I wrote articles for the press – I finally found some time to relax . The Association for Tourist Press was having their annual Congress in Athens, and I registered. On the Sabena carrier, I met several other delegates to the conference. The Managers of the Brussels TAP offices (Transportes Aero Portugueses) where a cheerful crowd. In Athens, they were joined by a member of their Embassy; a very handsome Portuguese who took a fancy at me and who followed me like a shadow. When the Congress was over the participants where invited for a trip to Olympia. I hate to travel by coach and my Portuguese friend offered to drive me. I got in his cabrio and everybody left.

At the Channel of Corinth the caravan made a stop over.. On both sides of the road souvenirs and drinks were offered on local market booths. My friend left and came back with a bunch of straw flowers, very fancy. Later I was told that we were in a kind of pilgrimage village where women came to ask the Madonna for fertility.

When I returned home, I hung those flowers against the wall. Four months later I was pregnant again.

99

Chapter 18
I Figured That
I Had a Daughter

It was rather funny. A great deal of my life I had linked sex with having babies, and had been terrified at the idea. When I started my sexual activities condoms were not very popular . My escapades were always followed by days and weeks with the sword of Damocles over my head terrified that something was going to happen that would change the rest of my life. In my family, there were several small children, and I had friends with kids but I cannot exactly remember that those small toddlers and myself were attracted to each other. I do not remember one picture of myself with a baby on my arm who didn't cry. My general practitioner, a client of Tele Call, who through a routine examination discovered that I was pregnant told me with a very worried face that I was going to have a baby. After all I was 47 years old. However, what I didn't expect anymore happened : for a moment, I was dumbfounded but seconds later I was full with joy. It was about five years, since I had a miscarriage. I couldn't say that I had been grieving a lot, but on the other hand, it had made me thinking .The couple of months that I had been pregnant had left a mark on me. When I was in a nostalgic mood. I often felt sorry, that although I was very surrounded I had nothing that I could call my own. Finally, I accepted with some kind of resignation that I would never be a mother. I was wrong. From the moment, I heard the news this unborn small piece of a human being took a definite place in my life. Another unbelievable fact was that nobody was negative about it.. Even the job students at my office urged me not to consider abortion. I did not even think of it. The months that followed didn't change much to my lifestyle. During week-ends, I was still sleeping between the telephones, but I wasn't alone any longer. During the daytime, I went hunting for new customers, and here and there I found one. My weight was not changing too much, it was hard to notice that I was expecting. On a bright morning, I had a meeting with a Jewish diamond trader. The discussion went well. When he was about to sign the contract, he mentioned my pregnancy. From behind his desk he asked me when the baby was expected . 'Today' I answered. He turned pale and led me gently to the front door. I had the feeling that he expected me to deliver on his coach. However, it was going to take another ten days before I was going to give birth. And after all it came rather unexpected. My sister who stayed with me overnight had just left when I felt that something was going to happen. I called a taxi to drive me to the hospital, my sister was picked up on the way and the taxi driver who noticed what was going to happen had the same grayish look as my Jewish diamond trader. Finally we arrived where we were supposed to be.

At the desk, they called for a nurse who put me on a stretcher with the intention to bring me to the delivery room, but we didn't make it that far. She dropped me in the first available room , a midwife ran toward me and screamed 'My God, are you lucky' and after a couple of minutes there she was.. I had a daughter. The nurse showed her to me, but I didn't trust it very much. The newly born was wrapped in a kind of a towel, and I was convinced that at least she was missing an arm or a leg, after the life I had been living. They were about to put her in my arms. Knowing how clumsy I could be I was sure I was going to drop her. So they put her between my legs on the stretcher and drove us to our room. Then I felt something that I never will forget in my life. Tiny little fingers who messed about my thighs. The first contact with her mother, with me. The most wonderful feeling I could imagine. I named her Alexandra after a Pelican, the mascot of Mykonos, who always followed me when I was on the Island. . Alternatively, maybe I gave her without realizing a Greek name on behalf of the straw flowers that were suspended in my living room.. Proud as a peacock I brought my daughter home. Meaning, I was convinced it was my daughter until, a couple of weeks later, when I received an official letter to point out to me that my child was illegal, that consequently, she was not mine, unless I should recognize her, adopt her and more of those ludicrous things and that, in anticipation, if I should drop dead, half of my belongings would go to her and the remainder to my sister. Hence before she was born, I could leave all my belongings to the zoo but now that I had a daughter I could not act anymore like I wanted. Not that there was much to inherit but there are limits. I was also invited to visit the Court of justice of the peace. I was furious. I did what I was told with the firm intention to make it clear to the judge, or whoever I was going to meet what my feelings were about those men and women in robe. I had to wait in the hall . I saw a young girl correctly dressed stepping out of one of the rooms, the kind of girl one could expect behind an office desk. Someone came to pick me up and introduced me in the room from where the girl had left. The Judge of Piece was waiting for me. It was a woman. She waited until I had poured my frustrations all over her. When I was out of breath she said that I was absolutely right. But, she added, the law is the law. It went back to the days of Napoleon, but we had to respect it. She mentioned the girl which I had seen before and who had left her baby in the maternity. Meanwhile a male registrar had entered the room and listened in on us. When I asked the judge if she was meant that I could leave my baby in the middle of the road without somebody could interfere. 'Indeed' she answered . Before I had time to explode the registrar said "women are always complaining, but they never act". I am not sure if this had a positive or a negative effect on me. One thing was for sure. I was going to do something. The problem was that I didn't know what.

Minister of Justice, Herman Vanderpoorten, made the same night, on occasion of Human Rights Day, a speech on Television that brought me the answer.

Chapter 19
Paula and Alexandra Marckx Against Belgium

December 10, the day when I returned home from the Justice of Peace, was, the United Nations Human Rights Day. Minister Vanderpoorten was asking attention for all the babies from the third world without rights. I was hardly listening. 'All very well' I said to myself but what about that little Belgian baby in his crib who, on paper, has no mother. And no father either, for that matter, but that at least was a personal choice. The end of the story was that I wanted to do something with that European Court of Human Rights to give my daughter where she was entitled to : a family. The boy friend of a law student, who worked at my Tele-Call office, was the son of Ricka de Backer, a well known politician from the Catholic Party. I asked Betty if she knew what the European Court was all about, and she did. She gave me a document called Convention for the Protection of Human Rights and Fundamental Freedoms, which just had been published and in which were mentioned the 66 points that the countries that signed the treaty had to respect. Minister Paul van Zeeland signed it for Belgium in 1961. Other subscribers where Robert Schuman for France, Konrad Adenauer for Germany, and Anthony Eden for Great-Britain .

It was rather dull material until I reached point 8, which said 'There shall be no interference by a public authority with the exercise of these rights except such as is necessary in a democratic society in the interests of national security, public safety or the economic well-being of the country, for the prevention of disorder or crime, for the protection of health of morals, or for the protection of the rights and freedom of others. Everyone has the right for respect for his private and family life, his home and his correspondence.' Which meant that according to the treaty the Belgian State had no right to interfere with my private life, and it was none of its business if I wanted to be an unmarried mother. I took a pen and wrote a letter to the Secretary General of that Organization telling him a few things about what happened in my country. The man replied that my rights had not been violated, because my link with my family was not denied.

Well, If that is the case, I thought, Alexandra will write him a letter. And so she did, with a little technical help from her mother. It started with 'I am a six month old baby and am putting in a complaint against Belgium' The letter ended with 'From the bottom of my little heart, I hope that a baby of my age can depend on an Organization such as yours to defend her Rights'. Before long an answer arrived. It said that the complaint was accepted, and that they also considered that my rights had been violated as well. An official file was opened : "Paula and Alexandra Marckx against Belgium".

The owner of a private garage where I parked my car happened to be the sister of Tilly Stuckens, a well known journalist who worked for a national paper and who specialized in women's rights. Tilly knew about the problems of unmarried women and was looking for a pilot case. When she learned where I was up to, she came to see me.

Next day Alexandra's letter was front page news and was immediately reproduced by every leading newspaper in the country. The ball was rolling.

Then followed a regular correspondence with Strasbourg. When it became to academic Tilly came to my rescue. She knew a Mony Van Look, a young trainee and Researcher for family law at the University of Louvain. She was going to help me out. The University of Louvain in turn was also offering support. The newspapers and magazines loved the baby and her mother attacking Belgium. A welcome item for their readers. As Mr. Nizet, who represented Belgium at the Trial, told me later 'When we learned that a baby attacked us in court we all smiled but when we noticed that her mother was a journalist we didn't feel like laughing anymore.

The Belgian State had a hell of a time to find a lawyer to represent them. Nobody was very eager to put up a fight against a baby. With the necessary financial rewards, they finally found one, a former professor of Mony. He tried to play it smart by offering her a job in his law office. She didn't even take time to consider it. She refused. Then they contacted me to ask to drop the case. Belgium was planning anyway to change the law concerning illegitimate children, they claimed And everything I had spent so far on the case would be highly reimbursed. I refused as well.

Lode, who adored Alexandra from the moment she was born, advised me to recognize my child. Through official channels, he had learned that, as long as in Strasbourg, there was no decision about her destiny, and this could take a while, Alexandra was not legally my daughter. Anyone could take her away from me. Herr Godfather, a divorced man without children was willing to recognize her together with me. We still had to find witnesses. Lode, bright as ever, advised me to find at least one witness who could not be accused of senility. The most obvious was Leona Detiège, an unmarried mother by choice, at that moment Alderman of Fine Arts in Antwerp. Later she was to become Burgomaster of our city. She accepted without hesitation. Then the merry-go-round started. I had the police force at my door to ask me if I was making enough money to provide for my child, if I had a suitable place to live in and more of those incredible questions. If I had been married, living on water and bread in an attic that had been of no importance at all. They send me the district policeman that I had known for ages. His inquiries were nearly hilarious. He asked me how much money I was making. I replied that I had no idea as I had no regular wages. What do you think about 100.000 Bfr a month ? I replied that it suited me fine. OK, he said, so it will be; He produced a favourable rapport, and we could go on to the next step.

After some months of corresponding , mostly between Moni and her French colleague at the Court, we were requested to Strasbourg to take part in the trial. The expenses involved were taken care of by the Court. Moni's boyfriend, Josse van Steenberge, who later would become Dean of the Antwerp Universities, and with whom Moni still lives in unmarried bless with their three children, went with us. They both belonged to the generation of the Flower Power people. We settled in the Grand Hotel opposite the station of Strasbourg. We went to one of our rooms and went to work.

The recognition had taken place in the municipal house of Wilrijk, a suburb of Antwerp where Alexandra was born. They obviously were not used to a situation like mine. When I showed up flanked by two citizens of indefinite age, my baby in my arms and the Alderman of Fine Arts the entire Municipality was nearly in shock. An Alderman of Antwerp should be at least welcomed by the Alderman of Wilrijk, but he was nowhere in sight. Leona Detiège saved the situation. She knew the law by heart. When it finally was over, and we went outside Alexandra was finally mine.

Moni and I are both Sagittarius and according to the zodiac we function at our best in stress situations. Moni had the choice between French and English language for her counsel's speech . However, none of them where her mother tongue. We had worked overnight . It was daylight when she was ready with her arguments. One of them was rather impressive : She had statistical proves that unmarried women were the only kind of women where numbers of births were improving. Without having slept, we went to the Building where the Court of Strasbourg was situated and in the very imposing hall, we saw a huge board within black and white.

Paula and Alexandra Marckx against Belgium.

...written in enormous capitals. It was quite impressive.

We entered the room where the Case was going to be pleaded. Mony had to sit on one side on a bench , I was directed to a bench on the right. All by myself but not for long . A young man took place next to me and introduced himself. He represented the Consulate of Belgium in Strasbourg. I pointed out that he was seated on the wrong bench because I had introduced a Case against his employer : the Belgium State. He replied that it didn't matter to him, he was convinced that I was right.

The judges entered one by one. It was not very encouraging. If compared to the youngest one Santa Claus looked like a teenager. One even fell asleep during the trial.

But they were good sports. The way some of them put their questions made me feel they want to help us. The north European judges were really astonished that Belgium still had that kind of law. Then it was Moni's turn. She was brilliant. At the end of the session we were told that the Commission, who was in command agreed with us, and that she was going to put a complaint against Belgium for violating the rights of their citizens.

When we left the Courtroom we were stopped by a judge of New Zealand, who happened to be in the country and who invited us for dinner. Because, he said, I want to telephone to my wife to tell her who I met over here.

The next day we returned home. All what we could do now was wait until the Commission made her official point. They did. Then they started in their own name a Trial against Belgium at the Court of Human Rights. They accused them for violating the treaty of which Belgium was one of the signatories.

Chapter 20
The Marckx Case

The day after the Marckx Judment was pronounced:
great joy at Alexandra's nursery class.
Alexandra, the little girl in cotton dress in front of me, becomes a star.

My company was doing very well. Rob van Dijck became our major customer. The man who, not that long ago, paid me with me an uncovered check was suddenly loaded. He liked our services. We were here to stay. The shuttle between the Telephone Company and our office took too much from our time, and we decided to buy our own equipment. Quite an investment but our mister Van Dijck opened new horizons to the company.

On a Sunday evening, I was watching the news broadcast on television when I heard that a terrible accident had taken place on the highway to the coast. A car went of the road, a family with two children was ejected. The woman was beheaded by her seat belt, her head landed on the lap of her little son seated behind her. They all died.

The next day the new furniture was delivered to my office. That is when I heard that the deadly victims that I had seen in the car accident where Rob van Dijck and his family. I was in shock. We had become close friends, and I lost a very important client when I needed him most. Incredible speculations where all over the newspapers. Millions of cash had been found in the car wreck, and it was suggested that it was linked with the mafia. However, I had fallen up to my neck in the shit.

One small bright light in a life of trouble I received a telephone call from Shehadeh. After more than ten years I was still living at the same address where he had come to see me, and he had kept my telephone number. He told me that he had fled from Jordan, he was married, had a travel agency in Thessaloniki in Greece and a four year old daughter. When he heard that I too had a four year old daughter, and that I was not married he said : you will never chance. He told me that he never had forgotten about me. That must have been nice to his wife . Later I moved and changed my telephone number. So that was the last I ever heard of my lover boy from Jordan.

It was very nice to know that I was still in the mind of a gorgeous man on the other part of Europe but that wasn't very helpful.

Lode, my very faithful Lode, suggested that I should return to my press activities. One of his connections, an art lover like himself, was Prince de Bourbon. The Prince lived in Paris. We went to see him, and he introduced us to a very well known Paris lawyer, Maitre Jean Violet. He was about to leave for his Summer residence in Bayonne and when he found out that Lode and me, and little Alexandra who was with us, where on our way to Spain, he invited us to stay in his residence for a couple of days. It was on our way and we agreed. We met his family, became friends and that is how I was almost sitting on the first row when not much later the scandal of the sniffing airplanes exploded with Jean Violet right in the middle.

A Belgian count and an Italian handyman swindled the French State for 800 million FF with an imaginary invention. The Italian came up with an equipment that he named "Vision Dirigée Selective". It meant to be installed in airplanes. When the airplane in question flew over an oleaginous piece of land it produced a whistling tome. The harder it whistled the more oil was to be found.

Master Violet was a close friend of President Valerie Giscard de'Estaing. Violet, who was the legal advisor of the two investors in the project knew there was a difference of opinion because Italian and Spanish interests were at stake. He advised d'Estaing to take his advantage of the quarrel and finally the President gave authorization to Elf – a French company – to buy the sole rights on the sniffle planes. What they did.

When we arrived in Bayonne Jean Violet gave me the scoop. I was delighted. It was published in newspapers and magazines all over the world. It was not before 1984 that the entire fraud was discovered. However, by then I was already busy with other occupations.

Nevertheless, we were not that far yet. I had to return home to put my company back on the rails. We would be out of business, unless we found new funds. I had a meeting with my English partners. They agreed to take over the majority of the shares and to take care of the daily business. On condition that I was staying in command. One of the managers of Pie, the English company, was going to settle in Antwerp to help me out. And that is how Tony Poole came into my life.

Tony Poole who I had met at the beginning of Tele Call was a look alike of James Bond in Dr. No. Charming, but dedicated to his company in a cowardly way . When entering our office his first action was to stick the map of Great Britain on the wall. The different branches of Pie, the company where he worked for, where indicated in red. Each time when he suggested something that I knew wouldn't work in Belgium – after all I had some experience in the field – he pointed with a dramatic gesture to the map saying 'They pay our wages, we will do what they say'. Years later when Great-Britain was reluctant to join Europe I often remembered that gesture. The second action he undertook was to make a pass at me. He was good looking, a little to sure about his abilities, but nobody is perfect.

We organized a party to introduce Tony to the local business authorities. He asked me almost politely if after the party he could stay overnight with me. After all he was English, and it were still the seventies. It was not quite my style to arrange what could be a one night stand two weeks in advance, but I decided to give it a try. I had the feeling that I'd better put some romance in my home to give it a push in the right direction. I decided on a selected choice of French cheese and a Château Margaux Grand Cru to commit murder for. When we arrived at home Tony told me that he didn't like cheese and that he wasn't much of a wine drinker either. But he felt a little hungry. Was there anything else? I looked in the fridge and noticed a guinea fowl. Would that do ? Yes, he said, he would. Meaning that at two o'clock in the morning instead of having sex I was preparing a damn chicken. I don't remember even what happened after we finished our meal but never again I was to invite a stranger in my home in the middle of the night.

It seemed that my Tony was clumsy in business as he was in bed. The disenchantment came at the General Assembly when the General Staff came over from London and Tony had to explain the dramatic losses we had suffered. It didn't happen to be my money. I didn't even chuckle, it was more getting rid of a frustration when I told him in the middle of the Assembly : Tony, I warned you that it would not work that way. Tony's reply was typical : Yes, but at least now we know that you were right. The General Staff didn't seem to realize how ridiculous this sounded.

They returned to their country and an economist came over to draw a business plan. Suddenly, I had in my office two Englishmen on my neck. One filled papers with letters and numbers provided by the other one who didn't have a clue how Belgian laws work. The end of the story was that they decided not to pay social security because this was not a custom in their home country. I didn't try to protest anymore . After numerous registered letters from official side, they decided to shut down the business. Just in time . At the moment, they arrived at the Airport of Deurne to take the plane to London our economist nearly was arrested. This was the end of Tele-Call.

Meanwhile I had learned that the Commission in Strasbourg was ready with her complaint against Belgium. That same year on June 13 the case was pled before the Court and in the evening I learned that Belgium had been found guilty by the Court of Human Rights in Strasbourg concerning the complaint introduced by Paula and Alexandra Marckx. The Marckx Case was a fact.

I didn't realize the impact this was going to have. From then on the Case obtained a steady place in the Law courses at the Universities.

111

Alexandra and myself had been recognized as a normal family and that was where it was all about.

Next day , when I brought Alexandra to the school where she was in nursing class the entire press was waiting for us. It was a respected catholic institute.

The nuns were interviewed and where stars of the day. They confessed that they had followed the entire Process on Television, and that they had prayed for us. No one seemed to care anymore that I was an unmarried mother and proud to be. I even don't recall that anyone asked me who was the father . I wouldn't have told it anyway.

At midnight on New Year Alexandra officially opened the Year of the Child and a little later I was elected by the Magazine Libelle Woman of the Year.

Chapter 21
An American Dream

For the time being, I was the Women of the Year without a future. I still had my journalistic ambitions but with Alexandra in nursery school I didn't feel like moving all over Europe.

In the beginning of Tele-Call, I had met a certain André Moermans who had his S.V.P. office at the World Trade Center Building in Brussels where I made an interview with Charlie de Pauw , a guru in the Building industry. De Pauw was the constructor and President of the World Trade Center in the Belgian capital. He invited me to a business lunch.. André Moermans was sitting next to me at the table of honor. André was from Antwerp, a playboy with style. He was managing the Belgian subsidiary of a daughter company of a French Television Station. They broadcasted the latest films with a human touch (f.i. Partir sans Laisser d'Adresse about a woman who ran away from home). During the broadcast, a text on the screen invited the viewers to send their comments to S.V.P. After the transmission a board of specialists responded. The Group was managed by Ghislaine de Marchand, a noble Lady by birth . André took me to Paris to meet her.

When Tony Poole was still around he became friends with the Manager of the World Trade Center, which had their offices near to the Town Hall in Antwerp. In England the name WTC was a concept . In Antwerp, it didn't came of the ground. It was through Tony that I learned about the Antwerp branch of the association. . As far as André was concerned as a tenant of the WTC in Brussels, he had links with the Antwerp section. They were regularly in need for guest-speakers for their business lunches and dinners and after Tele-Call was history André invited me as a guest. There were not too many women who could talk about their experience in business, so I was considered a welcome change at their table.

My speech was going to take place during dinner on a Friday night.

113

It was the hottest summer that we had in years. No one showed up, not a single soul. Most members of the Association lived in the country and didn't feel like going to listen, after long working hours, in a boiling hot town, to somebody they never had heard of . Finally I remained alone with André and as we both were optimists we managed to make it a very pleasant evening 'en tête à tête'. We talked about the WTC and where it stood for. André mentioned that Antwerp was not quite ready for it. The Manager had just given notice. With my new liberty in mind I asked him if I could not be considered as a candidate; André went to the telephone and called a Walter Osterrieth. the acting officer of the Association.. When he learned that André found somebody who was going to work for the moribund club, he invited me for a meeting next day.

Osterrieth belonged to the German business families that in the second half of the 19th century came to Antwerp and put their mark on the economic development of the city. Their names were whispered with esteem but nobody ever met them. Walter Osterrieth owned a shipping company. Fortunately through Pierre Grisar I had a fair notion of the shipping world. I was invited at Osterrieth's office. He was very distant and obviously aware of his importance.. To him. I was nothing but a shrimp that he could use someday. He gave me a brief summary about the importance of a W.T.C.and the problems they had in Antwerp. The end of the story was that they could use somebody to manage it but they had no money to pay for wages. At the contrary Antwerp had debts and owed money to the bank

My reply must have amazed him so much that I finally had his attention. . I suggested to work a year without payment at the WTC providing that they hired me for a serious fee if the year would prove successful. The idea came to me while we were talking – I mean when he was talking because I was unable to say one single word.. I had saved some money, and I could pull trough the year without being paid. Walter Osterrieth was a very stingy person. When somebody offered him to work one year free of charge he lost his voice for a moment. When he found it back he replied that it was worth considering. He suggested that I should meet as soon as possible Robert Dethier. Osterrieth made a call and next day I had an appointment with Robert Dethier at the buffet of the Brussels Central Station.

As soon as we met, Dethier asked me if I was ready to go to New York. The General Assembly of the World Trade Center was due in a week, and he wanted to introduce me to the Board of Directors. I had been traveling a lot in Europe, North Africa and the Middle East, but I had never been to the States. If I looked out of balance, he did not take any notice but gave me a brief history of the Association.

In the beginning of the sixties Dethier was in Tokyo in a meeting with Soichiro Honda; Guy Tozzoli and Paul Fabry. One of the items on their agenda was the necessity for a worldwide business network situated in sky-scraper's with a name in common : World Trade Center. The tenants of the Centers could interact with each other and with members worldwide who joined a World Trade Center Club. The four business men would be doing a marketing study in the towns where they were living : Tokyo, New York, New Orleans and Brussels.. The fabulous wealthy Soichira Honda, owner of automobiles and motorcycles of the same name had no problem to find investors for the project. He had a tower build in the center of Tokyo and with his private capital he financed a subway between his WTC building and the airport of Narita. Guy Tozzoli was a powerful man in New York, his brother was the President of the Port Authorities . They decided to build a World Trade Center in Manhattan, the Famous Twin Towers.

Paul Fabry had already a building in New Orleans that easily could be renamed to World Trade Center. Remained Robert Dethier. Dethier was a French speaking citizen of Brussels, who lost his heart to Antwerp. He had been living there during the war and made a fortune on the black market. His transactions had not passed unnoticed. Finally, he decided to return to Brussels where he was less known. The initial idea of the WTC network was to focus on harbors. To Dethier Antwerp was the place to be for a Belgium WTC. Dethier had friends in the right places. He formed a WTC and persuaded the most prominent Belgians, among which Paul Henri Spaak, to join the Board. Then he contacted his good friend Charley de Pauw, a very well known name in the building industry . De Pauw, was invited at the Town Hall of Antwerp to present his development plans.. That is where the problems started when De Pauw, who spook quite fluently the native language of the Flemish part of Belgium, refused to talk to the dignitaries in their language. He wanted to do the meeting in French. Quite unacceptable for the authorities. Exit De Pauw and also exit Dethier's dream to build a World Trade Center in Antwerp. The end of the sixties was nearing. The World Trade Center Association in New York was a fact . So where the World Trade Center Clubs, who had the same privileges as the tenants of the building who would soon be blooming all over the world, without having to own a Building.. A WTC building in Antwerp was only wishful thinking a WTC Club was installed in the building of The Chamber of Commerce which also became an Associate member . The business lunches would take place at the Restaurant Jacob van Galicie near the town hall. The World was not ready yet for World Trade Centers and Antwerp was certainly not. The Club was simmering along which left Robert Dethier, who considered the project more or less as had his baby, heartbroken.

This was the situation when I entered Central Station.

Robert must have been desperate to consider a perfect stranger, as I was, as his lifesaver. In about an half an hour time I was initiated in ten-year histories of the World Trade Centers .

In WTC circles Robert Dethier was still a powerful man. He was the buddy of Guy Tozzoli, who had become President of the World Trade Association worldwide . Robert immediately kind of adopted me.

A week after I met him, I was invited at a WTC meeting that took place at the Chamber of Commerce. I was introduced to the Antwerp Board members. I only knew one of them, Maurice Verboven, at that moment Manager of the Chamber. In my Tele-Call period, when the Chamber was still situated at the outskirts of the town Lode Seghers introduced me to Verboven in a desperate effort to bring my company to the attention of Antwerp business people. It had not been very successful but Maurice and I remained friends. It was in the beginning of August and the Board, after checking me out, asked me to return after the holidays with a business plan . I said that was no problem. No problem was the understatement of the year. When I went out of that meeting room, I had not a clue where to start. The nearest I ever had been to a business plan was when one of my English partners made one for Tele Call. Al I had noticed where a lot of figures on a couple of sheets of paper. And it nearly brought the one who had made it in prison. I had nobody to turn to for advice. I had to solve this on my own..

I went to our most important bookstore, looked for their section economy and noticed an American Book called Basic Marketing written by a certain Jerome McCarty. Americans are able to explain complicate matters in an uncomplicated way. I bought the book, took a seat at a terrace in the park and started reading. It was not exactly the literature where I was used to but through my journalistic background, I was used to lateral reading. I proceeded nicely, finally noticed a lead. and marked the examples that I could use for my business plan with a felt-tip pen. I went to a shop to photocopy the pages. Since years, I was a collector of thematic post stamps and had maps to put them into. Instead of stamps I inserted the sentences that I had cut from my photocopied sheets. Finally, I put them in the right order and replaced the word company by World Trade Center. My business plan came into shape.

Before I was going to translate it into Flemish and type it out I wanted the opinion of somebody such as Maurice Verboven. When he looked at my masterpiece, he said something, like 'I never saw anything like that it in my entire life'. However, the man had a great sense of humor, and he added : 'but after all it is not bad at all'.

I returned home, wrote my business plan and send it to the Board Members of the WTCA. A week later I was invited to the Chamber for a meeting. Everybody attended. My business plan was accepted. I was appointed manager of the World Trade Center of Antwerp. I just had to wait for a letter with instructions.

A week later Osterrieth called me panic stricken. A delegation of The World Trade Center Association planned to organize an Assembly in Antwerp. A delegation headed by Guy Tozzoli himself was coming to check how far our Club was proceeding. The Antwerp brigade had planned a dinner party for their important guests at the Yacht Club at the Left Bank of our River Scheldt, but they had no host to take care of the official welcome. I was called in a hurry. It was THE occasion for me to be introduced to the Top.

The first contact was excellent. Dethier introduced me to Tozzoli as being his 'crown princess' . The atmosphere was unique, to my eyes the Lights of the River Scheldt never had shone more brightly and our guests seemed to be convinced that Antwerp was doing well. At the table, I was seated next to a board member that I had seen at former meetings but never took notice of, Michel Plaisier. Osterrieth came to me and told me that Michel would help me to put our World Trade Center on the rails. When dinner was over the Belgians went home, and I escorted the foreign guests to the Waldorf hotel where they were staying . I was invited for a last drink at the bar. After the second glass, I was asked to provide them with some ladies in their hotel rooms. Not a very easy assignment in the middle of the night.. I had never done this before; Fortunately, the manager of the hotel was at hand and knew where to find them. When I finally went home I left my WTC delegation people in pleasant company. The reputation of our Club couldn't have been better..

Chapter 22
The Encounter. It Must Be Him

This successful week-end convinced Osterrieth that with the support of the Head Quarters in New York the WTC of Antwerp had a fair chance to succeed. Robert Vleugels, one of the managers and General Manager of the Port of Antwerp, who had his office had the town hall, invited every President of the Commercial Associations of Antwerp in the huge hall of the bench of Aldermen. It was a short meeting and only two questions were asked : is a WTC important to Antwerp and would the Commercial Associations support us? Nobody really seemed to know . Finally Captain Hubert of the C.M.B. (Compagnie Maritime Belge). said : it is worth trying. Captain Hubert was a very respected man in Harbor circles. Nobody argued anymore. They would give it a try.

No starting capital was offered , nor an office to function. The clerical work and what comes with it was going to be done in my living. A couple of days after I was in function Michel Plaisier called me. My 6 year old Alexandra just came out of her bad and I was drying her up.. When she heard the telephone ringing she ran to take the call and said in high spirit : Hello, I am standing here totally naked. I wonder if Michel, who didn't know about my familial situation, figured that I was on the line but he didn't give any comment when I took over. We agreed to meet at my home to draw out a strategy. I was about to meet THE love of my life.

We agreed that I would contact the Presidents of the Association whom I had met at the town hall. First I went to the economic associations of the Port .The first member I made was Captain Hubert and his CMB. From then on it didn't go as smoothly as I expected it to be but people from the harbor are in love with their city. Stefens Electro was one of those typical examples. It was a large family enterprise with father at the helm and his two sons managing the company. I first tried to convince Tom, the youngest one without a lot of success. I was convicted not to take no for an answer . I talked and talked and he replied that he would have liked to join but his father didn't think we had something to offer.. Whatever his father decided was law, he was a real patriarch from the old branch. I remained on my seat .Probably to get rid of me Tom suggested to ask his father to join us in the meeting. He arrived, in a very lousy mood. Clearly I had kept him from a far more interesting task and to cut it short he argued that Antwerp didn't need a World Trade Center. I do not recall anymore what I replied, but I did realize that I had to say as much as possible in the least possible time, because I was on the point to be thrown out of the building. To somebody from Antwerp his city is untouchable. I decided to touch that tender spot. Mr. Stevens I said what will become of our beautiful city without a World Trade Center? The man looked at me and replied: You give me a strong feeling that if Antwerp is going o miss the boat, it will be on account of me. Where is your agreement form? He signed it and that is how Stefens Electro joined our Association.

Meanwhile Robert Dethier had not been idle either. Robert had met Hubert Govaerts, a young entrepreneur from Antwerp, who was keeping on a family tradition in the printing business. A man with plenty of ambitions, rather introvert who could use a couple of introductions in the Antwerp Business World. Robert told him that if he bought the shares of the WTC in Antwerp – the building project that never went of the ground as far as Antwerp was concerned – he would acquire immediate respect in the economic life and elsewhere. Hubert bought the shares and for the time being, the public company was saved.

Then we needed a President for the Club. Jan Huyghebaert the Alderman for the Port, was young and ambitious, an up-and-coming star, his name was a symbol for dignity. He didn't have the really mentality of the Port people as we were used in Antwerp. In Antwerp, it was a tradition that the Alderman of the Port belonged to the Catholic Party (CVP) and the mayor to the Socialist Party (SP). Huyghebaert was a no-nonsense man. I suggested that I should ask him for an interview. Nobody believed that I could succeed. At that time Bob Cools, a socialist, was acting like mayor, my good friend Alderman Leona Detiège, a socialist as well, introduced me to him. Cools listened to my exposure and promised that he would fix it for me. I had my appointment with Alderman Huyghebaert and with some compromises. he accepted to become our President. He was the most correct man I ever met. Severe but fair as we were going to find out.

As more members joined our Club it was time to rent an office. We found one at the ground floor of a mansion at the Oudaen right in front of the Police headquarters. On the first floor was a caterer where the lunch meetings of the Club took place. We had an office but no furniture. Someone from the Board gave us a desk and a chair and that was that.

During week ends, when our office was closed the caterer organized wedding parties. When I came in on Monday morning, I often found flower pieces that the bridal couple had left behind, in the corridor; I asked the caterer if I could have them, no problem, that way my bare looking office had at least some kind of decoration. One of our members, who was in the vending machine business , was kind of sorry for me that I couldn't offer a cup of coffee to my guests. He offered me a coffee machine like the once to be found in railway stations. . It was a huge affair, but it helped me through. The problem was that I had no visitors, most of the time I was on the road to find them.

When I arrived in my office in the morning, I took a cup of coffee but preferred to remove the first ones that came out of the tap.. They had been all night in the pipes, and I didn't want to get poisoned. Because I couldn't get rid of the stuff except if I threw it through the window, which was rather risky with the police quarters on the other side of the street, I poured it in my plants. I took the habit to drink each morning a cup of coffee with my palm tree or whatever was nearest to me. The caffeine , or whatever was in it, proved to be excellent for their growing process because before I realized it, I was seated in a tropical garden.

A couple of months went by .We were beginning to see the light. I was accepted as a business woman, not that evident in those days of male superiority. In my case, they had not much choice. The men I had frequented until then for quite different reasons had mostly pampered me. Being the prototype of a mistress I never had been looking for a commitment in a relationship. This was also very true with my link with the World Trade Center. I had never taken orders from anyone and didn't get out of the way for a good argument. Those men belonged to the beau monde. I am not sure if they found me refreshing or scaring. However, they knew damn well that if they didn't give me the necessary respect in my work, I would close the door behind me and throw the key away. Besides I had found myself a fine ally, Michel Plaisier. He was the General Manager of the Monsanto branch in Antwerp . From the first visit at my home, we liked each other. We worked together, we had fun together, we became very good friends, we were growing toward each other without even realizing it and he guided me gently towards my new responsibilities.. Michel was from the Western part of the country, a straitlaced man, not a flirt, someone one could lean upon. As a fact a man like that was totally new to me.. The men in my life had always been very hard workers but with a past of drinks and girl friends. Michel was very satisfied with his wife and children. His mother used to have a little drugstore and after solid studies Michel had become an engineer and was heading for the top as a manager. Soon after I met him, he left Monsanto and became crisis manager at Barco. He fascinated me whit his stories about his business trips aboard and how, when his working day was over, he returned to his hotel room to watch television. However, the World Trade Center was something special, it was from the both of us.

To bring our Association on the rails we had to meet at least once a week.. When there were Board meetings Michel sat next to me to step on my toes, when I wanted to intervene, which was not appreciated. When one of the Board members came to visit me, they were mostly all right, but when they were together in a meeting it was an entirely different story. The ones who were the least important were mostly the ones who had the most critics. The victim to be attacked was the one that was supposed to be the weakest in the group : me. When I wanted to protest: Michael stepped on my feet under the table and it helped for a while.

The main problem was that we had no regular WTC Building. The regular member meaning Govaerts paid the fee just as if there was one . Hubert kept saying : I am a printer not a constructor. And we still had the Club.

We had to look for more income. The problem of most of the business clubs. Around that period, the Province of Antwerp was considering of making a Congress Centrum. Meetings were organized with Jan Huyghebaert to find out if we could sub rent the back of our office, we had only one room, so that we could share the expenses. I went to see our Governor Kinsbergen . While I was waiting for him in the reception hall, I watched the telephone operator who had started to knit. I was fascinated. When Jan Huyghebaert, during one of our Board meetings talked about a plan for cooperation, I asked if this meant that if I would be submerged with a lot of work and the girl was knitting, I wouldn't be allowed to ask her to help. He replied to that was the idea. I said that in such a case, I would take her by her neck , throw her in the middle of the street and make a call to the local paper to take a picture of the show. That put an end to the meeting.

A couple of days later I entered the office building when I saw Huyghebaert and Osterrieth descending the stairs. Huyghebaert came to me in a very bad mood and said something like :Madam, what did you do? I was called at the Governors' office to explain the incident with the Staff of the Province. He didn't give me time to react, I could have done it anyway, I was flabbergasted, I never had seen my President mad, and he walked outside. When he was out of sight I figured that he was right. After all I had caused the trouble. A week later I met Huyghebaert at a reception at the town hall. I went to him and said : Mr. President you were right. Please tell the Governor that you didn't know about it and that it was entirely my fault. He looked at me very seriously and said : Madam, I am responsible for you. Nobody has to blame you for anything, I am the one to take the blame.

I became friends with Hilaire De Wulf, who with his International Club of Flanders situated in Ghent was also Associated with the World Trade Centers. We wanted to start in Antwerp regular business lunches and dinners, but I needed some experience. Hilaire invited me on a Japanese evening at his Club. I knew the reputation of Hilaire, I was sure there would be a lot of eating and drinking, and I booked a room at the Holiday Inn. Michel was in his office of Barco in West Flanders, and we agreed that on his way home, he would stop at the Holiday Inn, so we could have a drink. I was almost ready to go out when somebody knocked at my door. I opened, it was Michel. By now we had become so used to each other that it didn't occur to him to wait for me in the bar, and I found it also extremely normal that he was entering my room. . And suddenly we were in bed.

Chapter 23
La Vie En Rose

For almost a year we had been working together very closely, we sat close to each other without someone watching us. We were not even flirting. Maybe it was much deeper. We became one without realizing it. What happened at the Holiday Inn was just a natural transfer to another period of our lives. It does not sound very romantic but romance had been with us for months. At that very moment, our bodies said what we never had spoken in so many words, that we were in love with each other. We did not need any words, it just happened. We entered in each other's lives and were tremendously happy. I didn't know it existed, and suddenly I was laying there next to the man of my life. Much later Michael told me that he had the impression that the sky was falling on top if him, he never had been cheating on his wife, but he didn't at all feel guilty that it happened. It felt so natural. His tender smile when he looked at me was totally new to me. Then we both dressed. He went home and I went to my Japanese dinner.

Next day he called me. It was the beginning of a fairy tale romance. We were made for each other but the fact remained that he has a wife and five children. And none of the two of us wanted to hurt them. It was rather a strange situation. Michel lived in a mansion in the country not far away from Antwerp. To drive to his office in West Flanders, he nearly had to drive by my house. Sometimes he passed by in the morning, sometimes at night. I saw him each day. And we made love. Before long he told me that in all the time he was married, which was almost twenty five years he had never made love to his wife as many times as he had made love with me in a couple of month's times. I knew that at nighttime he always went home, and accepted it. And just waited for another day to arrive. Just like a perfect mistress should. When we were at WTC events, we didn't try to hide our feelings. Not that we made a spectacle of ourselves. Not at all. It was the way he looked at me and the way I looked at him. From time to time, he took me out for a weekend. Just the two of us in a city abroad. Once when walking in Lille, he said to me : I should have met you much earlier. I asked him what he meant. Then we would be married and have five children, he replied. Me spending my life with one man ? Would it be possible ? But what was the use of wondering. The man that I loved was married and for his own good he had to stay that way. Did it puzzle me? Not really. I knew what to expect. The best things in life are free.

Our office had expanded. André Moermans, my WTC friend from Brussels who lived in Antwerp had suggested to work jointly with his SVP office. We accepted. He could take his quarters in our office, and in turn he would look after our service department. André had a special motive that had nothing to do with me. He was going to tell me, whenever he was ready for it.. I went through the most fantastic time of my life, I had a daughter, a man where I was very much in love with, a working agreement with the WTC , a dream job and on top of it André, a friend that I could trust with my most intimate feelings. Before long I was going to explore the entire world with the World Trade Center. The only shadow on my happiness was that Lode became very ill.

The first Assembly where I felt accepted in the close circle of the WTC top was in Switzerland. It was a very small group of people , from all over the world. I drove to the meeting with Michel, who had been elected Secretary General of our Antwerp WTC. The weather was lousy. Consequently, we arrived in Switzerland at the moment the Meeting was almost over. It was a small family, nothing likely to the kind of Assemblies with hundreds of people, that we were going to know later. Tadosji Yamada, a very respected name in the Japanese industrial world had succeeded to Honda. He promised to assist to the Japanese business dinner that we were planning in Antwerp, and he kept his promises. The people who I met that night were the real core of the World Trade Center and became friends for life.

Back in Antwerp we were ready for our first big event. With the support and in the presence of Yamada and the Ambassador in Belgium of the country of the Rising Sun, it was going to be a Japanese dinner that would take place in the Building of the Governor of our Province. The company that once offered a coffee machine to me was going to assist me. The Japanese restaurant in Brussels that had taken care of the evening in Ghent would prepare the dishes.. That should take care of everything, at least that was the general idea. I didn't realize by then that an English conversation with Japanese people is not to be taken for granted.

The response on the invitation was excellent. About three hundred guests registered , a big success. Everything went well until the delivery vans arrived. Everybody smiled. Japanese always do. They started with the preparation and the cooking. It smelled very nice. And the room was transferred in a Japanese garden.

My two nieces, students, where handling the wardrobe. Before the guests arrived, I wanted them to put the plates on the dinner tables. I asked the Japanese in command where we could find them. He looked at me and asked : Plates ? What plates ? We no plates. Finally, we understood that they had no china plates with them only something in cardboard that is used on picnics. It was a buffet where the guests were supposed to pick up their food from a large serving table. I saw the situation exactly in front of me, ladies and gents in a gala outfit with soya sauce leaking all over their dresses and suits. I needed desperately six hundred place in a minimum of time. My guests were arriving about an hour later !

I called Alexandra's school for help.. They sympathized with the situation but the refectory was already closed. Next call went to the hotel and catering school. All their plates were still filthy. The man in charge of the coffee machine and the catering was ready to help me out. He offered to drive through Antwerp looking for over 600 plates. The waiters should go with him to help them carry. Those waiters were supposed to serve cocktails but necessity knows no law. The next thing I know the waiters were gone. The only persons left where myself and my two nieces. The first guests had already shown up.. The program of the evening started with a documentary about Japan.It was projected in an adjoining hall. The guests were sent immediately in that direction. When the film started the theater was filled. And still no delivery van with plates, waiters and all what we needed to avoid disaster. Fortunately my twin nieces grew up in a family where they had guests all the time. They were used to serving them. We put the glasses on a serving tray, filled them up and decided to start the service on our own. Seconds before the film came to an end the delivery van stopped in front of the door. Out came the man with boxes full of plates just in time for my nieces to take over. The doors opened, the crowd of people came out, the waiters were waiting with their cocktails and my nieces ran to the table to put the plates in their places. Yamada, who hadn't noticed what was going on – nobody did, for that matter – joined me together with the Ambassador of Japan and said : "What a perfect organization". My first event for the W.T.C. was a fact.

By then half of the harbor companies had joined us as a member. It was time to move. The building Jacob van Galicië where it all started was for rent again. Hubert the Man of the World Trade Center took the building in command, with a restaurant at the ground floor and the Club on the first floor. The building was situated next to the Town Hall, and before long I was walking in and out of the building. Everybody knew me from the Mayor to the attendant . It made me think of my mother, if she could see me there', finally I had made it to the Town Hall., my mother's ultimate dream

When I needed to see the Mayor I didn't even have to ask him for an appointment. I walked into the office of his cabinet chef and asked if he was free to see me.

Someday we had a business lunch in the restaurant of our WTC. It was Santa Nicolas day the excellent man paid us a visit together with his black servant. Our lunches were in general very jolly, and finally we found our-selves with Santa and his black friend at the bar. They read a lot out of their holy book with regard to our members, which made them very thirsty. So was everybody. At the top of our euphoria, somebody suggested to pay a visit to the Mayor. At that time, it was Bob Cools. We crossed the street, entered the town hall and went straight to the office of Jules Trappeniers, the Chief of Cabinet. Jules said that we could not go in because there was a Television crew in full action. However, nobody can stop such a Holy Man so in we went. Bob Cools is not only a notorious Anglophile, but he has also their phlegm. The pictures that were taken from him and his black servant were later published in his official biography.

When we came out of the building I noticed that it was about time to pick up Alexandra, who after school time went to the Academia of Music. We crossed the street with the Holy Man and his servant, everybody with a drop too much and arrived at the class in the middle of the lessons. The pupils, still at an age to believe in Santa Claus, were totally taken aback. We fished Alexandra out of her group went back to the Volkswagen and drove back to the pub in front of the Town Hall. On the back seat, a solemn greeting Santa Claus with Alexandra on his lap and his black servant next to him . I was seated next to the driver. Dozens of cars were following us. The city was ours. Not one police officer stopped us. They wouldn't have dared. I supposed that they would have a received a trashing from the public crowd.

Chapter 24
Chicken With Popcorn

Meeting with the International Delegation of the World Trade Centers

I had moved to a larger apartment. Michel and I finally had a real home of our own where he visited me in the morning when he left for work or in the evening when he returned. However, he never stayed over. His wife and children were waiting for dinner, I made part of his business life. His wife was part of his daily routine. And he loved us both. I am quite sure of that. To put it cruelly : I had as much sex and good time as time permitted without having to wash someone else's socks. On the other hand, his wife wasn't that badly of either : she didn't' had to worry about her husband's business problems, he never told her, and she slept at night with the man I loved. He cared very much for Alexandra, and she loved him in return. When in Florence, Italy, where we entered a church where a Saint was devoted who was said to be favorable to girls wanting to get married Alexandra asked me who that Saint might be. I answered Saint Michel. She looked at me for a moment and replied : However, we do know a Michel, mummy, the real one.

Michel took me regularly to Barco. Before long I knew everybody, also Tanghe, the CEO from ACEC and President of Barco. Whenever Michel had a problem, he used to advise him : Ask it to your madam . The madame was me.

When Michel had to go to the States on business. he took me with him. My first visit to this great New World. And I was going there with the man I loved.. Barco was putting up a branch in Charlotte, North Carolina. Brochures had to be made, and I was going to make the photos for the illustration. It is a practical joke to tell that Americans visit Europe like a hurricane, 'if this is Tuesday this must be Belgium',' but I did about the same thing in the States . Michael had been several times to America. We went in and out of airplanes to arrive in our hotel in Charlotte in the middle of nowhere. We only left our hotel room to drive to his office where we met Nancy, the secretary in command. Michel was supposed to make some promotion for the American branch but Nancy told us that the local press was not interested . I offered to take care of it.

The Charlotte Observer was the local and the most read newspaper. I asked to speak to the chief editor. When he heard that I was a Belgian journalist he almost gave me the red carpet treatment. The good man had Belgian roots. His grandfather was born in the region where Barco had his head office. The end of the story was that we were on the front page of the following weekend edition under the heading 'We Belgians are gaining'.

I didn't see much of Charlotte actually., except for one lunchtime when Michel was in a meeting with a banker. He asked Nancy to take care of me. Nancy, very impressed to take out the collaborator of her boss made a list of all the fancy restaurants in town. Exactly, the places where I didn't want to go. I always had been fascinated by the America of the truckers and their road restaurants. I asked her to take me there. That was not exactly a place where ladies went to. However, in her opinion she could not turn me down either. She probably only could hope that I would back of when I was going to see where we would end up. No way. The huge parking was filled with dozens of trucks. The smallest had about the size of a railroad wagon. A fascinating view. A wooden hangar was acting as a restaurant. When we entered a crowd of corpulent drivers, real wardrobes, who matched exactly to their trucks were standing, seated and hanging around everywhere. When they saw us, with our summer dresses completely out of style, they stopped talking. Complete silence. The landlord arrived with a dishcloth to clean a table for us, but I asked if we could sit at the bar, on a stool. We could. The men who were seated moved so we could sit between them. The menu of the day was chicken and popcorn. It was great. Finally, I had the feeling that I was in the States. I asked if I could take pictures. Nobody minded, on the contrary. They took us in their arms, they pressed us against their sweaty breast, and we learned that they never had met such a fantastic ladies as we were. Everybody waved us goodbye when we left.

Next day we left for Washington. We stayed for the night. We had breakfast, went to a meeting in our hotel , stepped into a taxi who drove us to the airport. I mentioned that I would have liked to see the White House. The driver took a turn, stopped where I asked him to, I took a picture, and further we went on our way to New York.

In New York, it was worse. We arrived in the morning, took a taxi to the World Trade Center, went into one of the Twin Towers to the 77th floor to the offices of the President. He took us to the 101st floor from where I could see the Statue of Liberty, then we went to the Windows of the World on the same floor, we had a very pleasant lunch after which we returned to his offices for a short meeting; Then we took a taxi and drove to the airport and flew home. We didn't even sleep in New York.

In the airplane, I asked Michel if this was his manner of traveling. He said yes. No wonder he never had an affair. The man never came out in the open.

Chapter 25
Forbidden Games

We had promised Guy Tozzoli to take care of a WTC building in Antwerp. However, there was a major problem. Govaerts a very successful printer and publisher was not a building contractor and didn't know anything from real estate.. The Club in turn was doing so well that hardly anybody was interested in a building. And the building we had rented was very special. It dated from the Middle Ages. It was called Jacob in Galicie because its roots went from way back to the twelfth century when pilgrims from all over Europe went by feet to Santiago de Compostella in Spanish Galicie to abolish their sins and start a new life. On their way, they stopped at inns indicated with the famous Coquilles St Jacques to sleep and to take care of their wounded feet. Our Jacob van Galicie building was one of them. The brand on their hooded cloak was also marking our front poach.

Being next to the Town Hall was an extra asset for a World Trade Center but Robert Dethier was about the only person to believe in the concept. Even headquarters lost faith in him. He was leaning on me but what could I do? I didn't belong to the Association, I belonged to the Club. I was taken for granted as long as I brought members in but that was that.

Lode's health was declining. Nothing is more frustrating than seeing somebody you care for going downhill. The man that I knew for about thirty years was dying. He knew it and I knew it. Cancer was taking the better of him but Lode kept dreaming about what once had been. When I went on a holiday with Alexandra, he indicated the roads we had to take. It became his way of traveling. And suddenly he was dead. I missed him more than I thought it would be possible. He had always been there for me, and now he was gone.

I was fortunately enough to busy with the World Trade Center to grief for a man, I realized this much later, who had meant so much in my life. More so Michael was always there to lean on. My Michel, that is how

132

I thought of him, who took me as often as he could to Paris where we became regulars at La Mère Catherine, the well known Café on the Butte at the Place de Tertre . Where the piano players played when we came through the door our favorite tune : La Vie en Rose.

The first General Meeting of the WTC that Michael and I both attended was in Tokyo. Tadoshi Yamada insisted that we should attend. W e traveled with a delegation of fifteen members to the other side of the world. I was in command. In Copenhagen, we had to change planes and upon arrival in Tokyo, we noticed that our luggage was not on Board. It had remained in Copenhagen and was going to arrive with another plane. Meanwhile the members of our group had nothing more than the clothes they were wearing – and in which they had been traveling for over 24 hours. When we arrived at the hotel we were officially invited to attend the monthly lunch of the WTC of Japan. We had to leave immediately to make it in time. With the invitation in my hand and followed by the entire delegation, I went to the door of the five star hotel to ask the doorman to find us a taxi. He pointed to a taxi line a little further on the street.

With Michael and another passenger, I went in the first car. The others were to follow us with other taxis. I asked the driver to bring us to the WTC building. The man nodded politely but did not move. Neither did the taxi. The former experiment with my Japanese dinner in Antwerp hadn't learned me much about the linguistic capacities of the average Japanese, so I asked him once more in English to drive us to the WTC. Nothing happened. I showed him the invitation. However, it was written in English and the man didn't understand a word the language of Shakespeare.. According to me the only person able to solve the problem was the doorman of our hotel. Providing we could explain our driver what we wanted. My gestures in the right direction didn't have the desired result; I became so frustrated that I cursed like a trooper. In pure Antwerp dialect, I shouted to him that he had to drive us to the doorman. It helped ! Later I learned that it was the sound of my voice that had put him into action. Japanese people are used to be drilled.

Finally we made it to the WTC building, the pet creation of Honda in the first place and now from Yamada. We were given a VIP treatment; Yamada went on stage to welcome us officially. The speeches were in Japanese, so we didn't know where he was talking about. My table companion was a very friendly Japanese businessman who spoke rather well English. During our conversation I mentioned the problem with our lost luggage. I mentioned that our Group was expected that same night at a Gala Dinner and that we had nothing to wear. No problem, my neighbor said, come to my office after lunch. And so I did. His offices were in the WTC building a couple of floors below we had met. When I arrived in his oak wood office he asked me with how many people I was traveling and what we exactly needed. I told him. He made a couple of telephone calls, that I didn't understand either. When he finally put down the receiver a driver entered the room. My host gave some instructions and he disappeared. My new Japanese friend asked me to return after a couple of hours. Our outfit would be ready. When I returned the table was filled with tulle tied scarf's in which were dozens of evening dresses, shoes, handbags and jewelry for the ladies in our group. Dinner jackets for the gentlemen were to be delivered to their rooms. In the evening, we were a glamorous Belgian delegation in a Japanese outfit.

Next day our luggage arrived. We were so relieved that at night, we decided to draw a party in one of our rooms. The ladies in bikini, the gents in a bathing suit. Everybody emptied the contents of their mini bars. After we finished all the bottles we called the floor manager for a new load. When the man entered the room I suppose he wasn't sure he was seeing right. However, a Japanese being a Japanese he didn't even blink.

At the General Assembly of the WTC, I was elected member of the Committee of Communication. From that moment on I was going to attend the WTC meetings all over the world.

****

In Antwerp my best friend was André. He was a dear, the perfect gentlemen, a man of the world. Bit by bit I became his soul mate. Years ago he had been the manager of a store chain in Antwerp. He became acquainted, or to put it more correctly, to well acquainted with one of his sales girls. His board of directors finally ordered him to choose between his job and the girl. He chose for the girl and went for a new start with S.V.P. That is when we met. His family lived in Brussels, his girl friend in Antwerp. After I started to work for the WTC in Antwerp, he took an office in our building and worked as an independent broker. He intended to use his link with the WTC to take his girl friend with him on so called business trips abroad. In the beginning, it went on very smoothly. And then he took her for a couple of weeks to the States. They flew to San Francisco, traveled further to Las Vegas where they stayed for a week in the hotel Caesar's Palace. Then they rented a car and drove through the United States, to visit some family of the girl in a small town not far from New York. His wife believed that he was on a WTC mission. The trip was made on his own expense account so to me, there was no problem. A friend is a friend. I received a postcard from André in San Francisco with on the backside in his handwriting one sentence : Paula, every day when I wake up, I remember that it is the first day of the rest of my life, and I enjoy it.

Two days after receiving that message, on a Sunday morning at five o'clock the phone rang. It was the girl friend of André calling me from America. I never had met her. She was hysterically sobbing trying to tell me that André had died. He had told her that if ever something should happen to him, she had to call me for help. Everything had been going as planned, and they arrived safe and perfectly happy about the home of her brother. After dinner, she and André went for a walk in the garden when André suddenly collapsed. When help arrived, he was already dead..

It was quite a shock. I had lost a dear friend and moreover I had to return him to Belgium. He was supposed to be on a business trip for the World Trade Center meaning that it was our responsibility to bring him back. Nobody in our WTC, except me, was aware of the situation, I never even had considered that possibility. André was in his fifties, in very good condition, and now I was on my own to solve the situation and to notify his wife. It seemed hopeless and could mean the end of my WTC career. It was finally the girl's family that offered the solution. Her brother who was the manager of a Credit Lyonais branch in the States called me to tell me that André's son knew all about his father's affair. I called him and he was willing to help me out. I had met the young man quite often, he was a photographer and broadminded so he was going to talk to his mother. She started to call on me as she figured that the WTC had to pay for the expenses to bring him over. The manager of the bank took care of it. I was saved. André arrived back at the airport of Brussels at the very moment that I was leaving on the same Airport for my yearly holidays. Our paths literally crossed. His dreams had come to an end, but he had lived them his way.

Chapter 26
What Now My Love ?

To me, it was a little different. At least that is what I thought. We didn't have the feeling that we were cheating on somebody. It was out of the question that Michael should make a choice. I belonged to his business life, I was his business partner with whom he shared a great love. His wife belonged to his familial life that he also was in need of. He didn't want to leave that behind. Michael had always been a family man and that is not to be changed overnight. I wouldn't want that to.. I never could have been so deeply in love with him if he hadn't been like he was. He belonged to me during the daytime and our passionate business trips abroad. At home he belonged to his wife. I knew his children and he knew Alexandra. The nearest we came to an engagement was that he had a dream that his youngest son Geerd would ever marry Alexandra. That way we could become family after all. However, that was way ahead.

Meanwhile, as a bachelor mother I raised my daughter which with 47-year difference in age was not so obvious. The parents of her little friends didn't consider me differently in age. I was a young mother just as they were . And that was it.

Not for a moment she messed up my life. As a baby I took her with me when I had to go abroad. I cannot remember how many times she sat on the lap of a business acquaintance that I met somewhere in that great big world. More than once the caretaker of the Chamber of Commerce looked after her when I went there for a late meeting.

Problems started in primary school when I was supposed to help her with her homework. I always figured myself as a logical person but to understand the way they teach nowadays is not that simple. When I was at primary school it was impossible to divide seven by three, but suddenly I learned that you could divide it but there was one left. When I met the nun who teaches Alexandra she said it was odd that a child her age didn't know where the North Sea was, but that she did know where to find the Mediterranean Sea and the Dead Sea. To me, it was not strange at all.

136

Alexandra had never been to our North Sea beeches. However, we had great fun , both of us, When the weather was fine and other young mothers hurried home to prepare dinner for their husband, I lingered on a terrace with Alexandra. When I went away on business, and I couldn't take her, there were always family members who loved to take care of her.

Leaving her temporary gave me some remorse until I went to visit a niece where she had never stayed overnight . When se asked Alexandra if she wanted to stay with her for a couple of days Alexandra turned to me and asked : when is the next time you are leaving ? That took care of my remorse. Did she miss a father ? I do not think so. A child misses a father when she never had known one. In her immediate surrounding there was a normal contact with women AND men. Pedophilia was unknown to the general public – I suppose that there were exceptions to the rule – but it was nothing that was brought regularly to our attention. If a man was friendly to a child it was taken for granted. I had not in the least problems that men were fond of her, I thought it was a normal kind of kindness, and it was..

One morning a woman walked in my WTC office. She introduced herself and said that she had noticed my name in a register of Opus Dei members in Spain. It belonged to my C.E.D.I. past. Opus Dei was going to open an office in Brussels, and I was asked to take charge. I knew very little about Opus Dei, I didn't even realize that the members of our CEDI group automatically became members of that organization. What I did remember was that they were supposed to be extremely anti feminist.. Male members pretended that it was a women's fault that they were rejected from the Garden of Eden. In their book of truth, or whatever they called it, was suggested that to minimize their guilt complex women should offer themselves as carpets for males to walk upon. It was clear that I didn't want to trade my women friendly WTC – even with some up and downs during the General Assemblies – for an uncertain future in Brussels As diplomatic as I could I explained this to my visitor, and they left me in peace.

More so that I had more pleasant prospects in view. . Paul Fabry had invited Michel and I to the World Trade Center of New Orleans. In the middle of August we were leaving for our second trip to the States. I was taking care of the official formalities.. A couple of months before Michael became a grandfather for the first time. He was the happiest man in the world.. We decide to leave after August 15, day that in our country the mothers are honored. A day that he wanted to spend with his family. Finally, we decided on August 18. The night before my telephone rang. I was watching my favorite soap on Television and at first was reluctant to pick up the receiver. Finally, I said hello.. It was Michel; We went over some last details. I didn't realize that this was going to be to be the last time that I ever would hear his voice again..

Next day, in the late afternoon I went to pick up the airline tickets at the travel agency. It had been a very hot and dry summer and at that moment it was starting to rain. The girl at the counter needed some more information, and I called Michael at his office. His secretary came on the phone crying hysterically. I couldn't understand a word she was saying. A man took over. It was the President of the company. He told me that there had been an accident. I didn't realize what he was trying to tell me. Michel? He answered. Michael, I asked, is he hurt? No, he replied, he died . I could not understand what he wanted to clarify. Died, I asked ? What do you mean ? I stood there in a travel agency with a clerk who stared at me, I suppose that all color had left my face, and on the telephone line a man told me that the man of my life with whom I was about to leave for America was dead. I heard vaguely that Michel had taken a service car to attend a last minute meeting. He slipped on the wet asphalt and drove his car into something. He had been dead on the spot.

I had the feeling that they were talking about somebody else, it could not be, not my Michel. From the distance I heard Tanghe's voice. Madame, he said – at that time it was not customary to call everybody by their first name – may I ask you to inform Michel's family? It will take us a couple of hours to arrive, and you are practically on the spot. Of course, I replied and went out of the agency to my car. I remember that I started the engine, I do remember that I drove to the suburb where Michel lived or used to live. I also remember and never will forget the empty feeling within me. It was a miracle that I had no accident on the way.

I never had been at Michel's home before. I drove by several times. Walking past the street where you live, my fair lady, remember. I nearly drove there on an automatic pilot. I didn't wander even for a moment if I would be welcomed and how.

I rang the bell. The door went open. Michel's wife and his children stood in front of me. I opened my mouth, not exactly knowing what I was going to say, but they already knew. A policeman had just brought them the bad news. I wanted to turn back but Michael's wife stopped me and asked me to come in. They lived in a marvelous cottage. She took me to the garden and invited me to sit next to her. When the police had arrived, they had been in the middle of preparing dinner. Michel's wife called her son and said that I was going to stay . Just put another plate on the table, she said. To me, it was totally unreal. I was dumbfounded. I was sitting there in the frame where my love had been living, desperately unhappy, and the women with whom I shared her husband was comforting me. It is an experience that I never will be able to explain to anyone else. Much later I understood that she wanted to learn more about the business life of her husband that was totally unknown to her. And I was the one who had been part of it. Michel's motto had always been not to bother his wife with his business problems. That woman had loved Michel very dearly, and she wanted to make the puzzle of his life complete. She asked me to help her to send the death announcements.

Then I returned home. I tried to understand what was happening to me, but I couldn't. Alexandra was on holiday camp so fortunately I was on my own. It was not grief that I felt, it was far more than that . All my feelings had left me together with Michael. When I left my house, I heard the shopkeeper next door whistling 'La Vie en Rose'. Our song that was going to pursue me from then on. The ice-cream man who passed by, the Carillon of the Cathedral on the other side of the World Trade Center, and later when I took the elevator in my Hotel in Bangkok or when I had a real problem, everywhere I heard La Vie en Rose. Even the Restaurant on the Strip in Las Vegas where I was staying was called La Vie en Rose. The entire world played La Vie en Rose for me. However, Michel was no longer there to hold my hand.

The funeral took place in the village where Michael used to live. I was sitting on the isle. Jan Huyghebaert, my President and Alderman of the Port, came to sit to on the empty seat next to me and took my hand. When the coffin passed, I nearly collapsed. I only realized by then that Michael had left me for ever. I was sobbing for everybody to see that a simple colleague never could have had that kind of grief,. I looked at my

139

neighbor and asked him if I was not making a fool of myself. However, he replied very calmly : No child, it is OK.

The cemetery next to the church was much too small and only the nearest to kin followed the body. Some of the people left. Others went to the Inn where coffee was served. I went to sit on a table, Nobody talked about Michael or the accident that caused his death. Everybody talked about business. It seemed as if I assisted at just another WTC event.

As strange as it may seem for someone with my kind of life, I am a firm believer, Although I never attend mass.. A WTC member who took me out for lunch someday said that he couldn't understand that someone as bright as I was, could believe. Maybe I am stupid but it always has been a fantastic support to me. Audrey Hepburn expressed the feelings that were mine at that moment when in War and Peace, when her loved one died, she asked at his death bed : Where are you now ? That was the question that helped me going. A friend told me that I had been fortunate to know, even if it was only for a couple of years, this intense feeling of love, a feeling that not everybody was lucky enough to have experienced. I know he was right.

Stranger things happened. Except for the tune that I heard about everywhere there was also the question with the alarm clock. Each night at 12 o'clock it started to play. When I came out of bed to stop it, I always heard noises as if cars were driving on a high way . The following evening at the same time it started all over again. I thought that I went crazy. I had to pull the plug out to make it stop. When I turned in on the evening of All Saints Day, I had the chilling feeling that a skeleton took me in his arms. It was as if Michael said goodbye to me.

The year ended. Michel's wife called me and invited me at her home to spend Xmas night with her and their friends. She didn't want me to be on my own that night. A great Lady.

Chapter 27
Singing In The Rain

Nothing would be the same anymore. I regularly picked up signs from Michel but I figured it was due to my confusion. However, I found out that several of my friends had lived trough the same experiences; I read several books about the phenomena; One of the writers was Shirley Mc Lane. I send her a letter, and we kept corresponding for quite a while.

The WTC was doing well . With a President such as Jan Huygghebaert it was self evident; I was lucky enough to be there at the very moment that the booming of the World Trade Centers worldwide started.

When Huyghebaert left as an Alderman to become President of one of our most powerful banks he left his seat at the WTC to Walter Osterrieth. Osterrieth was also very respected in the harbor midst and had very important titles to come forward with. A man with a lot of class but in day tot day life he was a very 18th century personality.

He thought it very bizarre that I was a happy unmarried mother, and that I won a case in Strasbourg. He was brought up to be courteous . Nevertheless, he made me feel that I belonged to him but didn't belong to the high class circles of our members..

Robert Dethier kept on dreaming about a WTC building.. He was the only one to be at my side when I needed it. To him I was also his last hope. He saw to it that I became general manager merely to give me more power. I had to obtain the support from Osterrieth . I went to see him in his office. He looked at me as if I had gone raving mad and said : we will talk this over later, at this point you are no more than a maid for all seasons. And out he went. He left me speechless., Then I send him a letter to inform him what I thought of his reaction.. I remembered him of the condition the WTC was in when I entered the scene comparing with when he was in charge I requested an apology and insisted that he had to appoint me as general manager;

141

First time I saw him again was at a business lunch at the Holiday Inn Hotel. In the hall badges were waiting for a lot of members. Osterrieth entered, gave me a hand and went to the door to welcome the guests. I walked to him to ask if he received my letter. A cautious 'yes' came out of a half open mouth. I asked him if he was ready to apologize. An even more cautious 'yes' came out of the same half open mouth. And have you decided to make me general manager ? I continued. At first there was no answer . I said that I needed an answer on the spot. If not I was going to go on stage, while everybody was at lunch to tell them one or two things about his behavior.. He looked at me in amazement. I could almost feel that he was figuring out what was going to happen to him. More so I am still convinced that the man never had apologized in his entire life.

The first guests arrived. Osterrieth clearly didn't know what to answer so I decided to give him a little help. I repeated : what do you think? Am I going to become a general manager or not.. Almost inaudible but loud enough for me to understand he replied : All right, all right, if this is what you want. And that is the way I became General Manager of the World Trade Center of Antwerp. To be perfectly honest he didn't come back to his words. At the next General Assembly, I was inaugurated.

They send me to the different European WTC's to study the way they were managed. One of the most amazing persons I met was Maria de Silva, a distant niece of President Salazar and President of the World Trade Center of Lisbon. She welcomed me at the airport of the Portuguese capital when I arrived there in the late afternoon. She apologized that she could not take me out that night, but we were going to have dinner at her place. We jumped, to follow her, I had to jump; in her tiny red car and drove of. She lived in the center of town in an apartment filled with antiquities. The maid, dressed like maids had been dressed for centuries with laced apron was waiting for us . Maria threw orders around and we went back out to visit the WTC. When we returned cocktails and food were waiting for us in silver plates and serviced on a dining set that would have made a fortune at Sotheby's. At 11 o'clock at night, after finishing the main dish the maid prepared for dessert. Maria told her to wait because we still had a meeting at midnight with the Minister of Foreign Affairs at his office in the Ministry.

Maria drove through the streets of Lisbon, as if we were chased by the devil himself. Through one way streets in the wrong direction when needed When I timidly objected she replied that she had not time to consider such futilities. Finally, we arrived. at our destination. Several men were waiting for us, the meeting started – to my surprise, they all looked quite awake, they seemed to be used to such a situation – Maria was mostly talking, and about 1 am, we drove home, where the maid was waiting for us with the dessert.

When I returned to Belgium a huge problem was waiting for me .Until then non-profit associations didn't had to pay turn over taxes. However, suddenly a Royal Decision was published saying that non profit associations which rendered services, meaning us among others, had to pay those taxes with reactively back date. Our WTC existed for six years and had a lot of members. This meant disaster. We didn't have that kind of money, we were talking about a couple of million Belgian francs. This meant the end of our Association. By chance the Minister of Finance Willy De Clercq had traded his post for a function in Europe. Frans Grootjans was going to be installed as a Minister ad interim until Mark Eyskens was nominated. I knew Grootjans rather well and he did owe me a favor. In the sixties I worked as a reporter for his newspaper, the Nieuwe Gazet. I knew him not only as a politician but also as a business man and when I started Tele Call I visited him regularly to request his advice. Just before the elections he asked me if my staff could help him with his election mailing. They were on guard day and night, I didn't seem a problem, it was done and I was warmly welcomed at the office of the Liberal Party . End of story. Now that he was temporary Minister of Finance he could maybe help us out. When I suggested it to the Board it was accepted reluctantly as every suggestion would be accepted that could have pulled us out of hot water.

However, I was not supposed to go on my own – what could a woman do all by herself ? – I had to take at least one Director with me. Fortunately Armand, an elderly Board member with a good sense of humor offered to go with me. We were welcomed at the office of the Minister, and we left with the promises that the arrears from the past were not to be paid. Our duties would be collected from that day on. The World Trade Center of Antwerp was saved. Not one member of the Board of Directors expressed its gratitude.   .

Chapter 28
Between Brazil
and Amsterdam

WTC panel discussions.
On my right Guy Tozzoli, President of the World Trade Centers

When a few months later I took a plane to attend our yearly World Trade Center annual General Assembly in Brazil. I nearly ended up in prison. On the plane, I was seated next to an elderly couple. They were on their way to their son, who was doing field work in the South American country. His way to avoid being enlisted in the Belgian Army. The parents had been several times in Brazil and knew what was to be expected.. I had a ring on my finger who looked like a gold one but wasn't. They advised me to take it of as it was not unthinkable that my finger would be cut of to steal the ring. They told me to distrust the custom officers because they didn't joke with people who tried to smuggle things into their country.

Which made me aware I had stuff with me that could course trouble : 200 neckties, packed one by one with the logo. of the WTC of Antwerp. They were made to offer to the Congress people in Rio. The custom people

144

in Rio had a very special way to pick out people who were going to have a double check. They made them walk through a sophisticated engine and each time a passenger passed by a light went on, arbitrary green or red. When it turned to green, the passenger was allowed to go through, when it turned to red his luggage was checked over and over again. While I was queuing up the thought occurred to me that I was smuggling. It was quite a queue so I had plenty of time to think this over and it was not very happy thought. The wildest scenarios passed my mind. When I was with my car in the Egyptian desert I never had been sweating so much as when I looked at the light shining closer and closer to me. Finally it was my turn... The light turned to green. With my 200 neckties I had made it safely to the Brazilian territory.

Our Rio Palace hotel was situated on Copacabana. I haven't seen much of it . I was too terrified to leave the hotel. We were brainwashed about all the dangers that we were on the point to meet outside. The meetings took place at the hotel and the only walk that I took was to the swimming pool on the second floor

Our next WTC stop was Bahia . I wanted to inhale the local sphere and decided to assist to a Voodoo happening, not one created for tourists, the real thing. Bahia seemed to be known for his voodoo evenings but the driver who came to pick us up at the Airport was not very exited. It was only when he realized that our group could mean extra income he gave in. As long as we didn't put on jewelry, meaning no watch, no money, no credit cards or camera's. We agreed on every point.

He picked us up in the evening and took us to the slums of Bahia. From one small street into another one; The houses where all chalked in white. It looked quite clean. Our van stopped in the middle over nowhere . A black man came to us, looked us over and invited us without much enthusiasm to follow him in one of the houses. We were the only white people, white civilization hadn't ruined anything yet. If we felt safe is another question. We were invited to sit on the floor between several voodoo-worshippers, men, women, black and fat. On a kind of stage an aged negro woman was meditating. In the middle of the circle a young black girl was seated. She had been locked up for five days without food or anything to drink. This was supposed to bring her totally in trance . She was bending from left to right. From time to time, she received a kind of syrup prepared by the priestess on the stage. Finally, the young girl rose and disappeared with a man behind a very dirty curtain.

Our driver came in and sat next to me. I whispered to him that I would like to find out what was happening to the girl. He looked at me with wide open eyes. If he could have turned to grey, he would have. I noticed the disbelieve in his eyes but above all fear. To him, anything could be expected from a white woman who wanted to assist to a voodoo session, including that she would go on her own behind the curtain and be raped on the spot. After a sleight hesitation he turned to somebody who obviously was in command. That man looked at me for a second and beckoned me to follow him. My delegation probably thought that was the end of me but nobody tried to stop me. I suppose that they were in a kind of a trance as well. I entered behind the curtain. The girl I had seen before was seated in ecstasy in front of the man who had picked her up. To be more exact she sat in front of something that the man held steady in front of his trousers and that looked like a phallus in extra large. The child, because she was very young, started bending again from left to right in front of the man and his attribute while he was mumbling God knows what. I didn't see what came next because I was asked to leave.

Meanwhile the sphere had changed in the small room that I had left. Everybody stood up and was invited to go to the upper floor. Upstairs meant via a wooden staircase with a couple of steps. The members of my little delegation were all from Antwerp except two who were from Tunisia. Sla el Goulin, a man who intended to build a World Trade Center in Tunis and his wife. Sla had some problems transferring the necessary money for his admission fee to Headquarters and risked expulsion from the WTC happenings. Somebody told him that I was the perfect go-between between President Guy Tozzoli, and himself. Sla el Goulin, my salad as I called him disrespectfully had been Ambassador of Tunisia in Belgium and liked our country. He was small and didn't look like a hero, but he would have gone true a fire for me. That was the reason that he went with us to that Voodoo house without having the time of his life. Far from !

The staircase was to small for all of us. We were divided into two groups. El Goulin sacrificed himself and went with his wife and a couple of other people upstairs. I stayed behind with the rest . After five minutes they returned. When El Goulin noticed me he headed towards me saying

146

: Paula , for heaven's sake do not go up there. I thought that they were slathering chickens, or something like it, what I should have hated to watch but his wife told me what had happened. We had to drink something from a spoon, she said, it was awful. Did you drink it ? I asked incredulous. Of course, she said, what else could we do ?

It was my turn to walk up the stairs followed by the remaining once.. A man with spoons with a stinking liquid was waiting for us.. I refused to take one. Nothing happened until one of those men started to undress. To play it safe we hurried back downstairs and asked our driver to bring us to our hotel. No hard feelings. At the porch, we received a small voodoo house as a souvenir.

Our last stop in Brazil was at the Iguassu Falls where we flew over by helicopter to visit Paraguay. It was a relieve that we could stroll around the village without fearing to be assaulted. In the middle of a small village where our guides dropped us of was an Indian market where leatherwear was sold. At the booth where I was biding with a salesgirl a native Indian boy came crawling out of a wigwam. When he noticed me, he gave me a big smile and asked 'Donde?' , where are you from. I figured he even didn't know where Europe was. I answered 'Belgica'. Belgique, he answered full of enthusiasm and in French, je connais. My attention went from my suitcase to this French speaking Indian, and I said stupidly 'Oh, yes ?' . Of course, he said. I have been studying there, in Louvain-la-Neuve., a well known student city in my country.

A couple of days later we were home again.

Chapter 29
The Lord Of The Manor

I never stayed long in one place . It happened that Miek, the assistant of head shareholder Govaerts and I get fed up with all those men who took us for granted. The publishing house that employed her specialized in publicity campaigns, and they gave her far away trips as a bonus. On very short notice, she asked me if I felt like breaking out for a while, and I always did. We left without leaving notice, which sometimes led to chaotic situations. Miek's secretary contacted mine to ask her if she knew where her boss had gone to. Answer of my secretary : no, but mine is gone as well, and I don't know whereto either. My God they left together! The husband of Miek was not much of a help and Alexandra was safely in hand of a family member who didn't know where to look for us. And nobody knew when we were going to show up again.

Sometimes we stayed away for about ten days; It happened when we were invited at the performance of Aida at Louxor. Quite a show where only the very rich of this earth attended . Most of them Americans. The opera took place between the temples and the roman warriors playing in the Opera were recruited between the local citizens. Their arrival was impressive and amazing as , probably to please the American visitors they played in total devotion the Stars and Stripes in their outfit from decades before Christ, a very unusual combination. It was a unique experience. Nobody had claimed for us as Missing Persons. They knew we would be back someday. And we did come back. Everybody was happy. For a while we had the red carpet treatment. Even from our male bosses.

De Muynck became one of the managers of the World Trade Center on my introduction . He was larger than his boots . International trade didn't interest him at all. However, when he heard how successful and pleasant our WRC missions where he joined us to a mission in Atlanta. He had never crossed the Ocean. He took his wife and two children with him and insisted to fly in business class.

148

It was un unwritten rule that if one of our business mission members flew on economy we all did, but not De Muynck. We flew to London where we changed planes and took British Caledonian. After a few drinks on board we became friends for life with several other passengers and the air hostesses. When we learned that The Rolling Stones were on board we wanted to see them to have some autographs for our children. One of the hostesses disappeared and returned with the messages that we were welcome for a short visit. Th pop group was traveling across first class, in the large hump of the plane where a turning staircase let to . We had to pass through business class where De Muynck sat with his family. He was not thrilled that those worms from economy passed through his holy ground . We didn't care and went up. The Rolling Stones were playing cards with a couple of other guys. They didn't mind being disturbed and gave us the autographed picture where we came for.

From Atlanta, we flew to New York. We had dinner at the Windows of the World. Everybody was in a good mood until the head waiter showed up with the wine list and De Muynck ordered Champagne for everybody. French Champagne in an American five star restaurant! It was not quite what we had in mind but De Muynck told us to keep quiet. He was the only WTC manager on the table – apart of me but that didn't seem to be a problem – and he knew how to behave in a place like this! At least that was what he apparently thought. Until the bill was presented and everybody was asked to pay his share.

Back in Belgium the trip seemed to have gone to de Muynck's head. He bought himself a manor to live in, called everybody by name, by preference politicians whom he invited complete with a Chamber Orchestra in the hall of his new home.. He bought Francky, an international building company, traveled all over the world and became President of the Flemish Economic Union. It didn't take very long. Francky went bankrupt. Exit Johan de Muynck.

Our World Trade Center's monthly lunches had become very popular.. Since a couple of years they specialized in Antwerp themes. We had been in the Port, the Diamond Sector and were looking for something new. The solution came one day when I was waiting for a train in the Central Station of Antwerp . The terminal is situated in a beautiful classified building . The PR man who was in command, disposed of some very healthy sense of fantasy. I asked him if the WTC could organize a lunch in the huge main hall. It took him a minute to think it over before he said yes. My Board figured I was going out of my mind. As I happened to be their event organizer, and up till then everything was going well they reluctantly gave me green light. I talked to a catering company, the one that had helped me with my Japanese night and who had become used to me and my crazy ideas.. They promised to fill the hall with tables and to serve cocktails on the stairs leading to the platform. Minister Marcel Colla, our Minister of Communications had become a friend of mine. His Ministry was building a very large Post office with an even larger Parking at Berchem Station, one stop away from the place where we planned our event. He called me up and suggested to use the Parking for my guests. From there on they could take the train to Central Station. Colla would receive free publicity for his post office, and I knew where to park the cars of my members. We had a deal. Next act was to find a train . I expected about three hundred guests. The PR of Central Station helped me out. He would see to it that the train from Brussels would carry an extra compartment for our entire party. I didn't sleep a wink that night. In the morning the Central Station of Antwerp was in complete chaos. The kitchen of my catering company was installed in the room of the lost and found and the staff who had to dispatch the tickets for the travelers had retreated in the luggage room. Without their beloved computer, everything had to be done by hands for the day. Through a side entrance the travelers were guided to the trains. The WTC of Antwerp made headlines and wrote history.

Chapter 30
Visit to the Hookers

Our service department in the Antwerp WTC was in the lift. Although it didn't always went very kosher;

WTC member Marcel, who owned a company specialized in import and export from tapestry, was about to expand . From all over Europe journalists were attending his press conference. He had invited their partners suspecting that they would leave them home. However, they did not .They came along leaving Marcel and his team panic stricken. They had no lady's program at hand . Marcel almost begged me to look after the female sex in the afternoon, with high tea or something similar in our Club. A women party is not exactly the most exiting thing I have on my mind, and coffee or tea was not exactly my department either.

At the corner of the street between the WTC and the main square, is the worldwide famous Café Den Engel with an as well famous terrace . It had been a beautiful summer. Every evening, after work , when I went from my office to my parking, there was most of the time some one who called me in. It had become my favorite hangout. .

Practically at the door of Den Engel coachmen and their horses were waiting for tourists. From time to time we talked about the local gossip.. This could be the answer for my ladies problem. A visit to Antwerp in a carriage. However for my assignment I needed more than one carriage. The coachman made a more practical suggestion. In my stable I have an old tramcar with wooden wheels, he ventured. I will hitch two horses in front of the chart and that will do the trick. That sounded better. I went to our Antwerp Tourism Board and they booked us a guide. We were ready to take care of whoever wanted to follow us.

My unexpected guest who came from all over Europe stepped enthusiastically on the horse tramway that was waiting for them on the main square. I gave them the necessary information on Brabo and the giant Antigoon and of we drove to the Fortress at the bank of the River Scheldt.

While the ladies took pictures, and I was sitting there idly I was thinking that everybody could walk in the center of the city, they didn't need me to do so. The least I could do was to take them where the average visitor didn't go. . In a glance I noticed, on the opposite side of the road a row of houses, the quay and the red light quarters. I asked the coachman if he would be able to guide his tramway and horses through the Blood Mountain, the main street of the famous whore quarter. He was an elderly man who sat a little bended over his horses but when he understood my intentions he straightened up and his eyes started to blink. Naturally, he said, watch me. My women went back into the car and without a further word our driver staggered us trough the narrow streets to the infamous neighborhood of which I knew the history, as well as I was acquainted with Brabo, I literary grew up with it. Whorehouses, if you like it or not, are an important accessory to any harbor. How incorporated and taken for granted they were in my youth is perfectly illustrated with my first contact with them as a teenager. A little before World War II a military conflict broke out between the Soviet Union and Finland. The Burgomaster of Antwerp, a notorious socialist and fervent anti-communist decided to organize an action in favor of the Finnish people. He needed some money to make it work and asked help from the schools in the district. Their pupils should go with a collecting box through the streets to ask charity for all those little Finnish kids who were in danger. I was one of the children elected. The child who brought in the most money was going to receive, out of the hand of Huysmans himself, a book : Finland, the country with a thousand of Lakes. Frankly I didn't give a damn about those poor little children in a country that I hardly knew where it was situated, but I wanted that book. When it was my turn to receive the collection-box I asked the woman in command where I had to go to collect a lot of money. She looked at me with a frown, probably must have thought that I was gifted, and answered in the red quarters were the prostitutes settled. I did not had a clue what a prostitute did for her daily meal, but I asked the lady where I could find them. She said : "If that is where you want to go, I will go with you. A child is not supposed to go there on her own. And that's what happened. I was not in totally strange territory. My mother had taken me there when she went to her favorite spot, the harbor. It was her way to travel. Even those prostitutes where part of it. I even suspect that in some way she admired them. For my frigid mom, it was a total unknown and exotic world. So there I was going in and out all those "brothels" and collecting money as I never could have dreamed of. The lady in command was right. Those women are kindhearted and have some money to spend; I was the one who was invited at Huysman's home at the Belgielei and I received the reward, the book. The Finnish cause to be solved by the prostitutes from Antwerp. Stranger things have happened.

Back to 1985 and my female guests. With a deafening noise, caused by the wooden wheels, the cobble stones that they had to pass by and the stamping of the horses. we ended up where we intended to go meaning in the street with one brothel next to the other, with girls from different color who were sitting in their sexiest underwear on a cousin in front of the window where they offered their merchandise in a spotlight of red lamps. I told my guests about the thousands of seamen who had found their way to those streets after months at sea, how their oppressed passions had exploded and how that way they integrated with the embankment.

When we arrived it was early in the afternoon but in several of the showcases, as they were called, the curtains were down. The street was almost deserted. The passengers had disappeared at the other side of the curtains. It didn't need many explanations. A Dutch lady observed that we obviously arrived at the rush hour.

Our tramway proceeded slowly until we arrived in the next street. This one was more a cozy harbor street with also one brothel next to the other. Most of the seats in front of the windows were empty. It was burning hot and the whores stood in their working outfit, going from leather boots to girdles and everything between on the street near the ice-cream man who was in business. I don't remember anymore who was more surprised, my company or the girls who noticed a couple of horses coming toward them with an entire group of women. With the ice-cream man in the way, we could now go back or forth. So we stepped out to buy an ice-cream. The girls were from different nationalities and so were my guests. There were no communication problems whatsoever. Impossible to come nearer to the folklore of our city.

Our tram arrived back at the Main Square just in time to return the ladies to their hotel. In the evening, there was a gala organized by Marcel.

I was invited but did not feel much like going. We were in a period when a lot of hold ups were made on Delhaize, a chain store group. The restaurant where the party went on was right next to such a store, and I didn't want to drive on my own to that location in the dark of the night. I declined.

Next day Marcel called me to thank you for my intervention, but he also asked what I had done with his female guests. They were all wild about their lady's program.

Chapter 31
A Friend In Need
Is a Friend Indeed

All I knew about India I had read in the wonderful book 'La Cité de la Joie'. It tells the story of the slums of Calcutta and how the outcast dealt with their poverty. When I arrived for another WTC Assembly in Bombay. I went to the slums without fearing to be attacked. This was not like in Brazil. Entire families were living in the most horrible circumstances on the filthy, greasy soil and smiled at me.

When the Assembly was over we traveled with the Belgian delegation to Pushkar, in the North of India, where the yearly Camel market, the biggest of his kind in Asia took place. Everywhere around us where herds of camels with their shepherds who arrived from all over Rajasthan to be sold . Cars were banned in the fair area, the local taxi's where camels as well who brought the visitors to colorful tents where animals and people stayed together in perfect harmony.. Circus acts – always with camels, popular games, it was a colorful and joyful get-together. But above all it was a place of pilgrimage.

The story goes that Lord Brahma, the Hindu God of creation, was looking for a place to stay on earth. Lotus leaves fell down from heaven and fell on Jayeshta, the later Pushkar. Lord Brahma was ordered by a Godstath to purify the place with a yagna. To do so his wife should be next to him and Goddess Saraswati was invited to join Lord Brahma. She could not make it in time and as the moment of purification was nearing Brahma ordered his servant, Indra, to look for somebody who could replace his wife. Indra found Gayatri, a milkmaid, whose head was put in the muzzle of a cow (the holy animal). Brahma accepted her for his wife of that day. When Goddess Saraswati arrived she cursed her husband and ordered that he was not to be honored anywhere else than in Puskar and merely with Kaertika Poornina. Therefore to Brahmans Puskar is their Holy Pilgrims place and their purification takes place in the adjoining lake.

The four members of our WTC group decided to have a closer look at this Holy Lake. In the distance we noticed a small white village. Through a narrow gate we arrived in a kind of patio. A man dressed in a white gown welcomed us.. He bowed very deeply and invited us to follow him. Moments later we arrived at the lake. On his signal we sat down with our feet in the water. Another man, dressed in the same way, came forward. Both sat between. us . Each of them had one of us on his side. We understood that they were guru's and that they were ready to baptize us in their faith. They put Lotus leaves in our hands and he man next to me asked me if my father was still alive. I said 'No'. He told me that he was going to pray so that he could rest in peace. I didn't want my father to rest in peace. My memories about that man were not too good and that is what I told my guru. He was not alone an holy man but a diplomat as well. He asked me how I felt towards my mother. I replied that she died as well but that I had good feelings for her. He decided to pray so that she could rest in peace.

We had to repeat what he prompted, what it was I never would know because it was the dialect of the territory and even if it had been in plain Hindi I wouldn't have understood a word. Meanwhile the water of the lake had been poured over the Lotus leaves we kept in our hands. When the prayer was over a little colored ribbon was put around our wrist. The men helped us to our feet bowed very respectfully, both hand as if praying and brought us back to the gate. We left the ribbon on our wrist for a couple of days but when it became dirty we took it of and threw it away.

Before we had left for India the commercial manager of Air India paid me a visit at the WTC. His company was the official carrier of the WTC participants to the Assembly. He offered to give our group an upgrading to first class providing that we bought business class tickets. Everybody agreed. Traveling to India first class on a flying carpet was not to be underestimated.

On our return flight from Delhi the departure was delayed . We didn't care, we were treated like royalty, so what. A very important passenger was expected. The seat next to was reserved for the person in question. Finally an Indian walked in, the hostesses nearly bowed on to the floor, guided the man to his place and we were ready to leave. It was late at night, my neighbor didn't say one single word, closed his eyes and fell asleep. I did the same. Several hours later I woke up, my nose nearly touching the nose of the man beside me. It was a strange feeling to wake up next to a complete stranger. Slowly I became aware of the situation. After a while the man opened his eyes. Again he didn't say a word until he noticed that I belonged to a group seated elsewhere. I suppose that customs didn't allow him to talk to a woman traveling on her own. Now that he found out that this was not the case he introduced himself as the Minister of Foreign Affairs of India. He was on his way to an Assembly of Ministers of Foreign Affairs in New York. While he was talking I noticed a string around his wrist exactly similar to the one that I received from my guru at the Holy Lake. I asked him what it was and he told me that he was a Brahman and that it was customary that, each time when he went for a long journey abroad, a Guru came to his house to bless him and put such a string around his wrist.

I related to the Minister what happened to us and asked him if this was fake. He said no, and told me that everybody could become a Brahman without having to deny their own faith. The fact that I had been bathing in the Holy Water in the presence of a Guru made me a Brahman. If this was the fact and touching the Holy Water was a certain passport to heaven, I was doing very well.

The General Assembly of 1989 was planned to take place in China. On April 15 the revolt took place at the Tiananmen Square in Bejing. In every Committee, including the one where I was a member of, the question was raised if it would be proper to organize the next General Assembly in a city where the massacres took place. Most of the WTC members found it a to delicate and dangerous situation. There was no general agreement reached therefore a vote per correspondence took place. Headquarters sent us an inquiry formulary. We, the WTC of Antwerp, where the only ones from the 300 WTC's worldwide who voted in favor. My reasoning was that if we didn't organize the planned Assembly, the WTC of Being could be in trouble. For that matter there were only two alternatives. Or the existing Government was going to be overthrown, a new one was going to be installed and we had to meet them sooner or later. Or everything remained as it was and there were no problems. However the majority was against and the General Assembly instead of being held in Bejing was transferred to Geneva. In China nothing changed and the female President of WTC Bejing Guilin assisted with a very important Chinese delegation to the meeting in Switzerland. She expressed her gratitude for my support and told me that she and her delegation were traveling to Antwerp to visit me in my quarters. The following week she invited me for lunch at our WTC restaurant. I was considered a guest of honor and seated next to the Minister of Foreign Affairs from China. On my other side was the President of the Chinese Chamber of Commerce. Guilin toasted to me first in Chinese then in English. I said to my Honorable Partners, she told me, that we drink to the health of Paula Marckx, a friend in need is a friend indeed. She offered me a delicate Chinese porcelain plate. I still have it.

A couple of months later I received a phone call that took me back in time. When I started Tele-Call I had interviewed a lot of candidates who were looking for a job.

One of them was Marie-Rose Van de Put who was deadly nervous. She was in her forties, not that young for a job as a telephone operator, married to a business man and a mother of three. In her twenties she had been a clerk but had chosen to stay home to raise her children and had no recent references what so ever. The children grew up , she wanted an occupation and was depressed to find out that at her age she was out of the working market. As far as I was concerned I needed motivated people and she looked like one. I hired her and never regretted it for a moment. She was at my side when Alexandra was born and one of her daughters came to work for us as a job student. It was almost like one big family. When Tele-Call was over, our roads parted. I never saw her again.

More that fifteen years later I had her husband on the line. Marie-Rose just died. On her deathbed she had requested her family to contact me. She wanted me to be at her funeral. I considered it a great honor and kept contact with her children. In their mother's name.

Chapter 32
The Gulf War

One of the friends I made in the WTC circuit was President of the World Trade Center of Dubai. Whenever we met at some International Assembly he insisted that I should pay him a visit. In 1990 I planned to go and see him. Alexandra was going with me. Our timing was not very good. While we were packing our luggage ready to leave the Gulf War broke out. A Revolution stopped me once, the one in China, but there we had been voting hundreds to one. In this case, I was the only one to decide, and I wasn't in the mood to allow a War in the Middle East to cross my travel plans. I figured that when it was becoming too dangerous I was going to be stopped. First we went for a couple of days to Egypt where I didn't notice much of the war next door. After a cruise on the Nile, we boarded the Gulf Air plane that flew to Dubai. The airplane was fully booked, but we were the only white people on board. The other passengers where natives of the Gulf States who worked in Egypt and returned home to be with their family. After we landed, we attracted full attention. At the customs two rows were lined up, one for the Arabs and one for the rest of the world. The row with the Arabs was endless, the rest of the world where the two of us. Taxi's as much as we wanted. One of them drove us to the Hilton Hotel where we had booked. Except for a couple of sheik's in full dress there were no other guests in sight. Our room looked more like an apartment in an oriental palace than the rooms we originally were staying in. Before we unpacked I phoned the reception desk to tell them that they're obviously had been a mistake. The man on the line told us not to worry , we were going to pay for an ordinary double room. We were put in this suite because they didn't expect any other guests , apart from guests from Kuwait, the country where the war was all about , and where the Iraqis were firing at. . The hotel keepers in Dubai were forced to make several of their rooms available for the VIP guests from that country. .

The local newspaper didn't bring bright news at all. The American coalition was not there yet to help them out and the countries around the Persian Gulf, meaning where we were, were about to enter the conflict. When I was preparing my trip, I had found out that in Dubai an

159

Association of Oil Wives existed. The husbands of those ladies were working in the oil fields . The President was an English lady, and I had fixed a date to see her for an interview. After reading the paper I figured that no one with common sense would be left in this country, except myself as far as one could call me sensible. I called her and to my surprise, I had her at the end of the line. She seemed overwhelmed with joy that I did arrive and asked where I was staying. When I told her that I was at the Hilton She said : that is just fine. We will be there this afternoon to play bridge. I will see you then.

Meanwhile I went to the other side of the street, to the World Trade Center to see my friend who was at the origin of my trip. He seemed to have forgotten all about me and had returned to England. Away from all that shooting.

In the early afternoon, I met my female date, but she was much to much involved in her bridge game to have much time to spend with me. We agreed to meet for lunch the next day.

In the lobby of the Hilton, I had noticed a young Arab, a son of a Prince from Kuwait as I was to learn later. He stood there from top to bottom dressed in white looking with more than average interest at my 17 year old Alexandra., who obviously did not feel very easy with those jet-black eyes staring at her. On our way out, the man came to us. He had style but I didn't trust the situation very much. He invited us to step in the cabriolet that was waiting for him at the front door, but I declined. In my imagination, I saw us already disappearing somewhere in the desert or in the best case behind bars in a royal palace. Fortunately in that kind of country's daughters who are with their mothers are respected. For the time being, he left us in one piece and we went in town without any more problems. We had dinner and returned later in the evening to the hotel . When we arrived at the reception desk I noticed at the other side of the lobby red letters and a word that is to be understood in every language : bar. I asked if it was open and the bellboy not only said : yes but he guided us to a waiter who took over from him. Every seat in the bar was taken, mostly by Arabs in white dress and one crew of an airplane. A table was prepared for us in front of the stage where an English duo was providing sphere music like only English singers can do. Inter-acting they were talking with the public on a very charming way mostly referring ironically to the war situation around us. Something like (to the pilots) : didn't they fire to you on your way coming in ?; Answer of the pilot : no, but I believe that I will take another way to return home. When he noticed us the singer said : And now we are going to play for those lovely ladies. By the way, are you here to visit your husband . I answered : No. Are you here on business ? I answered no. Are you on a holiday ? I answered : yes. For a moment there was a silence. Then he said : What do you think about our weather conditions?

After a few moments, a bottle of champagne was brought to our table. The waiter pointed to the man who offered it : the young prince. It was his 24th birthday. I didn't know very well how to react. They brought cake and more champagne; Finally, the evening was over, and we went to the lobby. The manager, a lady and staff of the hotel were waiting for us. The lady asked if the Prince was bothering us. I said no and she went on : should he bother you. please tell us than he will be put at the door. I saw it clearly in front of me that because of a us a Prince from Kuwait would be expelled out of the Hilton Hotel. I was sure that his entire General Staff was staying there as well

Next day we went to the swimming pool for the meeting with our oil lady. I hoped to learn from her more about this war business, and if we were in any danger. She shrugged her shoulders. I asked her if it didn't frighten her. Well, she answered, my father was an officer in the British army. I traveled all over the world with my parents. When I was 18, we lived in Egypt for quite a while and on my 18th birthday my father called me. He said to me : Birgit, you are an attractive young lady by now, and it is not unthinkable that in one of the countries we will be staying in you will be sexually assaulted. Should this happen to do not defend yourself; Just let it be. As long as you cover your face so that you cannot see your attacker.

I never had considered it that way. However, she had Alexandra's full attention. Besides, the young lady continued, if the situation is out of hand there remains a way to leave the country. The boats on the river are from Pakistani, they are our friends .I will take my dog and my canary and those men will take us to the other side of the stream. It sounded like a silly question, but I asked : What about us ? No problem, our new friend said, we will pick you up. It didn't sound very reassuring, but finally we left for Europe without damage.

And our Prince ? I have a feeling that his father kept him in sight. We never saw him again.

Chapter 33
A Hotel In Town

Robert Maslen, manager of the Hilton Hotel in Brussels came to see me one day. He was assigned to do some marketing research on the possibility to open a Hilton Hotel in Antwerp. Since I was a youngster the name Hilton had a certain impact on me. As a teenager , just after the war, I idolized the first American movies and was wild about their glimmer and glitter that were totally new to me. Movie stars were semi-Gods to us. I watched Elisabeth Taylor make her first step into movie history when she performed in National Velvet.. The little child-star was a couple of years younger than I was, but she became my heroin . I followed her whereabouts, as if she was a member of my family. When she was 18 and married Conrad Hilton Jr, son of the Hilton tycoon, I lived to the fairy tale wedding, as if I was a maid of honor. It didn't end that well but that had been no reason to worship her less than I did.

And at this very moment a manager of a Hilton Hotel was seated right in front of me and wanted to know if there was place for one more luxury hotel in Antwerp. Of course I thought there was. A Hilton hotel in Antwerp ! No doubt in my mind. That same day Robert Masslen, Bob as I was going to call him later , visited the Chamber of Commerce and the Flemish Economic Union to ask them the same question that they asked me. A week later I called Robert Masslen to ask him for the latest news. He told me that the project was canceled because the Chamber and the Economic Association didn't believe in it. I didn't believe what I heard. One of the Board Members of our WTC was an architect, Hugo van Hoecke, who had several assignments in the hotel sector. I asked for his advice. He felt sure that Antwerp was ready for a Hilton Hotel. I suggested that we both should go to Robert Masslen in order to convince him. Masslen welcomed us with not much enthusiasm in his Brussels Hilton but my soul mate seemed to have the right arguments because when we left Masslen promised to pay us another visit in Antwerp.

When we arrived in the basement parking we found out that the exit was blocked by a number of cars . The levers where out of order. There was no employee in sight and the drivers were raising hell when suddenly the long silhouette of Masslen, a kind of John Cleese from Fawtly Towers, came out of the elevator. He ran straight towards us. He had the levels blocked to be able to stop us from driving away and to have some more information. When he had the answers, he went back to the elevator and a couple of minutes later the levels were working again. When we drove outside I said to Hugo : I think that he has changed his mind.

After the holidays, in the month of September Masslen called me. Another meeting in my office was arranged. He told me that the Hilton chain had decided to open an hotel in our town in a building at the Place Verte, home of a department store for years. They were on the point to sign an agreement with the owner, but they had one major and considerable problem. The City had to agree. The outer front had to remain as it was, which was not a problem, at the contrary, but on the dome on the third floor that had been restored in 1920 a magnificent crystal chandelier was the attraction pole. An unconditional requirement was that it had to remain exactly at the same place. An agreement had to be concluded with the department of labor of the city of Antwerp. The Alderman in command was John Mangelschodts. I knew him rather well. He had a cheerful mentality, typical to Antwerp people, we both liked to use our dialect, which sometimes led to conversations like when I called him for an appointment, and he suggested a date that I was out of town and unavailable he bellowed 'how can you find yourself a husband, you are never around.'

When Masslen explained his problem I took the telephone receiver and called John. To Masslen it was a surrealistic situation that somebody called an Alderman and had him on the other side of the line as well. Just like that. Fortunately he couldn't understand our conversation. John was swearing at me and said 'Goddamn Paula, why cann't you leave me alone, I am in an important meeting'. Normally, this should scare of any outsider, but I knew John to well and knew he was putting me on. If he hadn't felt like talking to me he wouldn't have come to the phone in the first place. 'John' I replied 'keep quiet for a moment. The manager of the Hilton in Brussels is in my office. He intends to build an hotel in Antwerp and you don't give the necessary permission !' 'Come again' Mangelschodts answered obviously impressed 'The Manager of the Hilton , and he is with you now ?' 'Indeed when can we meet ?' A couple of moments of complete silence, probably John was checking his diary. 'Wednesday, he said 'at 2 o clock' I turned to Masslen 'We have an appointment' I said 'What about Wednesday ?'. Masslen looked at me completely flabbergasted 'You mean this Wednesday?' he asked. I said 'Yes' and Masslen also said 'Yes'. And so we went on Wednesday to the Cabinet of Alderman Mangelschodts, who had drummed up his entire staff. When we went out Masslen had his permission in writing.. A couple of months later the agreement with the owner was a fact. Antwerp was going to have his Hilton Hotel. My name was all over the papers as a kind of life-saver. The Antwerp Hilton Hotel opened his doors in 1993. The crystal chandelier is still hanging on the same place.

Chapter 34
The Fallen Lady

A young man by the name of Peter came into my office. He just came back from the States where he finished his studies. He was a protégé of Charles Mulcahy, a Professor of the Marquette University, International Business Leader, Government Affairs Expert and President of the World Trade Center of Milwaukee, a personal friend of mine. I had stayed in Chass' home, I took his daughter under my wings when she was in Antwerp, and he had advised Peter to contact me, as soon as he would return to Belgium. We hit it of directly, whenever he was in the neighborhood, he came to see me . He was looking for a job, and I offered to help where I could. Some bright morning he told me that he had been offered a job as a trainee by Agfa Gevaert in one of their offices in Hong Kong. He asked my advice. Should I have advised him against it, he would have left anyway, but it was nice to be taken into consideration, Especially because our next WTC meeting was going to take place in Hong Kong. Peter accepted the offer, left for Asia and never returned to Europe except for holidays. He was assigned to different Asiatic countries, married a Korean girl and lived happily ever after. I stayed with them when I was in Japan. Later Peter became President of Agfa Asia with quarters in Shanghai.

I was still desperately looking for an investor/ promoter for a WTC building in Antwerp. I wondered if organizing a WTC General Assembly in Antwerp could help. However, to do, so I needed a sponsor, a big spender. The High Council for Diamonds was an option. I asked for an interview with Marc van den Abeele, at that time General Manager of the Council in question. I wanted an invitation from Antwerp to be on the agenda of the WTC Assembly in Hong Kong. I persuaded a bank manager to sponsor a videotape of our city and its facilities and Van den Abeele gave, without many difficulties, his agreement for the Diamond Council to become our major sponsor. It was about time for the World Trade Center of Antwerp to elect a new President, and I promised Marc that if he would bring in the necessary money I was going to lobby for his election as President of our Association. In Hong Kong, we were put on the waiting

165

list as an organizer for the next General Assembly. A first result was scored and meanwhile our Board discussed the change of Presidency.

A couple of months went by. In Summertime I decided to go with Alexandra for our holidays to Hawaii . We took our local airline Sabena to New York where we were going to change to another carrier. Above the Atlantic things went wrong. I stood up to pick up a magazine, stumbled and felt with my thigh on top of the arm of a chair. A thighbone fracture. It hurted like hell. The hostess arrived, saw that it was serious business and called for a doctor. No doctor on board. She decided to bring me to first class, to be more comfortable. No one from the crew knew how to handle the situation.

The chief hostess from first class asked me if I wanted some champagne. I shook my head as heavily as I could. I was totally conscious and realized that if I had alcohol in my blood the airline responsible could have argued that I had fallen because I had been drinking. I asked the girl to put ice on my leg. She brought me a champagne bucket . I explained to her that wouldn't work that she needed to put the ice in a plastic bag. Then I asked her to arrange for an ambulance upon arrival in New York . I don't knew if she did so but in New York, there was no ambulance in sight. The passengers left the plane , according to the staff, they had not been able to reach anyone to help me. At the end of my wits I asked to call Europe Assistance where I am a member of. One of the hostesses came to inform me that the coach that brought the crew to New York was ready to leave. I asked them what was going to happen to me and my daughter. They suggested that they would put me on a seat outside the plane so that we could wait until help arrived. A layman could know that this was impossible in my physical condition, I was screaming with pain – later when I put Sabena on trial, and I won the case , the crew argued that they didn't think it was that serious because they didn't see any blood. Finally, a steward decided to wait with me until an ambulance arrived. When it did the nurses took over. They brought me to the nearest hospital, with a complete black staff. The nurses were dancing in front of my bed to sheer me up. They took excellent care of me.

With all those aids- stories I didn't want to be operated and infused blood which I did not know who it had belonged to so I requested to be repatriated to Belgium. Not exactly what is to be expected from a holiday.

However, as mentioned before I won my trial, received financial compensation and two brand new tickets. As soon as I was out of the plaster, I returned to America.

Chapter 35
The First Attack at the World Trade Center

When I was hired by the World Trade Center, about ten years ago, André Moeremans introduced me to Yourie Demeure who had his office in the W.T.C. building. Youri was chief editor of the magazine Impact published by his friend, Charlie de Pauw, building promoter of the Word Trade Center of Brussels. After a while, he started a business of his own specialized in trendy business guides named. Who is Who in Business. The serial became very successful and a leader in his field . He intended to make a similar guide for female entrepreneurs worldwide and came to me for help. He needed my connections at the WTC in New York. Guy Tozzoli and my President of the section communications, Tom Kearney were in favor, and they invited Youry, his business partner. and myself to a business meeting in New York. The date of February 26 1993 was suggested but as Tozolli had to receive the same day a delegation of the East European countries wanting to discuss an eventual WTC building in the Eastern Block, our meeting was postponed for a week.

The day that we should have been in one of the Twin Towers it was bombed for the first time. Terrorists drove a rented yellow Ford Eccoline in the basement garage of the WTC and brought a 750kg ureal-nitrate bomb to an explosion. Six people were killed, over 1.000 people injured and the damage was far over millions of dollars. A group of terrorists who lived in New Jersey headed by a certain Yousef at first intended to use chemical weapons but didn't dispose of the necessary financial backing. Yousef had been trained in Afghanistan after having traveled all over the world, by the name of the Islamic Jihad. The WTC building had become a target for practical reasons. It was close to New Jersey where the explosives of the terrorists were stocked and one of the terrorists parked on different occasion his car in the underground parking of the World Trade Center. Most of the members of the group claimed that they had lost family in the Gulf War, and that they wanted revenge. At that time Yousef already had declared to the American Authorities that the original plan had been to destroy one of the Twin Towers and to kill as many people as possible.

We arrived in New York a couple of days after the attack took place. We met Guy Tozzoli and Tom Kearney in a restaurant. We feared for a moment that the meeting was going to be postponed. However, it wasn't . Youry made his point, questions and answers went over the table. After the business side of the meeting had come to an end, I brought the conversation to the attack of the previous week. I had seen the terrible crater left by the bomb. It was a small miracle that there had been not more casualties. I asked Guy how it felt being with his East European guests in his office on the seventy seventh floor when it happened.

He replied that the lights went out, a huge cloud of dust came to them, but there was no real panic. Everybody took the hand of their neighbor and made a human link to go blindly downstairs. When I asked him if he hadn't been frightened, he answered that there had been no reason to be. When, in 1968, the World Trade Center was build the building constructor knew that they were near John Kennedy Airport and that there always would be a possibility that an airplane in difficulties would bump into the building. That is why, he concluded that the inside frames were built in a way that there will never be a danger for collapsing.

Chapter 36
A Right and a Wrong Decision

René Uhrich asked me to follow him and I did

On my return from the States, I was nominated as Woman of Europe. It was the second time that such an election took place and the nominees from all over Europe, gathered in the Bank of Paris and the Netherlands in Antwerp. It was a very colorful but interesting lot. I was not elected but became close friends with other nominees, like Patsy Sorrensen and Lenie ' t Hart who was nominated for Holland. Patsy had made herself a name with her Payaoke Association, an organization that since a couple of years cared and fought for prostitutes and sexual abused women. In the years to come, she was going to receive international recognition as an expert on the field . Lennie 't Hart cared for seals who were washed ashore in Northern Holland and who were looked after in her nursery in Pieterburen. They had both something in common. Patsy started her work when watching a prostitute who lived in her neighborhood, Lenny started to care for a baby seal that she found ashore and kept alive in her bath tub.

170

Meanwhile my Alexandra had other plans. To polish her language knowledge, she left as an Au Pair to Atlanta. All of a sudden, I stood waiving my daughter good-bye at the Airport of Heathrow where the different Au Pair's met for a collective departure. The last I saw of her was when she waved at me at the gate. And away she went. For the first time traveling on her own. She had been a couple of times with me to America, so I didn't really worry. If I had realized that up to a certain point she had acquired my adventurous nature it probably would have been different. While I returned home and did what I had to do Alexandra arrived in New York where the entire group was staying in an hotel across Central Park to receive training instructions about the American way of life.

The first evening the girls were supposed to have an early sleep to recover from their Jet lag. Nevertheless, not this Alexandra. She wanted to enjoy at the fullest her first day away from home. She put **on** a cocktail dress that was made for her some time before in Thailand and walked into Central Park – a place that every tourist knew they have to avoid. Extremely exited with her new freedom, she lost her way and finally ended up in Harlem. Fortunately she remembered the name of her hotel and a helpful black man who told her it was much too dangerous where she was walking gave her some money and put her on a city bus who brought her to her hotel..

In Antwerp, I was again on my own. Before Alexandra was born, I had lived most of my life by myself. Even so, by now I had been used to have her around. Since Michel's death my sex life had never been what it used to be. There had been sentimental journeys, it had always been part of my life. I had spent years between more or less available men. A strange coincidence was that during my entire life professors had made passes at me. I believe that I have some kind of a Fair Lady syndrome. I was not the brightest in school, but I have a feeling that, with all I have learned on the way, I would finish cum laude if I should ever go for a degree.

Take René Uhrich. The man was Professor Economy at the University of Strasbourg, and member of the Bureau of the International Congress of French Economists. I never heard of him before but as an international authority in Economy, he was invited as a guest at the WTC meeting in Geneva. The local President and close friend, wanted to introduce him to

Guy Tozzoli. Professor Uhrich arrived when the session had already begun so I hadn't noticed him when he was coming in the auditorium..

Meetings took place in the same hotel where the members were staying . Lunch was served in one of the main dining rooms. There were no reserved seats and Uhrich sat down next to me. He introduced himself and the conversation went on like everywhere where strangers share a same table in business conventions 'Where do you come from?' 'What kind of business are you in ?' small talk that is forgotten as soon as lunch or dinner is over and everybody walks away.. Suddenly, coffee was not served yet, Uhrich took my hand, stood up and said 'Come along'. I stood up followed him out of the room, into the elevator, through the hotel corridor to his room. He took me inside, locked the door and took me in bed. We remained there the rest of the day, economy was far away and completely forgotten. Next day he returned to Strasbourg. Two weeks later he called me 'Paula, I am coming to Antwerp', he said. I picked him up at the railway station and drove him to the Crown Plaza hotel where he had booked for the weekend. On Monday, I brought him back to the train. In between we didn't come out of our room. For me, he was merely a heavy flirt, but to the WTCA, he was much more. Guy Tozzoli kept inviting him for all our further meetings and assemblies. Every time we met, we took the fiber where we left it. And this went on until I left the Association. When he took my hand, he was 59. I was sixty. Some attitudes never change.

But on business scale I had been making a big mistake. Finally, after lobbying quite a lot I pushed Marc van den Abeele into the Presidential Seat. First time he presided over the Board of Directors he suggested to get rid of me. He was convinced that only a man could be a representative manager of a World Trade Center. I had figured that Marc would be an asset, but I never realized that he was such an ass and a bastard. I should have known better. Once at a cocktail party I met Marc with his wife,. I had never seen her before. I told her that I was pleased to meet her, and that I hope to se her on a regular base.

Marc took me aside and snapped at me that I was way out of my duties by inviting his wife to the WTC events. She had no business being there.

Finally, I looked up André Gantman a friend and member of the same political party where Marc belonged to and complained about him being a liar and a no good so and so. When I finished talking André asked me: Do you think we are unaware of that ?

After the holidays, the question was put on vote if I should stay on or not.

Meanwhile Alexandra had returned from the States and went to work temporarily for Lenie 't Hart and her little seals in Pïeterburen. The foundation had made quite a name for himself. From all over the world students dropped in order to spend their leisure time working for the nursery. They paid for their transportation, were not financially rewarded and only received some money to buy food on condition that every other night one of them prepared food from their native country. Their duty was to play with and care for small and very big seals. Alexandra felt quite at home because she had been employed as a student for part time jobs at the Zoo in Antwerp where she looked after lama's, polo bears, tigers, night animals and more of that exotic fauna.

After her return from Pieterburen Alexandra left to Madrid for another year as an Au Pair. The day we arrived in Spain King Baldwin died in Motril.. Spain was in deep mourning. The family where Alexandra was going to stay with treated us as if someone of our family passed away. It certainly was sad but the way our King had been living, I felt sure that he was going straight to heaven. With a red carpet treatment included. I don't believe that is what I am going to get. However, I am sure that on earth I had a better time.

In my World Trade Center, the mood was not exactly positive. Marc Van den Abeele had done an excellent job to obtain what he wanted. Moreover, another Board member, Hugo van Hoecke, the man who had been with me to the Hilton Hotel had had taken my secretary away for his own business use.. The girl was South African and spoke fluently English. Hugo had signed a contract with an English company and was urgently in need of somebody who spoke and wrote the language, which, at that time was not that easy to find. He offered her more money than the WTC could pay her, plus an extra bonus and that was that. Van den Abeele hired a new secretary, somebody he knew who was going to support him.

In September at an assembly Marc asked if I would be allowed to stay as a manager. He put it on vote. He was the first to vote against, most of the Board members followed him, some withheld – those were the worst. Marc was still at the helm of the High Council for Diamond Trade and the Board members were hoping to receive sooner or later a piece of the cake. I was dismissed. Not immediately. I was going to receive six-month salary and I was able to choose, I could leave or finish my time. I stayed. But not for long. A couple of weeks later a jurist came into my office and asked me to leave immediately. I never knew why. I suppose that I worked on their system.

When the news went around Eliane Achten, the most important lady of the Association of the Port, told me that the entire harbor industry had the greatest respect for the way I had handled the situation. Meaning that I had not presented the WTC as a bogeyman. There was no need to do so either. I am convinced that when somebody put someone else a knife in the back sooner or later he or she has to pay for it. Not by me but by unwritten laws. As a matter of fact, Marc Van den Abeele was not so much later dismissed in a similar way by the High Council for Diamond Trade.

Just before I left the WTC of Antwerp a WTC Spring Meeting took place in the Argentines. I was not supposed to attend and my expenses were not longer covered by my Association. When Désirée Huysmans, wife of one of our WTC members learned about it she invited me at her Castle in Meer. François I am going with Paula to the Meeting in Buenos Aires, she said to her husband, you pay our tickets. Which he did. Unfortunately, Désirée broke her foot not long before we had to leave so she had to stay home. Nevertheless, she insisted that I took my ticket, and I left on their account.

Probably, WTC Antwerp had notified WTCA headquarters about what was going on so nobody expected me anymore at their meeting. When I did arrive at the Congress hall I received a standing ovation. . What my future would be, che sera, sera. Meanwhile I went in the evening on my own to the tango bars in the slums of Buenos Ayres and in the daytime to the tomb of Evita Perron.

Chapter 37
The Jungle Beat

The last meeting with my WTC buddies made me perfectly aware that I was not ready to retreat from the kind of life I was accustomed to. Before everybody forgot about me, I had to act fast. I made a couple of phone calls to people I still trusted and started an event office in my own name. Sam Sasportas, the Jewish manager of the Carlton Hotel, offered to use his hotel as my hangout. I wrote to my former WTC members. More that half of them followed me in my new venture. Carla ten Cate, a Dutch woman who had a PR office not far from Antwerp was ready to become my partner. If I needed contacts from abroad, I was just a phone call away from my former WTC colleagues worldwide. They didn't care that I didn't work for the WTC any longer, to them, I still remained Paula from the World Trade Center. My event bureau became a successful fact. I contacted several Embassies and organized each month a roaring festival from some magic country. We were on our way.

In summertime Alexandra returned from Spain. Two months later she became 21. I wanted to make it something that se always would remember so we left for Kenya. We had been there before and were hooked. In Nairobi, we took the train to Mombasa where we had booked at a hotel owned by a Belgian. The man had worked for an Antwerp freight forwarding company . He was in command of the African lines and his work had brought him to Mombasa. He decided to stay there for the rest of his life.

When I told him about my problems with the WTC and my new company he advised me to contact Jean-Marie Denis. He felt sure that he would support me and is what happened. At the time being who cared about the future? I was having the time of my life under the tropical sun. My new friend took care of us like a baby and warned us not to go too far away from the hotel. A gang of thieves were operating in the neighborhood, and I had better stayed away from them, He called for a taxi stationed in front of the hotel when I wanted to spend the evening in another hotel on the beach. Those men were to be trusted so I kept him with us.. We

175

decided to make it an entire day excursion and came back late at night. Our driver decided to take a short cut through the jungle. He was driving rather fast, and suddenly it happened. We drove against a tree. From every side, I saw branches and leaves coming towards me. We turned over upside down, the car was a total loss. The first to crawl out of it was our driver, loudly moaning about what he saw. Finally, he helped us out of the wreck. I seemed to be all right, Alexandra thought she had a broken nose. A car crash is never a pleasant experience, but in the jungle in the middle of the night it is extremely scaring.. I heard all kinds of noises where an average European is not directly accustomed to. And my black driver kept on moaning. He was in shock and not a great help. From the distance, I noticed a tinny light coming in our direction. It could be anything. I have no idea how wild animal eyes look like in the dark. It was no animal. It was a flashlight and it was in the hand of a man who spoke English. He touched us all over. But didn't seem to have dubious intentions. He told us to follow him. Step by step, because apart from the tree where we had driven into there where lots of other ones. In the distance, we saw a house where all the lights were shining brightly. It belonged to an Indian family who had heard the crash. Their son, who found us, was a veterinary surgeon. The nose of Alexandra was not broken it just happened to be a bloody nose. The young man drove us back to the hotel.

Next day we took a plane to Masai Mara and arrived in one of the most beautiful wild reserves of the world. In the early morning, a guide fetched us at the tent where we had spent the night and brought us to a bright colored hot air balloon that was waiting for us. I have never been very lithe and to crawl in that kind of a basket only helped by a couple of Negroes, who pushed at my bottom was not so evident. Finally, I made it. Alexandra followed me. The balloon went up in the air. It was in the middle of October and bellow us the annual migration of millions of gnu's and thousand's of zebra's between Kenya's Maai Mara National Reserve and the neighboring Serengeti National Parc was in full swing. The stamping of the pawns of all those animals was as deafening as impressive. We were gliding south, along with them. I never felt closer with nature than on that moment. Left and right lions were having their early meals, we were flying so close that we could watch the prey in their muzzles. After a while the balloon landed in the middle of the savannah. A jeep with breakfast arrived. The wild animals watched us from a distance. A couple of guards took care of us with their arms ready to fire should any of our four legged friends should come forward with an idea that was not programmed.. We sat on the ground and were offered a champagne brunch with a birthday cake for Alexandra. Happy birthday , baby. We made it so far !

Chapter 38
A New Opportunity

Before we left for Africa, Alexandra and I agreed that she should spend another year as an Au Pair, this time in France. Since she was a little girl my daughter wanted to have a dog. With all the traveling, I had to do I didn't think this was a good idea. However, this time we could join the business to pleasure. After her baby sitting experiences in America and Spain, we were going to give it another try in France, this time as a puppy sits. An advertisement in a French dog magazine brought in dozens of offers. One was outstanding. Tom Caldwell, an American breeder living in Paris expected a puppy for his breeding ambitious. The little fellow was in urgent need of a nanny.

Tom's kennel was in a restored farm in Lhuys, a tinny winy village not far from Reims. He stayed there during week-ends with his boy friend Nicolas, his ex-boy friend Philippe and about ten Tibetan Terriers. My Alexandra was in good hands. Tom, born in New York and an outstanding piano player, had been living for several years in France where he gave piano lessons at the International School. The pupils of this school where children from diplomats and celebrities .He was the one who gave Carlo Ponti Jr, the son of Sophia Loren, by now a celebrated conductor, his first piano lessons.. Tom was a good friend of the star. One of the first Tibetan Terriers of his breed found a home with La Loren.

Jigme, the puppy from London that Tom expected, and where Alexandra had to take care of was going to arrive two days later by plane. Alexandra went to pick hem up. It was an instant commitment. They never separated anymore.. A week after her arrival one of the Tibetan dogs in the kennel gave birth.. I requested to be the godmother of the first born. In that year, all puppies had to have a name starting with the letter L. I called her Lara. A name that had a special meaning to me. The story of Dr. Jivago, especially Lara's destiny which I understood but too well, had moved me. Now I had my own Lara . I wanted her to be christened. Friends from Antwerp thought it was a splendid idea and decided to be part of it. The male household of Tom didn't dispose of the necessary equipment to look

178

after so many guests. One of my lady friends in the group was the secretary of Sam Sasportas from the Carlton Hotel. Consequently we left with cars filled with guests and pots and pans from the Carlton Hotel in the direction of Lhuys. The people of the villages must have thought we escaped from a madhouse . The entire village was upside down. But Lara had a fantastic birthday party with the necessary birthday candy to go with it.

Apart from the monthly theme events and its involvement in my social life, I organized meetings in the Carlton Hotel that were going to send my life in a new direction. A new Commanding Officer had been appointed at the Airport of Antwerp, a man by the name of Paul Paridaens. One day he asked me to join him at his office. He referred to the extended network of outstanding relations I happened to have. The Socialist Party was not too happy with Antwerp having its own Airport, and Paridaens liked to raise the matter with the President of the Fraction of the Party, Marcel Colla. Did I know him well enough to arrange a meeting. Indeed I knew him well, and I could arrange a meeting. But it had to happen on a neutral territory. The most neutral territory where I could think of was the Carlton Hotel. We arranged for a meeting Colla, Paridaens and myself. A table was reserved for us in the breakfast room but to take care of our privacy we were installed behind a huge curtain far from indiscreet eyes. I do not recall anymore what had been the conclusion, but I do remember the astonished regards from the people having breakfast when at this early hour I appeared from behind the curtain with a well known Alderman and the Commanding officer of the Airport.

My Godchild was doing fine. Lluys had become my home away from home. For a woman it is great to live between gay people. They are so specially charming and tactful. Should I have another child, which is next to impossible, I definitely would like him to be gay I also learned a lot. Dogs where the main theme of our conversation followed by very animated discussions about French wine. And connoisseurs they were and so was I.

I was after all the one who had worked for the Wine Department of Christies in the sixties. Through Lode Seghers I had met Michael Broadbent , who was responsible for the wine auctions of Sotheby's. I had been at its wine tasting, a very traditional English wine tasting meaning that several from the best wines on the market were offered, not to drink but to keep it for a couple of moments in your mouth after it was spat out in an enormous beaker. The wines I have tasted at Christies were priceless . When they were about to open their wine department at Christies Brussels at the rue de l'Abbaye I was asked to do the translation for their wine lists. Needless to say that good wine remains one of my passions, which came in very handy in the circles that by now had adopted me.

France is a very dog friendly country unlike other nations where dog owners attending a dog show have certain difficulties to find hotels where pets are accepted On the internet I discovered that in the States a dog friendly hotel guide was published. With the idea in mind that Europe needed this as well. I looked up the author, and we arranged a meeting in New York. The lady I met liked the idea of a European publication. It started very smoothly. I remembered my experience with English partners but to Europeans Americans are not that evident to work with either. I traveled a couple of times back and forth and an agreement was drafted But that is when the problems began.

The lady wanted more of the benefits, she argued that it was her idea. I replied that Europe was on the other side of the Ocean that I was going to concretize the guide, so it was my idea. The last conversation I had with her ended by her saying : If you know better, why don't you do it on your own. Obviously, she was sure that I was going to crawl on hand and knees back to her for assistance. This is the last I saw of her. After returning home, I looked up a friend who was in the printing business and asked hem where I could find a publisher for my guide. He answered 'You found him. I am a publisher and I will take care of it'. Meaning that I had been crossing the Atlantic a couple of times to find myself a publisher practically around the corner where I lived. All I needed was a written text and thousand of addresses all over Europe. A job fit for Alexandra when she returned from France. Which could be any day now. However, we had a major problem. Alexandra and Jigme, the puppy that had become a grown up Tibetan by now could not live without each other anymore. I decided to pick up my daughter and drive to Spain for a holiday. Returning home we had to drive by Lhuys anyway, and then we should check how the dog was doing.

Since I came the first time to Spain I had been in admiration for Don Quixote Fighting against windmills sounded very familiar to me. We drove through la Mancha , noticed the world famous windmills and decided to follow the Camino de Don Quixote . It brought us to a small village where it was said that Cervantes had lived for a while. His house was to be visited by going to the government office in the village and request for the key. It was a Sunday hen we arrived in the typical castellani village of Argamasilla de Albe. The peasants were everywhere on the streets having a chat after mass. I stopped and asked 'Donde e el casa de Cervantes? '(where is the house of Cervantes ?) I didn''t think that they had many foreign visitors, let alone two women who asked about Cervantes. At once we became the attraction of that day. Men and women pointed out that we should follow them, they walked in front of our car, and finally it was quite a procession that arrived in a narrow street before a modest house. Someone came hurrying with a key and someone else preceded us to a modest room with a bed and a table. If what was said was right this was the bed on which Cervantes sat while he was writing Don Quixote. Much later, after Internet came into my life, I read that Cervantes had written his masterpiece while he was in prison in Seville, but I am much more in favor of the house that I visited in la Mancha. After all it was close to the Windmills, and I had been sitting on his bed.

Our trip did not solve the problem as far as Alexandra and Jigme were concerned. What I had feared happened. During the holidays Alexandra was grieving about her dog and Jigme was whining at Tom's. A year earlier I brought Alexandra to France, and now I returned to Belgium with Alexandra and two tri-language dogs , Lara, the niece of Sophia Loren's pet was also joining us as a playmate.

That those dogs understood fluently three languages had to do with their education. One American and two French masters and a Flemish foster mother, our Tibetans could sit in all those languages. This came in handy as we were going to write our dog travel guide in six languages. From the moment, we returned home Alexandra was e-mailing day and night to ask European hotels if they accepted dogs. There were finally more than could have been expected.

And I had still my event organization to keep me busy. More and more members had joined our club.. It was time for a roaring thank you party. However, that meant money and we were not exactly loaded. The Bank of Paris and the Netherlands had remained loyal to me after my WTC adventure. I asked the manager if I could use the ballroom in his medieval building for a party. I could. All we needed was drinks. I had learned to like wine from Chili while in America. Quite normal once you learned its history. A couple of centuries ago winegrowers from Burgundy immigrated to Chili. They took branches of the vine with them and found themselves a place with a temperature very much similar to one of the places they left and where they could raise grapes from the same quality as in their homeland. I considered Chili as a possible sponsor and went to see Fernando Gonzalez, a Grande like I had met in my Spanish period, and who happened to be commercial attaché of the Embassy of Chili.

He welcomed me gracefully in his office at the Brussels' avenue Louise and asked me how he could help. I told him that I was giving a party for business people in Antwerp, and that I wanted to offer them wine from Chili. Of course, he said without hesitation, took the telephone receiver and called a supplier in Liege. He told the man that he had a very important person in his office – that was me – and that he wanted to make sure that she should have enough wine to serve to her guests. In the middle of his conversation he looked over the receiver at me to ask how many people I was expecting. Three hundred, I replied , trying to look as much at ease as he did. He didn't blink and continued : white and red wine I presume. I nodded . You will have it, he went on, just tell me where and when you want it.

When that point was settled. he insisted that I should stay a little longer. He wanted to know if I ever visited his home country. I hadn't. Gonzalez unfolded a very large map of Chili before my eyes.. I asked him where he came from he put one of his fingers on an island and said, that is where I come from. Yes, I replied but from which spot. He looked at me amazed that I didn't understand . I own this island, he said calmly, it is mine. Then he informed me about import and export in Chili, mostly fish. I do not like fish, so I wasn't very interested in his explanation. Then he mentioned a certain kind of white alcohol Chili produced. That was more likely. He asked me if I wanted to taste it and conjured up a bottle from somewhere behind him. I liked it and asked him where I could buy it. He asked me where I lived; I told him and he replied that he was going to bring me a couple of bottles. As this would be after office hours, and he would have to come from Brussels to Antwerp, I asked him if he would care to stay for dinner. He liked the idea. A date was settled It was the craziest conversation I ever had in an Embassy.

A few days later he arrived with his bottles. Alexandra and her dogs where home . Gonzalez seemed to enjoy our company. After dinner Alexandra prepared herself to go out. Where is she going ? Gonzalez asked. She is going to walk the dogs, I replied. I go with her, he decided. He insisted to take the leash of one of the dogs. They went out. At first sight the man was not used to walk a dog, right away he was in trouble. In front of my house, there is a lane with several trees. Morales kept Jigme, our male dog, on line. Before he realized what happened to him Jigme pulled him to his favorite tree. He turned a couple of times around it, still with Morales hanging on to him, and suddenly the commercial Attaché from the Embassy of Chili was sticking against a tree in front of my house..

However, this did not put an end to my adventures with Morales. When I told Coppieters, the manager of the bank, how generous Morales had been with his wine from Chili, he suggested to invite him for lunch . I telephoned to Morales, he agreed, we made an appointment, and I gave him the address where he was expected.

The day in question, upon my arrival at the bank, Coppieters asked me to wait for Morales in the main entrance hall. I was the only one to know how he looked like. The appointment was at noontime sharp. Twelve a'clock, no Morales. A quarter of an hour later, sill no Morales, half past twelve, no sign of Morales . I became worried.

The intention was that Morales, Coppieters and I were going to have lunch in the splendid dining room on the top floor of the bank, a caterer had been especially ordered for us .I called the Embassy, it was during lunchtime, nobody responded. Around one o'clock when I was on top of my nerves Morales walked in, in full splendor a large, black cape dressed around his shoulders.

'My dear', he exclaimed, 'you don't knows what happened to me. I parked my car somewhere and asked for the Mayer avenue and nobody knew where it was' . I didn't try to explain that the name of our main street Meir, had nothing to do whatsoever with the Minister of Foreign Affairs of Israel. We had not a minute to spare. I introduced him to Coppieters. Morales went to the washing room to be fresh up, and finally we could sit down for lunch. Later I learned that Morales forgot to turn the water tap to his normal position. The floor was soaking wet, and they had to renew the entire parket floor.

I met Morales later. Each time when he organized a special event I was invited. One of the highlights was a dinner reunion in Bruges with several of his guests. On the program was a boat trip on the local canals. It went on very well until we had to stop for a closed lock. Morales asked the guide why we couldn't proceed. The man answered politely that it was late at night and that the lockkeeper went home. Out of the question, said Morales, go and get him, I want to sail on. The guy went to fetch him, the lock was opened, and we proceeded as planned.

When his duty was over at the Embassy Morales returned to Chili where he became a Minister in the Government.. However, he bought an apartment on the Avenue Louise to be able to return at our country as much as he could. We had made ourselves a mighty friend.

.

Chapter 39
The Love Boat

The management of my company had changed. My partner, Carla, had been offered a full time job as an employee, and she needed security . Being self employed is always a risky business. She was replaced by Marc who was a member of our association and whom I knew since a long time. Circumstances had put him out of a job, and he decided to join us. He seemed a nice fellow. We made a fresh start. The 75th birthday of the Airport was nearing, and I had asked the commanding officer, the one from behind the curtain, if I could organize the festivities. He agreed to rent me an office at the Airport. It was a little to much of an assignment for me to do it on my own . Now that Carla was gone, I was glad to have Marc on hand. We had an office of our own, we needed orders, and I went to see my club contacts to find out if they could use my services. A manager of an insurance company gave me a tip. He had his office at the outskirts of the docks. Nearby a steamship was moored. They had them under insurance contract. The name of the boat was Hakon Kari. It had sailed as a postal ship around the coast of Norway. From north until south and back it had anchored in little ports around the famous fjords of Norway to transport travelers and post to where ever they had to go to. The ship was sent from Oslo to Antwerp to be sold to a Dutch couple . Not for sailing. It would remain on the docks as a party boat. My insurance friend figured that they could use some public relations. He called them and I was asked to come over straight away. No problem.

It was an imposing steamer but apart from Jo and Connie van Aarle, the owners, there was nobody else aboard. The couple was seated in a kind of galley. It was noontime. After a first introduction Connie said that they were about to have lunch, and she invited to share it with them. I said 'yes' and she arrived with the greatest plate of sandwiches with ham and cheese that I ever saw. They all were piled up one above the other, a tackle which one wouldn't present to a dockworker. While we were eating Jo told me that they originally had a second hand car company somewhere in the Netherlands. Some weeks before, on a day trip to Antwerp , they had noticed that the boat was for sale and had bought it immediately. About

185

the same time, they read in a Belgian newspaper that in Geeraardsbergen, not far from the French border a castle was also for sale, and they bought it as well. To have a home away from home. .Connie showed me pictures of the manor, the park around it and several exotic animals playing around. It made me feel at home and I asked if I could bring my daughter to see the pictures . 'Why pictures' asked Connie ' come over and stay for the weekend'. We agreed to arrange something and went to visit the ship. Jo explained to me that they planned to open a hotel boat with a restaurant and disco bar. It was due for October. I could take care of the show. When I went down from the gangway I had an agreement in my pocket for the entire organization and an invitation to stay with them the following week in their castle in Geeraardsbergen.

In the castle, we had an entire apartment at our disposal . In the park, we walked between zebra's, ostriches and lama's and in the evening we were invited for dinner in town. In the three stars restaurant where a table was booked the Van Aarle's were so to see, and in the short time, they had taken their quarters in town, regular and appreciated customers. When we had breakfast in the morning in the rural kitchen the zebra's put their heads through the window to beg for a piece of bread. I had found myself a farm in Africa but then on Belgium's soil.

While in Antwerp I took care of Connie . For some reason, or another she seemed not to be able to make friends in my city. We were in the middle of summer, Connie adored Antwerp, and the terraces around the Cathedral in the old part of town where I introduced her to. Little by little we became close friends.

As far as the boat was concerned everything went smoothly. I ran back and forth; The staff had accepted me as belonging to the Van Aarle family. The ship was named the Diamond Princess. At the opening in September the entire Who's who from Antwerp and other Belgian and Dutch regions attended. The sun was shining brightly. Prospects were excellent. It was front page news. as well as the end of our contract. However, my friendship with the Van Aerle's lasted. Alexandra and her girls' and boyfriends were regularly non paying guests at the disco, and I went into town with Connie as I was getting used to. Money, a fantastic husband, a company to be proud of, children, she had it all. She was in her prime, in her forties, beautiful, lady of the manor. What more is there to want. A couple of weeks later she committed suicide. She hung herself up with the leash of her dog in the kitchen of her castle.

I learned the news from my newspaper . I was in shock.

I tried to contact Jo but didn't succeed. The telephone operator of the Diamond Princess told me that Connie had spent the weekend with her husband in Geeraardsbergen. When he was ready to return to Antwerp on Monday, she didn't feel to go . When Jo returned home at night, he found her hanging, death. I never saw him again.

A couple of weeks later the lady in command of room service on the boat called me. She was completely in panic . While desperately sobbing I finally understood that she and the room maids were forced by Jo to prostitute themselves. She begged me to help them. I knew the state police officer of Antwerp very well. I called him and told him what was going on. He said he was going to take care of it immediately. I never heard anything anymore about what had happened with that Love Boat. It is still anchored at the same place the inside dock.

Chapter 40
Sex at the Airport

After the 75th anniversary of the Airport of Antwerp and the festivities that went with it our activities slowed down for a while. Marc and I were not complementary. Most of his life Marc had been used to work for a salary .As an independent he regularly panicked. Sometimes he was way out of a line. However, the money had to come from somewhere, my business relations were as far as he was concerned the ideal targets. That is not my style; I was no longer interested in a collaboration. Before long I was on my way.

As long as I had been in contact with the Airport of Antwerp it had always been a problem child. Because I had already an office at the Airport and was on hand, I was asked to start an Association with some high achievers of our city, to support and lobby for what to us was the right course. An antipode for the green girls and boys who with their frustrated ideas were doing more wrong than right. It was about time that our politicians became aware that citizens who paid most of the wages in the country, the economic sector from the Antwerp harbors, deserved an Airport. I went to explain my point of view to Jean-Marie Denis , he called his economic adviser and a quarter of an hour later the three of us started ABACI, an Association, who would fight for the conservation and the extension of the Airport of Antwerp. We took contact with a couple of entrepreneurs who joined us in the Board of directors. We needed also somebody important for the diamond sector. We decided to ask Dilip Mehta, an Indian , and in Antwerp a household word. He was a very discrete person. Only on a rare occasion he organized events which, for the average Belgian, seemed to come out of the fairy tale world of that distant India.

I never had met Dilip Mehta, I wrote. him a letter to explain him our plans, that we needed his help and that I was going to telephone him the following Wednesday . On Tuesday his assistant called me to tell me that Dilip Mehta was expecting me. The room where I entered was crowded with men who were very busy with diamonds laying in front of them. The girl that introduced me asked me if I would prefer to wait in the parlor but I was far too fascinated by what I saw. I preferred to remain where I was. After a while Dilip Mehta came to me and lead me to his office. A very sober one for somebody of his standing. I explained where I came fore upon which he asked : 'do you want to make a lobby group for the Airport of Antwerp'. I said 'yes' and he replied : I am your man. The most important man in the Antwerp diamond trade entered into our Board. Before long a lot of harbor companies joined us and politicians became aware that the Airport of Antwerp had a group of watchdogs that would not take no for an answer.

One of my business relations came to my office and told me that he had become the consultant of the Amro Bank of the Netherlands, who would consider to build a WTC building in Antwerp. Steven knew I had solid contacts in New York, and he told his client that I was the one to see. The past was catching up on me. We met . The group took the entire situation very seriously. One of the major problems was that they didn't dispose of any land nor an idea where they would like it to be. I called Guy, the President of the WTCA in New York. We hadn't seen each other for a couple of years but our friendship remained. He was thrilled at the idea that Antwerp after all had a chance for an own WTC building. I should call him, whenever I needed and gave me his private telephone number at home . For a leader in American not that self-evident.

I was completely integrated at the Airport . It is a rather small building, all the tenants knew each other, it was one happy family. I was very close with Christian Heinzmann, manager of the VLM, the Flemish Airline Company. One fine day Patsy Sorensen called me. Patsy with whom I once had been nominated as Woman of Europe and who had made it in politics. She belonged to the European Parliament by then and had become an internationally recognized authority on the field of fighting against women trade. She asked me if I was aware that on the Website of VLM there was a porno connection. This was not exactly the first thing that came to my mind when I thought about our Airline Company and our Airport. It reminded me vaguely of the period that I was a pupil of the flying school at our Airport, and while I was taking my first practical lesson way up in the air, I felt more than ones the hand of my instructor going in my panties. Even if I had wanted to struggle, there was no way. Somebody had to keep the rudder in his right position. However, this was clearly different. Patsy asked me, as an inside job, to find out what was going on. She was very Airport minded and knew very well that our Airport had enough problems of its own without having to be linked to the sex industry . What happened ? A lady had been seeing Bob Cools, our former Mayor who was in command of the Social Working Association of Antwerp to complain about the working conditions of her husband, an employee of VLM. He did to many hours overtime without any extra reward. At first she taught that he was seeing another woman , until she went to the airport in the middle of the night and noticed his car. What he said was right. He was at work. I knew the story was impossible. The airport building closes from 11 at night until 6 in the morning. Except for security personal nobody is supposed to be there at night. There is no air traffic what so ever.

However, the woman kept insisting. She returned to Bob and showed him porno pictures on paper with VLM heading. She had found it in the pocket of her husband's coat. Bob Cools called Patsy, she came to me, and I went to Christian who nearly had a heart attack. Nevertheless, when he heard the name of the employee he began to understand. It had occurred to him that in the morning the man in question had always been slow and sleepy. They found out that he locked himself in the evening and amused himself during the night facing the VLM computer. When Christian opened the file, he discovered an entire VLM porno site . It was deleted at once, the man was fired, and the VLM offices could function again in the same way as they did before.

Chapter 41
The Albanese Mafia

After a couple of years of hard work our hotel guide for dogs was a fact. We had a publisher, an international manufacturer of dog food agreed to sponsor, the text was translated into 6 languages, a dog magazine was going to sell it, we were on our way. We had a very attractive cover page with Lara and Jigme in a passenger seat of an airline served by a real air hostess.

A brewery situated not far from Antwerp offered to organize a dog party on the premises. The manager adored his dog and had a special feeling for dogs in general. Meaning that we had beer as much as we liked to serve to the guests on two feet and our local water supplier made a water bar for our four legged invitees. Our dogs were hosting. Hundreds of dogs received a beautiful personalized invitation. And they came. All kinds of breeds without any problem. Our guide was a best seller and Jigme and Lara were seated as real authors behind a table putting their paw mark on the first page. We were front page news. Before long we were out of print and our pets had become VID's, very important Dogs. I needed a company to make it perfectly legal. Mundus Canis was founded. Jigme our Tibetan Terrier, became one of the board members. It is always fancy to have a nobility in a Board and our Antartica Jigme Gyalpo had a pedigree. Pierre Grisar's mother would have been proud, at least one of us was born and fit to enter the upper world.

ABACI was making it to. Where possible, politicians were reminded that due to electoral willfulness the neighboring countries were taking advantage of us.

In my private life Patsy Sorrensen took care of some unexpected incidents.. Due to her activities, denouncing women trade, she was up to her neck involved with revenge of the Albanese mafia, Menaces were more routine than the exception. In the criminal atmosphere of the white slavery trade Patsy had found out about cases that were not intended to see any light. Some day she asked me to arrange a meeting with a friend of mine who had a high function in the tobacco trade. She had something to learn him of major importance . The man I had in mind worked in Brussels, so did Patsy, we decided to meet in the Hilton Hotel . She insisted that I should attend, a question of being a kind of neutral go-between. I suggested that I should take the train to Brussels and return with her car to Antwerp. Which would give us time for a chat? She told me that this was impossible because for a reason of her problems with the mafia, she used an official armored car filled with bodyguards. No one else was allowed in that car. She offered to send her own driver to the hotel to pick me up when the meeting was over.

On a Friday night I found myself waiting with Walter, the man of the Tobacco federation in the hall of the Hilton Hotel. Patsy came in, a tiny little woman, surrounded by four Chippendales. She told me that after all I would be allowed to ride with her to Antwerp My whereabouts had been checked by national security and they had had discovered that I was not a public danger. But from that moment on it was as if I was in the hands of the security office as well. The four men were seated on a table not far from us and eight eyes were constantly watching us. Even to go to the ladies a guy followed me.

When it was time to go home, same scenario. We were surrounded by the four. The more I looked at them the more insecure I felt. The road we had to cross to arrive at our car seemed endless. Two men went in the car with us, the two others went into a car that was about to follow us. We crossed Brussels through areas where I never had been before. For sure not the fastest way home. It gave me the impression that we were trying to avoid criminals who were about to attack us any minute. How the other car kept up with us remains a mystery .Finally, we made it to the highway. It was not long before we ended up at the end of a traffic-jam. An accident had happened somewhere in front.. Consequently, we were forced to stop. We were surrounded by lorries. Impossible to describe what someone with my kind of imagination fears in such moments. The probably total innocent truck drivers appeared to me as dangerous gangsters armed with bazooka's. Patsy didn't blink. She must have been used to such kind of situations. After what seemed an eternity the queue dispersed, and we could continue .

When the car stopped with screeching ties in front of my house, the second car stopped directly behind us. They hadn't lost us out of their site for a moment. All the men with us were fantastic boys and attractive to, but for the first time in my life, I was glad to be delivered of the whole lot of them..

Chapter 42
September 11, 2001

With Miek, my friend from the WTC period, I was spending a wonderful holiday at Mykonos, the lovely island in the Greek Cyclades In the hotel where we were staying, we became friends with two gay boys who called themselves 'the Crazy Americans'. One was a Hollywood producer, the other one was also in show business. On Tuesday September 11th when Miek and I returned from a shopping day in town John and Mike ran toward us completely shaken. When we asked them what was wrong they didn't seem to know where to start. Then they broke the news : an attack had taken place on the World Trade Center in New York. I remembered the former attack and supposed it was something similar. John took us to a corner of the hall in the hotel where I saw on CNN what really was going on . Again and again, it showed the airplanes flying into the second building, moments later we watched life the building collapsing. It seemed incredible, I had the feeling that a part of my life was disappearing at the same time. I knew so many of those people who were caught over there. Not merely those of the WTC headquarters on the 77th floor but also so many of the employees of the shopping mall at the street level. I regularly had stopped buying something or for a short chat. However, at that moment I clearly saw their faces in front of me. The lively coziness of the book shop, the spectacle shop, my first stops when I entered the building. And now all this was gone. Each time when I went to New York, and a taxi drove me from Kennedy Airport into town I was welcomed, in the distance, by the Twin Towers. New York was never going to be the same again.

****

It was not easy to return to Belgium. Every American staying in Mykonos wanted to fly home, airplanes where out of schedule . It was a chaos in Athens. Security was next to none existent. Everything that could cut was confiscated by the Greek customs but on board of the plane and in the tax free shops manicure sets were freely on sale. More than enough were available to cut the throats of an entire crew.

194

When I arrived home I called Guy to ask him if there had been casualties in his office. There were none. The attack took place before office hours and Guy who was supposed to be there to attend a meeting had been held up in a traffic jam. Like anyone else I spend the next days in front of the television but was unable to grasp it.

An immediate consequence was that the group of the Amro Bank was not longer interested in building a World Trade Center. Nobody was in the mood to build World Trade Centers. The general idea was that it was the end of them. However, that was not exactly true. New York nursed his wounds but my WTC people had immediately rented an office near Central Station.

The airport in Antwerp had some brighter news. The Flemish Government had liberalized their point of view and recognized that a decent business plan could help.

To lobby for an extension, Ernst & Young were going to take care of it. The man they appointed for the job had his office next to mine. We went along fine. To him, it was handy that I could give him all inside information he needed. I believe that I was the first one to know in detail about any of his plans . They became very concrete in the months to come. He was convinced that, to make the airport more profitable, we should have a business center incorporated. It rang a bell. I suggested a World Trade Center. He liked the idea. I asked some building promoters for advice. Their reaction was positive. I telephoned to Guy in New York. He was all for it and suggested that I should work it out with his vice-president, a Herbert Ouida, a total stranger to me. He provided me with the necessary information. I had to consult Hubert Govaerts, the man who owned most of the shares of the Antwerp Association.

I knew that Hubert had financial problems but had no idea how this had affected our WTC situation. When the financial troubles of Hubert started, he could not pay the fee in New York anymore. This meant that the Club was on the point to be expelled and the Club wouldn't be allowed anymore to function under the WTC name. To avoid this the management of the Club asked Hubert if he would allow them to pay arrear dues. He agreed. Years later when he wanted to sell his shares he learned that the

195

Club never had paid for the fees, and that he was in serious debt. Guy invited me to New York to clarify the situation.. An international assembly was going to take place in the Roosevelt Hotel on Park Avenue and I could join. I looked forward to meet Herb , my e-mail friend who was always there when I needed him; and whom I had never seen.

The room where the meeting took place was partly crowded when I arrived. Most of the guests were familiar , some others were new to me. It had been years, since I assisted at one of those meetings for the last time. But even the new faces seemed to know who I was. When I went for my badge at the reception desk the young man in command said : Paula, you don't need a badge. Everybody knows you ! Tozzoli had married once more and introduced me to his wife. He hugged me for a while and said : this is the famous Paula Marckx.

I was talking to a couple of congress goers with my back to the elevator when somebody behind me said : I know it was you ! I turned around and was flabbergasted. The man in front of me was not Herb Ouida but Michel Plaisier, my boy friend who died in that car accident. And although Herb Ouida had never seen me, he picked me out of the crowd without seeing my face. It was scaring.

During the entire congress Herb staid beside me. He told me about his son, Tod, one of the victims of the September 11 attacks. That disastrous day Todd, 25 years of age, had taken with his father the train from New Jersey, where they lived, to go to the World Trade Center where Todd worked for Cantor Fitzgerald on the 101st floor of the building. Herb went out of the elevator on the 77th floor where his office was. When the airplane went into the building Todd called his mother to put her at ease. In his office, everything was fine. Herb made it outside where he waited for his son. Seconds later the building collapsed. He never saw Todd again.

Todd had remained a very important part of Herb's life. He made a foundation to honor him. It intended to help financially children who were victims of fear and depression. An illness that affected Todd in his youth. Destiny was not pushing Herb out of balance.

My contacts with the WTC top went not smoothly. Before talking about new agreements the old debts had to be paid. That was the message

I had to deliver to Antwerp. Not the Association nor the Club wanted to be blamed. If there was no agreement the WTC of Antwerp was going to lose its license, and I was never to see the World Trade Center again.

It was Xmas time. New York looked fantastic with his Xmas tree on Rockefeller Center, **R**adio City, where our entire group went to see the Xmas show. It was a privilege to be part of it. When the Congress was over, I remained for a couple of days in New York. That is where I belonged. Much later Herb told me that somebody born in New York always recognizes somebody born in that city. He was born there and told me that the only one that could fool him was I. The day before I returned home I drove by taxi to my favorite spot, Pier 17. When I sat at my usual table at the top floor of the shopping mall in South Street Seaport overlooking the Hudson Bay and Brooklyn Bridge, with Xmas ornaments around me and with Bing Crosby singing in the background Jingle Bells all my problems with the WTC disappeared. This was perfection. New York, New York, it's up to you. I do love you.

Chapter 43
Uncle Sam

Different parties were fighting for the WTC name in Antwerp. Herb helped as much as he could. ; However, he was on the point to leave the World Trade Center for a totally different reason. He wanted to spend the rest of his life working for the foundation that he had established in honor of his son. American celebrities joined in. Herb was invited , as a Professor, to join a university . He kept in touch with the WTC's worldwide and the man that reminded me so much of Michael became my friend and advisor. We were only an e-mail away from each other.

Some day a Michael Goldhaber called me to ask if I was Paula Marckx from the Marckx case, When I said 'yes', he said that he needs to see me. He happened to be an American journalist and lawyer with an office in Fleet Street in London where he worked as a European correspondent for the official magazine of the American bar. In America, they didn't know much about the European Court of Human rights and Michael wanted to write a book with witnesses such as, I, Alexandra and Moni van Look, the lawyer who pleaded for me in Strasbourg.

We agreed to meet in Antwerp. As he arrived by plane, I suggested to meet him on the tarmac. You will easily recognize me, he said. I look like a real Jew. This was more of a difficulty. Most of the passengers arriving in Antwerp by plane from London are Jews and look like them. However, apart from the staff I was the only one waiting on the runway, so we had no trouble finding each other. Michael stayed with us for the entire week. After he returned to London, he sent me the file with the first chapter of his book. It was all about me and had a fantastic title : Why bastard, referring to King Lear. After a while, Michael left for New York where I visited him – when we met in Antwerp, he insisted that I should learn to know his dog . His book was published by Rutger University Press. This is where it can lead you to be an unmarried mother.

The license of our WTC was annulled. To keep the name in Antwerp a kind of agreement was made with the States but as a fact Antwerp had no

198

real WTC anymore. Dethier's ultimate dream of having a WTC building in Antwerp was never to be realized. That part of the story was put in the fridge. My attention was focused on the Airport . Flemish Government lost interest for as far as there ever had been any.

I still had my dog happenings and a grown up daughter who could do with a job. Together with a couple of soul mates I wanted to establish a company. I was confronted with a sort of inquisition official at the Chamber of Industry. Fist question asked was about my diploma. I had none. Business experience. 15-year general manager of a World Trade Center. This was a non profit company, this didn't count. For over 30 years I had been a journalist, that counted even less. Then I involved my daughter who was coming into our Board. Nevertheless, she had graduated in Spain, this was not taken into consideration either. To help me out of my publisher offered to enter my company.

We introduced ourselves at the Chamber of Industry and were welcomed by the same inquisition. My publisher owned a company in a building on the industrial field and had a large staff working for him.. But he had no diploma either, he had started his career from scratch. Out he went. The last in the row was my bookkeeper, my friend Miek, who had years of business experience. However, in her teens she had been in a car accident, had been unable to attend school for a while and had obtained her diploma before a special jury; She was not classified either. . However, Mundus Canis existed already in my own name, so I was allowed to proceed. Friends at the local newspaper brought the absurd story in the news.. Two days later the inquisition informed me that after all they accepted my fifteen years experience at the World Trade Center. I was allowed to form a company with several partners and could move on. In the same period of time, before and after, the same Ministers were one day Minister of Economy and the next day Minister of Public Health without any problem, without any special skill and without having to pass through an Inquisition.

With all my administrative adventures, I had made the press. An Alderman of the city came to me with an interesting suggestion. According to a famous novel written by an English author , a boy named Nello and his dog Patrasche lived in a suburb of Antwerp near the river Scheldt at the end of the 19th century. Nello had found a dog almost beaten to death and called him Patrasche. Nello and Patrasche became inseparable and like most stories situated amongst the poor in those days it was very melodramatic and ended with the boy and the dog frozen to death in the Cathedral of Antwerp. For some reason, the story became very popular in Asiatic countries and Alderman van Campenhout aimed to make an attraction pool for his city by building a Patrasche village at the place where the story had been situated. Me and my brand new company could make a business plan. First of all, I had to contact the owners of the place we had in mind. They had their office in a prefab building near the River. First I met the father and then the son. Two very attractive men from the north. They were very much in favor of the project, and we met several times, mostly in restaurants and taverns somewhere in the city. They knew how to live. The father often told me that his son had a crush on me. I took it as practical joking. Koen was forty years younger than I was, a very handsome playboy and very, very wealthy. Finally, the deal was never made, but we kept our telephone numbers at hand.

At our Airport Ernst and Young were not longer welcome, I suppose they were too good.

Elections were in view. I had mentioned on several occasions that I wanted to go on TV in a debate with politicians. I had a couple of items that I wanted to make public. The opportunity came when I was invited by our national broadcast to take part in the special election program / Your word against mine. The general idea was that politicians and business people would discuss hot events. In my panel was Minister Bert Anciaux, moderator was Siegfried Bracke, a TV reporter. I replied that I was willing to join them providing, I didn't have to drive with my car to Brussels. That didn't seem to be a problem. A driver with a limousine was going to pick me up.. The full red carpet treatment .I was supposed to go on the air at 7 in the evening, the broadcasting would take place an hour later. Meaning that I was not going to have time to check if somebody messed around with my answers. When the broadcasting was going to take place, I would be probably on the road between Brussels and Antwerp. Unless...I asked Alexandra to take the transmission on video. I made a couple of phone calls to editors in chiefs of the most important papers and to politicians from different parties and told them about my problem. I asked hem if they would be willing, providing, I should discover that someone had been cheating with the program, to spread the word. Each of them gave me their mobile numbers and said that for such an information they would be available day and night. The morning that the broadcasting took place a telephone operator from the TV station called me to tell me that I wasn't welcome any longer – but they were willing to pay a presence fee . When I mentioned this to an editor in chief he replied that I was not the only one who was removed. Somewhere there had been a leak.

****

Herb asked me to come to America. Every year at his son's birthday, the one who died on 11/9, he organized a kind of a party. The presents were auctioned for the benefit of Todd's foundation. Herb made me his special guest. In honor of the firemen who died in the attack I brought an outfit of the fire brigade of the Airport of Antwerp . . I took the opportunity to find out if there was a kind of interest for our Patrasche project. About five meetings in three different American States in six days, this must be possible. Herb took care of the contacts and where ever I went to a WTC , the manager was waiting for me. One of my meetings was in Manchester, Vermont. To arrive there coming from New York, I had to fly to Albany and from there on a drive with a taxi to a place a hundred miles further north. Arriving at the airport of Albany my driver was waving a billboard within huge letters the name PAULA on it.

While driving, he asked me if I had visited the tomb of Uncle Sam. When he learned that I was not aware that the man ever existed he told me the story : Samuel Wilson was a butcher during the war off 1812. He delivered meat to the US forces. It was packed in crates on which Sam had put the name U.S. But Sam also supplied the troops in the vicinity. While bullets flew around his head, he drove his horse and carriage to the barracks where the soldiers were waiting for food. When the commander in chief noticed him, he said : there is Uncle Sam. A reporter from New York wrote a text about the man in his newspaper and this together with the fact that US on the barrels were thought to be Uncle Sam made him to the personalization of the free spirit of America.

My driver was not yet finished with his anecdotes. About half an hour later he stopped asking if I ever heard of Grandma Moses. Yes, I had.. For some reason, I suppose I read an article about her, when someone asked when I would retire, I always replied : when I will be 80, and then I will learn how to paint like grandma Moses. And there I was, in front of her home that had turned into a museum.

The story was a little different than the one I remembered. Grandma Moses hadn't learned to paint when she was 80, but she was discovered when she was 80. She had been painting her entire life, just for fun, at the corner of her kitchen table. Naïve paintings about things that she saw in her surroundings. She lived in a village between New York and Manchester – the place where I was driving to – a very fancy winter sports center for rich people from the Big Apple. When grandma Moses was about 80 a new drugstore opened in her village. When she needed some medicines the new owner passed by to bring it. He noticed in her kitchen what she was doing and asked if he could put them for sale in his store, She agreed . He didn't have that much furniture and the painting gave the entire setting a brighter look.. A tourist on his way to his winter vacation stopped a couple of days later to buy something in the drugstore. He noticed the paintings and bought all of them . The customer was Mr. Kalir, owner of an art gallery in New York. Back home he made an opening with Mama Moses' paintings. This was the beginning of a fantastic career. One of her paintings won in 1991 the Price of the State of New York. When she was 90, she painted for a public on TV. For her 100th birthday, a TV station organized a tremendous party for her. She thanked them by dancing the jitterbug life. She died when she was 101 and painted until her last day. Her paintings are now in the most important art galleries of America.

After my meetings in Manchester, I flew to Saint Louis. I was looking forward to a boat trip on the Mississippi. Ever since I heard for the first time singing Paul Robinson Old Man River, I had a kind of nostalgia to that River where I never had been. Those songs of slavery had always touched me . As soon as my first meetings were over, I went to the river on board of a River Boat.

It was about dark when I decided to return to my hotel and to another meeting. On the highway next to the river, lots of cars passed by but not one taxi. I was staying there for a while when I noticed a horse and carriage obviously waiting for tourists for a ride along the stream. To me, it was the only possibility to arrive at destination. When I explained to the female coach woman where I wanted to go to she looked at me doubtfully. My dear, she said, that will cost you a lot of money. You want to go in the center of town. My horse is not used to traffic.. When she noticed my disappointment, she said : Come on, step in, I will drive you to one of our casino ships, there you will find a taxi. . I took place in the white carriage, and step by step we were driving next to my beloved Mississippi. My driver was charming , we talked about our family, her name was Helen. Suddenly, she interrupted herself and screamed : a taxi ! The taxi that she pointed at was on the other side of the street, but that was no problem for Helen. She talked to her horse that promptly turned around , cars on the road tried successfully to avoid us. Helen stopped her carriage, in the middle of the road, so did all the cars including the taxi. Helen went out of the carriage, talked to the taxi driver and beckoned to come near by. This lady has to be in the center of town, I heard her saying to the driver. She opened the door, kissed me, said 'Bless you honey', went back in her coach , drove her horse back in the right direction and of, she went. All the cars moved again. And I drove to my meeting.

Chapter 44
No, No Regrets

Me in front of the house where I dropped my clothes when I was 17 (picture taken by my daughter Alexandra) photo Alexandra Marckx

In Conrad Hilton's biography, he explains that his mother was very devout. When he had a problem, he went to her for help, and she didn't know the solution she said : Pray, my son, and while looking to heaven, ask Him, and he will help you. His father only went to church when he had to. However, he was a hard worker. To him seven o'clock in the morning was about in the middle of daytime. When Hilton went to him with his problems and the man had no advice ready he said : Work my boy, work brings the solution to every problem. Much later when Conrad Hilton was a father himself one of his sons asked : I have met a lot of people who were regularly churchgoers, they worked very hard, and they never succeeded, what is the key to your success? Hilton answered : in life, you must never stop dreaming and see to it that your dreams come trough. Fortunately dreams are never far away from me.

A couple of weeks before I went to America Prince Rainier of Monaco died. I had met the Prince in Turin but my interest went to a couple of words in the newspaper . Referring to his wedding in the fifties ,it said

204

that from three legendary persons of the fairy tale in Monaco, Grace Kelly, the Prince and Oleg Cassini, there was only one person alive now, Oleg Cassini. Cassini was of Russian noble birth and had made himself name and fame as an international fashion designer. Later in life he was going to dress Jacqueline Kennedy when she became the wife of the President of the United States. In the fifties, he was the favorite designer of the 'cream of the cream' in Hollywood .Joan Crawford, Joanne Fontaine, Marylin Monroe and Grace Kelly, they all swore by Cassini and his dresses Kelly and Cassini were on their engagement trip to Monaco when she met Prince Rainier. The rest is history. A couple of years later he married the gorgeous Gene Tierney. He was a Don Juan and was a habitual in the news.

Like for most of the young girls he had been my dream Prince together with Clark Gable and Eroll Flyn. The unreachable Gods there somewhere in America. The article I was reading said also that now Cassini lived in his mansion in New York where he kept a lot of pets, about ten dogs, twenty two cats, a couple of potbelly pigs, donkeys, horses, you name it. That was a man I wanted to meet. I asked Herb for an introduction.. He could not reach him

Two weeks before I left for the States, I looked through Internet to find some indication. It was easy to find the address of the Oleg Cassini Collection , but his e-mail address was an info@ address, and I figured my request for a meeting would be lost in the thousands of e-mails send to this same box. Moreover, it was a Sunday.

On my e-mail to him, I had mentioned as a subject : Mr. Cassini and his pets; I explained to him that I would like to interview him on his four legged friends. Not more than a quarter of an hour later his secretary answered that Oleg Cassini was ready to welcome me. She asked me to call her for a meeting upon my arrival in New York. So I did.

When I had Peggy Nestor, Cassini's assistant on the line she asked me to come to see them in their fashion house the following Wednesday at 3.30 in the afternoon. I told her that I would be arriving the same day from Washington, and that I was only going to land an hour earlier. She answered that was not a problem.

I went first to Toronto to attend to the yearly Woofstock Fair, and to meet some people who could be useful for my Woefstock plans in Antwerp. There I met the Chief Editor of the very fancy Canadian magazine Modern Dog. When I told her who I was going to meet, she was immediately ready to publish my article.

The day of my meeting with Cassini my plane was delayed. I arrived in my hotel room on Times Square at the very moment Oleg Cassini expected me in his Fashion Atelier in Central Park. I called Peggy supposing that they would take the opportunity to cancel my appointment. I was wrong. Just take a taxi and come over, said Peggy, Oleg has canceled his next appointment to see you. For a moment, I panicked. I had been in America for 11 days, there had been no time to go to the hairdresser, from Washington, I had been airplane in, airplane out, taxi in, taxi out, it was burning hot, I felt dirty and filthy, had no time to change or to take a shower. The rest of my clothes were all crumpled in my suitcase. That was the state I was in, in order to meet the man who was a figure icon in the fashion world and where I had been madly in love with about fifty years before.

In front of his fashion house on East 63rd Street his assistant was waiting for me. She took me to the first floor, and there he was, in the middle of a small group of people, the great Oleg Cassini, 91 years old and still leading his company. He was as charming and elegant as ever. He apologized for himself to his party by saying that his visitor had arrived. He came straight to me. I said that I was sorry for being late, but he replied that it didn't matter, that where we were going to talk about, pets, were far more important than his entire industry. He knew I came from Belgium and insisted that we should talk French. It was obviously important to him to communicate in the language in which he had been raised. To me, it came as an additional problem. Since my Pierre Grisar period, there were very few people where I had to speak French to. . My knowledge of the language had improved since then, but I was deadly tired, since eleven days I had spoken nothing but English so all this was not very evident. However, finally it went on smoothly. I had been in more complicated situations than this one. .He started to talk about his dogs, all of them came out of shelters. His enthusiasm was contagious. He ran back and forth to show me their pictures, he promised that more pictures were going to be send to my hotel When I left, he asked me to keep in touch. I made a story about him 'Oleg Cassini, a pet lover and a Gentleman'. The last time I heard from him is was when he wrote to me that he had read the article, and that he loved it. A little later I heard that he died. He was 92.

Back in Antwerp my company took a license on Woofstock. It would come in handy.

Chapter 45
I Start All Over From Scratch

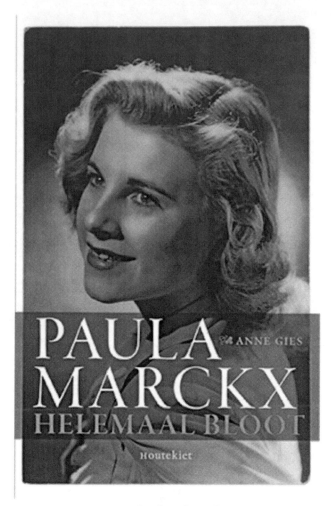

My book is for sale

My daughter Alexandra was in her early thirties, she had a boyfriend and four dogs. They needed a place of their own, and they found one. It took a little while to realize that I was again a full time bachelor, that I could do whatever, I liked without having to take someone else into consideration, and that I had no dogs on my bed at night. To be perfectly

208

honest I missed it a little. I wasn't exactly lonely, I had my friends at the Airport, my business partner Jean-Marie to talk so I wasn't complaining.

Walter, Alexandra's boyfriend invited me to a get-to-know-you party at the Hilton Hotel. One of the other guests was Walter's friend Johan van Herck, who worked for a company with offices not far from where I lived. He was a pleasant guy. We had a lot of common interests. Between lunchtime it happened that he came over for a drink and a chat. Little did I realize that man was going to introduce me to another part of my life.

One of Johan's lady friends, Anne Gies, was a reporter for radio and TV. She had a regular program and was always in need of interesting people for her interviews. With my Marckx Case in mind Johan found me worthy enough to introduce me to Anne who invited me for a life interview. Anne was a professional and her questions finally brought us to other incidents in my life . When the broadcasting was over, I learned that she was interested in writing my biography. I figured that I had not that much to tell, but the idea was rather amusing, and I thought 'Why not,'. We made a publishing agreement with Veerle, the manager of a publishing house where Anne had already worked with. Before long my life would be common knowledge...

We planned it to be ready for the next Book Fair, meaning there was no time to lose. First of all, I needed an attractive title to hang on to. According to Anne my name should be in it, that was the easy part, and according to me, it should show that I had nothing to hide. After some brainstorming, it was Alexandra's reply over the telephone when she was for the first time talking to Michel that put me on the track . Coming out of her bad tub she had said : Hello, I am totally naked. That is what it was going to be : Paula Marckx, totally naked. Anne started by asking what the first act was that I remembered in my adult life – for as far as I ever acted like one – and that was related to my nudity. And that's how it all started. The first act I remembered at that moment was when I dropped my clothes for a painter when I was seventeen.

The first chapter brought me inevitably back to my youth. I didn't realize it by then but, what I did was exploring how a well educated girl from a very catholic family – at least until the time my biography came to live, I thought I was -in the middle of the forties, was bold enough to

209

show her virgin body to a complete stranger. One thing was for certain that while doing, so I didn't realize that I could have been attacked, deflowered, and that I was at the complete mercy of a very attractive man. Those days young girls were not supposed to think like that. Sex – that horrible word, nobody used it, it was replaced by 'dirty manners' – was an action that was whispered about between schoolgirls, while giggling about what was happening to male and female between the sheets. What we did know, after all I was going to a catholic school, was that if a boy touched a girl between her legs before they were married the girl – and probably also the boy but that was not my problem - would be banned from heaven, when her time came to leave earth, and that for sure she would be sent to hell after having passed through purgatory. If she was lucky she could remain there for a while and be granted a second chance to enter in paradise. One option was left, she could go to confession and ask for absolution. The priest could than decide how many Hail Maries she had to pray to be considered free of sins. Nevertheless, even so, this was not a solution. In the confessional box, she was confronted with a man, before whom she had to kneel, and who's eyes were watching her through a kind of fly framework. I still remember when one Saturday – Saturday was the confession day – I tried to confess that a boy kissed me – according to what I heard from my classmates when a boy kissed a girl on her mouth, she could become pregnant – and cut of from the rest of the world in a box with the eyes of a priest on me, he asked me such unexpected details that I was seized with panic and decided not to go ever again in such a box with a priest or with any man for that matter. We were still far away from liberation day when the Americans arrived and any girl would commit murder for silk stocking and condoms that the allies from over the ocean had with them as barter trade.

****

When I came to the chapters relating my entrance in the world of 'the grown up people' a very strange thing happened to me. It started with Pierre Grisar, a man who disappeared out of my life more that forty years ago. Similar to a film in his developing procedure the man slowly came back to live, I revived our most intimate moment with more passion then when he still was alive. I felt madly in love with him all over. I even didn't try to reason myself, it just happened. With Lode Seghers it was different. I had never really been in love with him, but now I was sorry. I realized what a wonderful man he had been, how much he had loved me and how I had let him down. I wanted to repair, my fantasy took over and made me realize what a wonderful time could have been ours if only I had more sense. The couple of months I needed to write with Anne the story of my past, I lived in trance being each day possessed by the men I happened to focus on. I also started to realize what a hard time I gave to the man who were in love with me. Not that I felt like if I had been cheating on them, they knew where they had been in for. I didn't deceive anyone, they cheated on their wives, that was totally different. They were all ready to have an extra marital affair, and all things considered their wives were lucky that they fell for me, I never would have thought to steel their husbands. I just happened to give a surplus value to their marriage, and I feel sure that they were all bright enough to understand. But still. It was above all Lode who came to my mind. The faithful Lode who stood next to me, whatever. I recalled specially one moment when a very popular movie was released in Antwerp, Jamais le Dimanche (Never on Sunday) with Melina Mercouri who was going to become later Minister of Culture of Greece. Melina played a young girl in the harbor of Piraeus who gave herself to the sailors who boarded in her port. Except on Sunday when she danced and had fun with her friends. An American historian who visited the place wanted to change her but her friends told him that was an impossible thing to do. Because she liked the way she was, she was honest about it. Finally, it was the professor who changed his view of the world, fell madly in love with her, and was more than happy to accept her as she was. Lode said that she reminded him of me. .

When the book nearly came to an end I happen to read an interview with a Dr Hoeyberghs, who was also about to finish the book he was writing. He pretended that human beings are not by nature monogamous, he compared us with Pygmy Chimpanzee's and their lifestyle. I recognized myself in every word he had written and in whatever those chimp's or bonobo's as they also are called were doing with their sexual feelings. I realized that I was not monogamous either, that I was not the only one on this planet to feel that way . As a matter of fact, I was not so abnormal as some fellow man or woman may think I was. I was so relieved that I brought it to everybody's attention in the last chapter of my book. I suppose by then every reader may have noticed it already.

And then it was finished and Anne and I were presented to the press. "Paula Marckx, totally nude" was a fact. I do not believe that my business partner, Jean-Marie, felt much at ease. He supported me, like he always did, but he was not very sure about what was going to happen to me after my not so common lifestyle was revealed. However, it went on very well. I was all over the press and the most catholic oriented Belgian newspaper put in block letters on his front page that I, a rather well known business woman, was not monogamous and that my book was to be highly recommended. I didn't realize at that moment that I was on the doorstep of the second part of my life. What normally was supposed to be the end of a lifetime period was the beginning of an unexpected future. At the age of 79 going on 80? You must be kidding. Even so, nobody was kidding at all.

My biography was introduced at the Book Fair of Antwerp, my entire life in three hundred and two pages was exposed on a couple of shelves. Not exactly the literature to expect from a former pupil of a very Catholic institute. However, this was it , and if it would damage my reputation, so what ? The satisfaction had been mine.

On a Saturday afternoon, I was thrown in front of the lions. Meanwhile I had discovered that the man who had inspired me with his bonoboo's was under contract with the same publishing house as I was.. The man intrigued me. After all he had stepped into my life in the last chapter of my book. But, as everybody else in my country I knew him from TV. Dr Jeff Hoeyberghs, a plastic surgeon, had become an overnight celebrity when he had to face in a talk show, two women who attacked him on his knowledge. With his no nonsense replies and his roaring laughter he had charmed the audience. Not much later National TV offered him is an own soap serial that took place at the Wellness Clinique where he was stationed. I never watched it. I do not like soaps to start with. However, now I was intrigued. My editor not only introduced me to Jeff but put him next to me when autographing our books. Every TV reporter came to our stand for a shoot of Jeff. He drew their attention to me, He autographed his book to me . On the front page, he had written : There should be more women like you. I had never figured that he knew who I was. Nevertheless, we had some work to do , people were queuing up.

At the end of the session he walked away after we exchanged our mobile numbers.

Chapter 46
Sex At My Doorstep

Next day I was back at the Book Fair for another session of autographs. Jeff was not there, he was on duty later that week. It must have been a little after noontime when I saw, in the distance, a man racing towards me. Before my desk he made a full stop. I was sure I never saw that man in my entire life. Paula, he exclaimed at last I see you. He noticed that I had no idea where he was heading at. Have you seen, he asked me, how many times your name appears on Google and Yahoo? I said I didn't. It is incredible, he went on. He bought my book and said : Write something in for me. The name is Frank. I did what he asked me to do, and he gave me his business card. I would like to see you again, he said, on business. The word business is a word, I never neglect, so I replied that he was welcome to see me at my office at the Airport. My office is connected with other offices with a huge window glass. Should I be attacked by a stranger help would not be far of. Frank gave me a strong handshake and left.

The next day, I wasn't quite awake when I was called by another man I never heard of. What the man said was very indistinct, but I heard a lot of moaning and gasping at the other end of the line. It woke me entirely up when I became aware of what the man was doing. I hung up and poured myself a cup of coffee. During the morning several calls of the same nature came in on my steady telephone line. Impossible to verify where they came from, and I couldn't very well ignore them either. My publisher could need me for the Fair. Finally, I was nearly relieved when I received a call from someone I knew. It was Koen, my wealthy young friend that I had been in business with at the time of Patrasche. He called me from Holland to say that he bought my book. At first I was pleased with his interest but then he continued : I think that you are even more naughty now than you were before. Can I see you ? I remembered the different times I had dinner with him and his father, so I thought that it was that where he was referring to. Where do you want to see me ? I asked. Well, he answered what about in the late afternoon at your place. Not again, went through my mind, and I said : Koen, I may be older than I am on the cover picture, but I am certainly not cheaper. It didn't scare him of. He kept on phoning. He told

213

me that my book with my picture was laying on his big executive desk so that he could look at me whenever he wanted.

I went looking for some peace at my Airport office. Not long after I arrived at my office Frank, the man from the Book Fair called me and asked me if he could come in and see me. As far as I was concerned. I was at the Airport, and they have security service. And Frank at least hadn't gasped. Moreover he came on business. He was properly dressed with a briefcase to match. He asked me to be guest-speaker at a lunch of an organization he presided. We talked a little more and agreed that he would come up with a date. He stood up, opened the door to leave, and said over his shoulders : you know, I always fall for older women. It left me speechless for a moment while I wondered where the catch was.

Some days later I had a lunch engagement in Brussels. Luc van Raemdonck, a man that I had been introduced to by a mutual friend wanted to meet one of our foremost journalists Luc van der Kelen. When the first Luc learned that I knew the second Luc he suggested a lunch with the three of us . Van der Kelen accepted. The meeting suited me very well. I knew that Luc, the journalist, had read my book, but I hadn't received any reaction. I had and still have the greatest respect for the opinion of that man and due to his silence, I figured that he didn't like my literary experience.

The door of the Restaurant where van Raemdonck and I were waiting opened and there was Luc. He came straight to me, ignoring his host, and said : Paula, your story is an Hollywood story. He greeted his host, took a seat next to me and said. You really where the example of the libertine women of the fifties, your life could be compared of the one of Marlene Dietrich. He ordered himself a drink, turned again to me and continued : you had sex appeal, and after a few minutes he added, and in a way you still have it. So that must have been the explanation off my bonoboo behavior.

Frank had called again. He asked for a new meeting, and I gave him one at my office in the late afternoon. Shortly before the time agreed upon he called me to tell that he just heard that there would be a story about me and my book the same night on TV. I wanted to see it so I suggested to postpone our interview but Frank said that he was on his way to see me, and he wanted to see that interview as well, could he come to my home to watch it. I must have had a kind of a blackout because I said yes and gave him my address.

Where Frank had found the time I would not know but less than half an hour later he stood at my doorstep with a fantastic bunch of flowers. He gave me a discreet kiss on my cheek and declared that he had no intentions to cheat on his wife. I asked him if his wife knew that he was bringing flowers to my apartment. He said : No. Then you are cheating already on her, I observed, sit down. . The broadcasting started. In my living, there is only one place to sit to watch Tele, it is on my couch. When the show was over, or maybe when it was still on air, I was not focusing on what was happening next to me, Frank was drawing closer. Fact is that when I turned of TV, he was sitting quite close to me, he gently took me by my shoulders and asked me if he could kiss me. That is not exactly the kind of approach where I am used to. People who don't knew what they want give me the creeps. He was younger than me – but after what Luc van der Kelen said that was no problem material anymore – he was kind of attractive so I said : Listen, either you want to kiss me or you don't. If you don't go back to the end of the couch where you were before. If not, go for it and see what happens; He not only did, but he exploded ! Threw me on my back on my coach and kind of raped me. I said kind of, because I wasn't really against it, it was only a miracle that I didn't break my neck. I hadn't known before that I had remained in such a good physical condition.

We left in good harmony, and I figured that it was the end of an awakening friendship that went out of hand. Nothing was less true. Boxes of chocolates arrived, biography books from Marlene Dietrich , amorous telephone calls, e-mails in the middle of the night with publicity pictures showing appealing lady's underwear that I should be wearing next time when I was going to see me. But in each message he sent to me, he confirmed that he didn't want to betray his wife. In the beginning, I was vaguely charmed, it is quite exciting that a man cannot sleep because of you and send messages in the middle of the night to prove it , but finally it was very stressing. I was fed up with him, send him an e-mail that he was pathetic, and I never saw him again.

At the Airport, a surprise was waiting for me. I found a letter from Any, the daughter-in-law of Lode Seghers. I had been very close to her before she immigrated with her family to the South of Spain. After Lode passed away, I kept seeing his wife, Maria, on regular occasions. And so I kept informing about what happened to his children and grandchildren. From Marie, I had learned that their son Paul, Annie's husband, died at an early age in Spain, and that she had been invited by Any to live with her and the children. She wanted my advice and I told her, it was a sensible thing to do. She left and that's the last thing I had heard from her until I read in our local newspaper her death notice. Annie's parents still lived in Antwerp, and she came regularly over on a visit. On one of those visits she had noticed my book in a press shop. She tried to contact me at my airport office, but at the time I found her letter, she had already returned home, with my book. She wrote to me that they had loved to know more about the faith of Lode, their father and grandfather, who they adored. Before I knew it I was corresponding with them in Tarifa near to Gibraltar and especially with his grandson Alexander, whom I hadn't seen anymore since the age of ten and who was by now in his thirties. He had read my book and observed that he had the same good taste as his grandfather for good wine and beautiful women. He started his following letters always with : Ciao Bella, or Hola Carina. It was quite confusing. And in a funny way exiting. A month later he mailed me that he wanted to see me. He was going to stay with a former school friend somewhere in Belgium and was going to do a day trip by train to Antwerp.

The day of his arrival I was waiting for him in my car opposite the station building.; I didn't notice him until he opened the door on the driver seat and said : Hello, Charissima.. He gave me goose pimples. He had about the same age as his grandfather when I first laid.eyes on him. And he looked exactly like him. He went in on the other side, kissed me and said : Let's find something to eat. I started the car and we went to a tavern near the docks. He ordered wine, he asked a lot of questions, I gave a lot of answers. It was fun. We were not that far of the house where I was undressed for his grandfather, and I suggested to show it to him. He thought it was a great idea. I became acquainted with the present owner of the building. Just before my book was finished. I showed Anne where it all began. Then I went with my daughter, an excellent animal photographer - but what's in a name - to take a picture that was going to illustrate one of the chapters of my book. She must have had a sense of reality because when she noticed my shirt, she said : come on, mom, open a couple of those bottoms. This must look real. And now there was Alexander, pushing the very same house bell that I had rang more than sixty years before.

In the evening Alexander left not without the promises that we would see each other again.

Chapter 47
Modern Times

*Frie and I assisting at a lesbian pink wedding
at the Town Hall in Antwerp*

Around New Year Ann and Johan, my Naked Paula animators, came to my place for a New Year drink. Our book had been selling well, but it was written in my native language, Flemish, meaning it was restricted to the Flemish part of my country and Holland. Readers, also a lot of pro's, advised me to bring an English version on the market but that proved next to impossible. Anne suggested to contact The Gazette of Detroit, a Belgian Newspaper published in the States and ask them for advice. So I did.

The Editor, Elisabeth, replied very friendly that it was impossible to take care of my request because they were in the middle of a restructure of the paper, and they were rejuvenating the staff. I replied that in that situation it was me that they need, and by return I received a message 'welcome aboard'. At 81 I was on my way to an American press card.

Only I didn't know very well where to write about. Roots were not exactly my specialty. I found the answer when on an official dinner, I met Minister Leo Tindemans, a friend whom I knew from the sixties when we both attended C.E.D.I. conventions in Madrid. I asked him for an interview for the Gazette van Detroit, and he accepted immediately. Because I knew him so well it was more a chat than an interview with a lot of personal anecdotes what made it very lively. I had been a journalist for nearly fifty years and only now I found my lead. Doing what comes naturally.

Patsy Sorrensen called me one day. A lady friend of her who had read my book was very keen to meet me. Frie and her husband invited Patsy and I for dinner. Girls nor ladies had ever shown much interest in me. And it was reciprocal. Somehow I had the premonition that females would reject me after reading about my sexual experiences. I was a little curious if Frie would prove the exception to the rule, or if she just wanted to have a good look at that eccentric animal with rules of her own. Nothing of the kind. Frie, and her husband, happened to be charming persons as broadminded as I was. When later, after lots of other similar positive experiences I asked Patsy why that suddenly I was accepted in that female world, she replied : we all are jealous about you, at least you have no problems to tell everybody where it is all about.

However, let's return to Frie. We spend a fantastic night together. It was January; She told me that she planned a party at her flat for St Valentine's day on February 14, and that I would be the guest of honor. Before I went to see them, I wanted to know more about my unexpected friend. Frie belonged to the very high strictly catholic society of Belgium. She had a husband and two children and probably would have remained this way until the end of her days if faith hadn't turned up in the person of two gangsters who wanted to kidnap her for a ransom. Frie and her family lived in a beautiful villa at the outskirts of Antwerp, home to the rich and the wealthy. One day in the middle of the night, she was drying her hair after taking a shower when two men broke in to her bedroom. Frie who had always a gun at hand – with regard to her job - fired, and they ran away. However, security thought her attackers could come back – indeed a week later a neighbor was kidnapped – and gave her a n underground address in the North of France. She was sixty six by then. In the hotel where she was staying, she met John, a handsome Englishman, thirteen years younger than she was, who was staying there while restoring a castle nearby. In the past Frie's gynecologist , who knew that her marriage was not exactly what a girl like Frie needed, had advised her to look for a younger man. Frie took a good look at John and figured that he could solve the problem. They liked each other from the first time they met, so much was clear. She decided to take the bull by the horns and ask for his opinion. He fancied the idea. She added that if it shouldn't work right away she would show him the door for good. He agreed. Not that it went always that smoothly. Every day the party went on. When finally it was time for Frie to return home, she wanted to make a full stop with her affair and return to her civic duties. After all she realized that her boyfriend was so much younger, and she figured that not much good could come out of it. However, John did not give up that easily He telephoned her each night, she never responded. This went on for about a year. Meanwhile Frie had acquired a taste for extramarital delights . One of the high class hotels in Antwerp was called the Rosier. It was kept by two very popular gay antiquaries. When an international star had to stay over in Antwerp. he or she stayed at the Rosier. Some of the rooms were named after the VIP'S who had been staying there : Marlene Dietrich, Tina Turner among others.. Two rooms were booked on a daily basis for the 'Rosariennes', upper class married women who in the afternoon came, while their upper class husbands where meeting in order to win the money they need for their upper class life, to find comfort for being neglected, by not so upper class but very attractive young men. Finally John's mother called Frie and pleaded to come and see them. She gave in and when they saw each other again they could not say goodbye anymore. She asked her husband for a divorce.. He refused . She had the money and he wanted a piece of the cake. He suspected she had a boy friend but didn't realize who it was. Frie, a very talented classical pianist and very cultivated person wanted to start a new life by opening an antique shop with the new man in her life.

Frie had a friend by the name of Patrick , an antique dealer, and a very fine looking man.. He helped her to move around in his specialized world . Renaat, was watching the two very closely under the impression that Patrick was the villain ; Little did he know that Patrick was gay with lover problems of his own. One day when Frie and Patrick were going on to a visit to the niece of the young man they had to pass by a well known place of pilgrimage called Scherpenheuvel. They were both feeling miserable and decided to call the Virgin Mary for help. They went to the Basilic and bought all the candles they could find. They spend about 50 dollars went to the Church with their arms filled with candles , about 700 of them, light them and put them all over the place. The Basilique went nearly on fire.

That same evening Frie spent the night with John in Fries' apartment at The Eglantier Residence. At about 6 in the morning – they were not allowed to come in while it was still dark – policeman forced the door and took the couple in 'flagrant delit' It must be about the first time that police-men had to make such a statement in a n environment that was not exactly the place to discover a couple in full action. However it was exactly what Frie needed. Miracles do happen. Now Renaat could ask for a divorce him self – he was the good guy – and asked for alimony of his wife. Two days after her divorce Frie married her beau and was for the first time sexually happy in a married life. She was 66. When I met her, she was seventy five and she and John were. still naughtily in love.

There were several guests at their Valentine's party. Couples, singles, Patrick, Patsy where there to. Copies of my book where all over the place; While we were at the table young man in his thirties –he came especially with his own plane from Geneva to join us – told us that he was about to divorce. When he had said so to his mother. she , a very devoted catholic, had replied that he was no longer welcome in her house when he did so. I never heard anything like it. Frie told me that she had experienced similar reactions when she left her husband. And that is why, she said to her guests, you should read Paula's book. She is an example to us women, she knows where she stood for .

I was speechless. I never considered myself as an example for the Catholic Feminist Movement . Nevertheless, I did secure myself with a new and powerful lady friend. Who in the future was going to introduce me to the most unexpected guests for my Gazette of Detroit column.

Chapter 48
Men! We Can't Live With Them and We Can't Live Without Them

Jeff Hoeyberghs and I meet at the Book Fair
Photo Veerle Weverbergh

I never had seen anymore Jeff Hoeyberghs, the Wellness Doctor, since the Book Fair, but we became friends on an e-mail basis. I knew he was working on a new book, and had returned to Andorra where he lived. He had invited some friends to brainstorm about the contents. It had a lot to do with sex, sex was never far away from Jeff, and just before my Valentine party, he asked me for second opinions on e-mail. I suppose we were both intrigued with each other and our chaotic life stories, sexual freedom and all that. Before we knew it our e-mails were loaded with high voltage literature. I suppose we would have eternally banned from church if someone with more moral than we have, would have read it. Jeff turned me on with every mail he sent me and the bastard knew it.

My column for the Gazette of Detroit took shape. I realized that I had been a journalist for over fifty years and that it was not until now that I found my way. I could dig into Jeff I figured it was about time to put him on the grill. He invited me in his hometown for lunch. Since our first e-mails, I had the curious feeling that we had grown very close at a distance. I could not explain exactly what it was, maybe the man was just playing a game, or maybe it was just his way to handle women. I wouldn't know. However, it was very appealing. It could also be that my imagination took the better of me. Anyway, when I left for my appointment, I took a suitcase with me with things for the night. I was sure that I wouldn't return the same day.

Jeff finished working at two o'clock. We had decided to meet in a charming restaurant next to his Clinique. I had a feeling that Jeff was a bon vivant, and I was right. He offered champagne, but it was not to charm me, it was clearly his way of life. Conversation started exploring each other until I started with my interview. Before we finished our main course and the first bottle of wine, he was interrogating me, mostly about my sexual habits. It was a very strange conversation. It didn't even feel like flirting. After all he was a doctor, and he talked like one. I did not really know where he was getting had. His colleagues came in for a drink and the conversation didn't stop. Before I knew it I was discussing my sexual life with total strangers. Jeff's conclusion was that I need a man that was forty years younger than me. I still didn't know if this was meant to be an invitation. His friends went away and others came in. Meanwhile lunch was over and according to Jeff it was time for a 'digestif'. Before I went to meet Jeff, I made a solemn vow that I was not going to have a drink after dinner. However, Jeff ordered a grappa, he didn't ask me if I wanted one, he just ordered one for me as well.. The problem is that I like white alcohol, any white alcohol, it could even be distilled in a farm. Not that I need one every day, I am a social drinker. With the life, I have been living, I could hardly ask for a hard boiled egg, when I am talking about business in a café or a restaurant. So I couldn't say no to that Grappa of Jeff. Other doctors from the Clinic kept coming in and offered a grappa, the boss of the restaurant as is a custom for that kind of clients offered us a grappa, I stopped counting when I was at number eight.. By that time Jeff felt hungry again and decided to order dinner. We started from scratch. Champagne, wine at dinner, grappa after dinner. At three o'clock in the morning we decided to call it a night. You, said Jeff, pointing at me, are going to sleep in the Clinic. I must have said something like as long as nobody cut my breast away - with all those plastic surgeons in my neighborhood anything may happen – and between Jeff and another surgeon, the last one of the Mohicans, we left for the Wellness clinic. We went on upstairs and Jeff brought me to a room. He asked if he should help to undress me, but after a quick look at him, I said 'no'. Obviously, he was not in a state to do pleasing, sexual performances, and although I was not exactly in a clear moment I realized that if this would turn out to be a fiasco this could mean the end of a beautiful friendship. And I wasn't ready to take that risk. Before Jeff went out, he turned around to ask me if I had my mobile phone with me. I had. If I needed anything at all I just had to call him. I promised I would. However, all I needed at that moment was my bed. So I went under the sheets and slept like a log.

When I woke up in the morning I didn't realize at first where I was. Slowly, I remembered but didn't know exactly how to act. After all the staff in the clinic didn't know. who I was. If I walked out that door I didn't know in what direction to go and who I could meet on my way. Vaguely, I remembered that Jeff had promised to bring me breakfast in bed, but the question was, where was Jeff? I had my mobile with me, but Jeff's mobile number was in my car. I could call the clinic but didn't have the number. So I decided to call the national information service . They gave me the number, and I was connected to the telephone operator of the Wellness Clinic. When I had her on the line I asked for Dr Hoeyberghs. She answered. Is it for your hips or your breasts? Neither one of them I answered, I am a friend of him. Anyone could say that, the girl replied, I am not allowed to connect you to my boss if I cannot tell him why you want to see him. She started to work on my system. If you know what's good for you, I nearly shouted , you better get him right away on the phone. I think this scared her of. OK, she said in despair, where are you calling from? From upstairs, I answered. That did it . She must have thought I was a lunatic. I got Jeff on the line, and my breakfast was served on my bed.

Back home I realized the situation I had been in. I send a mail to Jeff asking him if I didn't misbehave in that bacchanalia. A couple of days later Jeff left to Los Angeles where he had some shooting to do for our television. While he was waiting on the Airport to check in, he sent me a mail saying : Paula, whatever you do you remain a lady. The perfect gentleman. I liked that man..

End of act one. I saw Jeff again several months later at the following book fair. He introduced me to a young woman who was his new girl-friend. I did not like her from the moment, I saw her. I did not mind that Jeff had a girl friend, but at least she should have class. Which was not the case with this Evelyn. She predicted misery. Jeff hardly kept contact with me in the months to come.. I had the feeling that his new conquest kept him on purpose away from his friends, but so what, life went on. I forgot about Jeff. He no longer had that strange effect on me.

Chapter 49
The Perfect Mistress

One of my meetings for the Gazette van Detroit, left Alderman Philippe Heylen, on my righ Prince Laurent, son of our King
Photo Ruth Huysentruyt

Stranded on American Highways :
Wilfried van den Brande, Dirk Baert and me.
Photo Harald de Bruyn

226

Months went by mostly devoted to my column in the Gazette van Detroit. Elisabeth became my soul mate. Every two weeks another one of my articles was published, every other week I made a new friend, all top levels; While surfing on the internet for some extra information one day I notice a Hilary Marckx, a Californian Photographer. His biography said that he used to work as a dairy farm, hauled hay, driven tractor, picked peaches, pears and apricots, sold brooms and brushes door-to-door, and worked for the State of California as a clerk. I send him an e-mail and yes his grandparents came from Antwerp and yes, we were related. He suggested to introduce me to the rest of my American family and before I knew what was happening to me , I was corresponding with thirty tree American nieces and cousins, mostly living on the West coast. I received a book with a family tree and a family history that I even didn't know it existed with pictures to match. I learned that one of my paternal grand-aunts had arrived in the States in the 19th century and was taught by the Indians how to hunt and to fish in order to feed her children. Another one saw a man killed in a saloon and went with her baby on the arm to the neighboring city to testify against the bandits. They were planning to organize their yearly Marckx Thanksgiving party and I was invited to be their guest. They were nearly fighting to give me shelter. And so I left for Seattle to meet the American branch of my family . They were very colorful indeed. One of the women, a heavy smoker told me that she was living all by herself on a ranch with her six horses and when winter arrived, she put al of them in a van and drove to Arizona for the season. After a week of relating all their colorful adventures . Some of them drove me to the Airport and I took it as a very big compliment when one of the men observed that I was a real 'Marckx'.

On my way home, I stopped in Detroit to get acquainted with Elisabeth and her family and my colleagues at the Gazette. When I had left for the States I only left my daughter behind, when I left America I said goodbye to an entire new family. But I wasn't home yet.

As I always do when I go to the States I make a final stop in New York. Before I left I had sent a mail to Oleg's Cassini's secretary, the one who had been standing by when I had visited the master. Now, that he had died I figured the poor girl had lost her job and I wanted her to know that to me that made no difference and I had invited her for lunch which she accepted. Upon arrival in my hotel I called her. She told me that she still was working for the Cassini fashion house, she had no time to lunch with me in town but she invited me to come to the Atelier. Which I did.

Peggy was waiting for me in the lounge . She offered me champagne but I was too thirsty and I asked for a beer. After she served me she told me that someone wanted to meet me, Marianne, the wife of Oleg Cassini. She came in with a crystal paper holder and gave it to me saying : I am so glad to meet you, Oleg was very impressed by you. Quite a compliment coming from a man who dressed Jacqueline Kennedy and Marylyn Monroe. Then I learned that Peggy Nestor, Cassini's former secretary was not only his secretary but also his sister in law. They both took me to an Italian restaurant near Central Park were they were, so to see, home. You serve us well, Marianne said to the waiter, if you know what is good for you, Paula is one of the most famous journalists of Europe. I was certainly not, but it is always nice to hear. So I was sitting there between the rich and the mighty, and Marianne made me promise that next time I was going to stay at her place.

Through a Belgian Magazine I had learned that Jeff Hoeyberghs was in trouble. He was involved in a battle divorce with his wife, he had left his Wellness clinic and his girl friend expected a baby. He was a welcome pray for the press, every move he made was largely analyzed. But somehow it was not my problem. It was only after I learned that he left his girlfriend for his wife , I thought he should know that I felt that he was doing the right thing. When I called him in Andorra he seemed to be on top of the world again now that his life was coming back into shape. He invited me to look him up with as many friends I would like to bring along. I said that I would think about it and spread the word. Anne, Patrick and Alexandra were willing to come along, but the only week that I was free they could not make it. So finally I decided to go on my own. In the month of August I had to travel to Detroit for the 95th birthday party for the newspaper and I thought that I might as well join Jeff in his wine yard after my return for some rest.

But first I had some commitments to attend to. Thirty years had been gone since the Marckx case had become a fact. Television and radio brought extra spots. At the same time Antwerp, or to be more specific the Zoo of Antwerp, had become the center of attraction with the birth of a baby elephant that was called Kai-Mook. He became Antwerp's little sweetheart and I decided to celebrate the 30th anniversary of my Marckx Case for broadcasting in company of his mother. After all we had something in common. We both were single mums. When a trip to the celebration of the 95th year of existence of the Gazette van Detroit was settled, I decided to take with me the biggest Kai-Mook reproduction in velvet I could find to offer at the Party to Ambassador Portocarero, the Belgian Consul General in New York who was going to be the guest of honor.

We were all looking forward to the trip. We that were Wilfried van den Brande, baritone, who was about to leave on a Cole Porter Tour around the world, Dirk Baert, conductor of the Nurnberger Symphoniker, Harald de Bruyn, photographer of the Gazette and I who was supposed to do a speech. Everything went spotless and in the best of mood, until we arrived in New York. There we managed to miss our connection flight to Detroit.. Our luggage including Kai Mook did make it to the plane. Imagine the sight : one singer, one pianist, a photographer and a reporter disheveled and sticky after a nine-hour flight, without a change of clothes, at the loose end in the city that never sleeps.

We hardly found hotel rooms and when we finally were installed, which was not that difficult, we had nothing with us, we went looking for a decent dinner. Last time he was in New York Wilfried had stayed in the Waldorf Astoria and that is where he wants to take us. When we entered nobody even looked up. The staff must have believed we were notoriously rich and odd character to enter in such a classy hotel dressed like vagrants. But the food was great. The mood was below zero. We had already found out that the next days there were no airline tickets available anymore to Detroit. And we had no idea how to arrive at our final destination. It was Thursday evening and the gala night took place on Saturday. I could not even shower. My make up was in Detroit and I preferred to run around filthier than without blush on my cheeks. Our consulate tried to help us, even the management of our hotel tried to help us out, mission impossible. On Saturday morning at five Wilfried was knocking at my door. Get, up, I heard him shouting, we are leaving. It seemed that he had found a car for rent at La Guardia Airport – in New York there was not one car available- Wilfried went behind the wheel and then we drove through four states to arrive , still wearing the cloth we'd left home in, close to 9 pm in Detroit. The party where we were expected had started at 6.30 pm and our problems were not yet over. Kai Mook, the stuffed elephant entrusted to me by the General Manager of the Antwerp Zoo as a special gift for Mr. Porrtocarero, was waiting for us somewhere at the Detroit Airport. After driving 633 miles, it became of major importance to us to find that animal. With some difficulty we tracked down Kai Mook (and the rest of our luggage)and once that impossible mission accomplished, we made it to Fraser by 10 P.M. Wilfried sang, Dirk played the keyboard, Harald made pictures and I handed over Kai Mook to Ambassador Portocarero. When we returned to Belgium we were all absolutely exhausted. However none of us would have missed it for the world.

A couple of days later, still in full Jetlag I flew to Spain to meet Jeff. I wasn't very sure what I was to expect. I hadn't read a Belgian Magazine for some time and I was not very aware of the last movements in VIP country. On the other hand what if my imagination was feeling things that did not exist. What if he didn't turn up to pick me up at the Airport of Barcelona. All I had with me was his mobile phone number. I didn't even know where the man lived. But he was at the Airport and he drove me to his home. A couple of hours to the north of Spain. That is when I discovered that Jeff and his wife were both living, in the best of understanding, in different houses, she in Andorra, he in Spain, a couple of miles past the border. There I was for a week, in the middle of a vineyard, living under the same room with a man I happened to like very much but very uncertain about his feelings. After all there was that large difference of age and it could be that he only needed someone to talk to with a wife next door and a pregnant girlfriend miles away. But it wasn't exactly some one to talk to that he needed, but someone willing as I was. Obviously Jeff was a barrel of frustrations and my presence and the past that he knew from my biography didn't help him to relax.

The first day we both played for time, a visit to Andorra, a tour on his squad between the vine shoots, dinner in a parador, just enjoying each other presence. On Sunday Jeff had organized a barbecue. His friends from the village were invited with their wives ; Jeff's wife and their children would attend as well. He was rather early in the kitchen to prepare the vegetables, the spices fresh from his garden and the meat, I joined him for breakfast in the garden at the swimming pool. We cleaned the table and returned next to the water and then for no reason at all – he blamed it on the sunshine, so be it, he threw caution to the winds and took me right there.. It was fantastic and in a way surrealistic. I had nearly given up on him but how wrong could I be ! It didn't even feel as it was the first time, it was a chemical reaction that had been simmering for quite a while and that now exploded. We had just returned to our senses – or what was left of it – when the first guests arrived.

It was also a kind of relieve. The guest that I had been not so long before suddenly belonged to the household. And I had the feeling I was considered as such. Jeff's wife arrived first. A lady with a lot of class. She welcomed me with a charming smile. When the other guests arrived she mixed with them and saw to it that they all felt at home. Like is to be expected from a hostess. I was glad that I had met her after I had made love to her husband, I believe that I never could have started an affair, be it a short one, if I had met her before. Jeff was busy at the grill. He was not only a good lover , he was a good cook as well.

It was a wonderful afternoon. I was back in the Spanish atmosphere that had been my second country decades ago. It was clear happiness. After the last guest left, Jeff and I made love again. It was the beginning of a fantastic week with a man who had put himself in a terrible mess and as men usually do in such a situation blamed everyone else for the jam he had put himself to. Married for over twenty years with his childhood sweetheart with whom he had build up a solid business empire and with whom he lived in Andorra, he had traveled back and forth to Belgium where he exercised his duties. He met a younger girl, his wife threw him out his home and his practice of which she was an important shareholder. He went to live with his girlfriend and although he told me it was a disaster he made her pregnant. As far as I could judge he did it to needle his wife. According to Jeff everything would have turned out well if he could have kept them both. The big mistake that Jeff made was to take a girl friend instead of a mistress. Girl friends of married men are eager to take their boy friends away from their wives. A mistress keeps marriages together . I for one felt sure that Jeff was still in love with his wife; And that it was mutual.

It was rather frustrating to find out how weak and puzzled the man was where I had always looked up to as a rock. He asked me for advice, but what advice could I give him in my new position. He could think I took it personal. Nevertheless the last days I spent with him on the vineyard and around where fabulous. I was to return to Belgium on August 20,

Jeff's birthday. He had planned to go with his wife and daughter by car to Belgium one day later. His wife called him up to suggest that he should stay with me at their place in Andorra on the night before my departure. That way he could drive me next day to the Airport in Barcelona, return to their place in the evening, in order to leave to Belgium the next day.

While making my luggage in his house in the mountains, packing my clothes and my souvenirs, Jeff came to my room. We made love for the last time, it was total, it was heaven, it was complete and it was goodbye. When it was over Jeff looked to me and said : you should write a book : the Perfect Mistress, for Small men with Large Ambitions.

And then we drove to the villa in Andorra, where Jeff's family was waiting for us. Jeff fitted right in the picture. His wife, an ambitious woman of the world, charming teenager children, a fantastic house in the green, even a dog to make the picture complete. I don't know if she could cope with his sexual desires, I didn't ask, but somehow he answered my question by referring to me as the perfect mistress.

We spend a wonderful night at that house. When we were back on the road next day Jeff wondered why that she hadn't noticed what was going on between him and me. I told him that I wasn't sure that she didn't notice, at the contrary, but she was a smart woman, and she realized that I was at that moment more an ally than a menace to her. It had nothing to do with my age but everything with who I was, an unconventional woman with an ethic code : a Mistress.

****

After several hours we just made it in time to the Airport of Barcelona. We stopped on the way for a drink and a bite to eat, we talked a lot, mostly about Jeff's near future. I didn't feel involved but on the other hand I cared for this man and I knew that if he wasn't going to be careful he was going to ruin his entire future and everything where he ever cared for. But I didn't know how to get trough to him. When I was back home Jeff called me several times but I felt that the situation was gliding out of my hands. Finally his wife left him, his girl friend had a baby and he went to live with her. When I told him that he was making the biggest mistake in his life he called me a so and so, I called him a so and so and that was that.

After all who needed him. I had my interviews with very interesting people, a new circle of very attractive friends, a lot of entertainment, even a very unexpected proposal of marriage. For some reason, or another I had always been very popular with gay human beings. I feel sure that hetero creatures have no idea how many gay's they are dealing with. One of them is Patrick, Frie's friend who went with her to the Basilique of Scherpenheuvel to get rid of her husband, remember ? We were circulating in the same circles, we had a similar view of life, we just plainly liked each other. Full stop. One night we went together to Brussels to attend to a preview of a book written by a mutual friend. It was a fantastic autumn evening. The building where the reception took place was near to a lake. When Patrick and I left, he noticed a French fry booth and decided that he was hungry, and that he wanted a portion. I wasn't hungry but thirsty and asked for a can of beer. We sat down on a bench near the lake, Patrick with his fried potatoes, I with a can of beer from which I had to drink which I had never done in my life, and after a moment of silence Patrick said : Paula, after all why shouldn't we marry. I tried to look in his eyes, which was impossible , it was too dark, and asked ; Is this a proposal ? Yes, he said, it could work. He hadn't stopped nibbling on his potatoes, but it was indeed a very romantic atmosphere, the moon was shining right on top of us, and I replied : Why not ? You are gay, I am an unmarried mother, we have no reason to be jealous of one another, and as far as the difference of age – he was thirty years younger – I am getting used to it. We can give it a try. We launched it the next day in upper circles, and consequently, it started to live its own life. Fashion people wanted to dress us, everybody wanted to walk in the bridal procession. Stranger things have happened. All that was needed were two sensible people who had seen it all – or most of it, a small bag with French fries, a tin of beer, moon over a lake and the liberty of throwing over board all valid rules. It sounded like fun. However, let's go back to reality.

I was about to put my short love story with Jeff between the classifieds when I received an e-mail from Marly-Ann, Jeff's wife. She had found my e-mail address and wanted to thank me for my visit. She wrote what a great lady she thought I was, full of great spirit, an example for all of us. The feeling I had is hard to describe, it was not guilt, not at all it was a kind of solidarity, from two women who cared for the same man.

The correspondence went on, she presumed that I was nearly the only one who was by her side. And this was so true. When I told her that I was no longer in writing terms, nor in any other terms, with Jeff she pleaded not to let him down. She went as far as to say that I was the only one to keep him on the right track. Which was easier said than done. After all I had never replied to his last mail and I didn't want him to think that I was crawling back on my knees. But one of my books from the Gazette van Detroit was published and Jeff had been a great help so I send him a thank you note. He replied and at the same token asked how the Perfect Mistress was proceeding. He could either have referred to me than to my book. I didn't take any risks and talked about the latter. And we were back in business.

In a way it is rather amusing. I am over eighty , live a very unhealthy life, make love, sometimes war and a man forty years younger calls me a perfect Mistress. Am I an exception? No, I am not.

Take Yahoo and ask for Young at Heart by Dean Martin or Frank Sinatra and you will hear them crooning :

Fairy Tales can come true, it can happen to you
If you're young at heart
For it is hard, you will find, to be narrow of mind
If you're young at heart

You can be damn sure those men knew where they were talking about.

And what about my beautiful daughter Alexandra ? How would a youngster, 37 year at the time, react when she learns that her 84-year old mother had made love to a man forty year younger than she was. The least I could do was to let her know before she read it in my book.

One afternoon when she came on a visit, I told her. I didn't know what her reaction would be. However, I think we all could learn a thing or two from her. I certainly was not prepared for what I was going to hear. She stared at me for a moment and replied "You and Jeff?". Then she smiled at me and with a twinkle in her eyes she asked me : "And how was it, mom?"

CPSIA information can be obtained
at www.ICGtesting.com
Printed in the USA
FSOW01n2116090317
31757FS